MATHEMATICAL METHODS IN ECONOMICS

Mathematical Methods in Economics

NORMAN SCHOFIELD

NEW YORK
UNIVERSITY
PRESS

CROOM HELM
London & Sydney

Croom Helm Ltd, Provident House, Burrell Row,
Beckenham, Kent BR3 1AT
Croom Helm Australia Pty Ltd, First Floor,
139 King Street, Sydney, NSW 2001, Australia

British Library Cataloguing in Publication Data

Schofield, Norman
Mathematical methods in economics.
1. Economics, Mathematical
I. Title
330'.01'51 HB135

ISBN 0-7099-2337-6

New York University Press, Washington
Square, New York, New York 10003

Library of Congress Cataloging in Publication Data

Schofield, Norman, 1944-
Mathematical methods in economics.

Bibliography: p.
Includes index.
1. Economics, Mathematical. I. Title.
HB135.S36 1984 330'.01'51 84-11502
ISBN 0-8147-7842-9

Printed and bound in Great Britain

CONTENTS

Biographical Details

Norman Schofield obtained B.Sc. degrees in both Physics and Mathematics at Liverpool University and a Ph.D. from Essex University. His principle research interests are in social choice, game theory and mathematical applications in political economy. He has published about thirty articles in these fields in a number of economics, mathematics, political science and sociology journals and edited two books - Crisis in Economic Relations Between North and South (Gower Publishers, Aldershot, England) and Data Analysis and the Social Sciences (Frances Pinter Publishers, London, and St. Martin's Press, New York). He is currently reader in economics at Essex University. During 1982-83 he was Hallsworth Fellow in Political Economy at Manchester University and in 1983-84 was the Sherman Fairchild Distinguished Scholar at the California Institute of Technology. He has previously taught at Yale University and the University of Texas at Austin. He is on the editorial board of the new journal Social Choice and Welfare. His book, Social Choice and Democracy, will be published by Springer Verlag (Heidelberg and New York) in 1984, and he is currently working on books on International Political Economy and General Equilibrium Theory.

FOREWORD

In recent years, the usual optimisation techniques, which have proved so useful in microeconomic theory, have been extended to incorporate more powerful topological and differential methods, and these methods have led to new insights into the qualitative behaviour of general economic systems. These developments have necessarily resulted in an increase in the degree of formalism in the publications in the academic economic theory journals; a formalism which can often deter graduate students. My hope is that the progression of ideas presented here will familiarise the student with the geometric concepts underlying these topological methods, and, as a result, make modern mathematical economics and general equilibrium theory more accessible.

The first chapter of the book introduces the general idea of mathematical structure and representation, while the second chapter analyses linear systems and the representation of transformations of linear systems by matrices. In the third chapter, topological ideas and continuity are introduced, and made use of in solving convex optimisation problems. These procedures then lead naturally to calculus techniques for using a linear approximation, the differential, of a function to study its "local" behaviour.

The book is not intended to cover mathematical economics or general equilibrium theory. However in the last sections of the third and fourth chapters I have introduced some of the standard tools of economic theory, namely the Kuhn Tucker Theorem, some elements of convex analysis and procedures using the Langrangian, and provided examples of consumer and producer optimisation. The final section of chapter four also discusses in a fairly heuristic fashion the smooth or critical Pareto set and the idea of a regular economy. The fifth and final chapter is somewhat more advanced, and extends the differential calculus of a real valued function to the analysis of a smooth function between "local" vector spaces, or manifolds. Modern singularity theory is the study and classification of all such smooth functions, and the purpose of the final chapter has been to use this perspective to obtain a generic or typical picture of the Pareto set and the set of Walrasian equilibria of an exchange economy.

Since the underlying mathematics of this final section are rather difficult, I have not attempted rigorous proofs, but rather sought to lay out the natural path of development from elementary differential calculus to the powerful tools of singularity theory. In the text I have referred to work of Debreu, Balasko, Smale and others who, in the last few years, have used the tools of singularity theory to develop a deeper insight into the geometric structure of an economy. Review exercises are provided at the end of the book, for the use of the reader.

I am indebted to my graduate students for the pertinent questions they asked during the course on mathematical methods in economics, which I gave at Essex University during 1979-1982. It is a pleasure to thank Mike Martin of Essex University and Peter Lambert of the University of York for the helpful suggestions they made, and Pam Hepworth and Nancy Tobbell for typing the manuscript.

I am grateful to the Economics Department of Manchester University for the opportunity provided by a Hallsworth Fellowship in Political Economy in 1982-83 during which I completed the book.

I hope that this book awakens an interest in mathematics for the reader, just as mine was by Terry Wall, Mike Butler, Ian Porteous and Tom Wilmore at Liverpool University.

Pasadena, California
January 1984

MATHEMATICAL METHODS IN ECONOMICS

Chapter 1.

SETS, RELATIONS AND PREFERENCES

In this chapter we introduce the elementary set theory and notation to be used throughout the book. We also define the notions of binary relation, function, as well as the axioms of a group and field. Finally we discuss the idea of an individual and social preference relation, and mention some of the concepts of social choice and welfare economics.

1.1. ELEMENTS OF SET THEORY

Let U be a collection of objects, which we shall call the domain of discourse, universal set or universe. A set B in this universe (or subset of U) is a subcollection of objects from U. B may be defined either explicitly by enumerating the objects, for example by writing

$$B = \{\text{Tom, Dick, Harry}\}$$
$$\text{or } B = \{x_1, x_2, x_3, \ldots\}.$$

Alternatively B may be defined implicitly be reference to some property P(B), which characterises the elements of B, thus

$$B = \{x: \ x \text{ satisfies } P(B)\}.$$

For example:

$B = \{x: \ x \text{ is an integer satisfying } 1 \leq x \leq 5\}$
is a satisfactory definition of the set B, where the universal set could be the collection of all integers. If B is a set write $x \in B$ to mean that the element x is a member of B. Write $\{x\}$ for the set which contains only one element, x.

If A, B are two sets write $A \cap B$ for the set which contains only those elements which are both in A and B, and $A \cup B$ for the set whose elements are either in A or B. The null set Φ, is that subset of U which contains no elements in U.

Finally if A is a subset of U, define the <u>negation</u> of A, or complement of A in U to be the set

$$\bar{A} = \{x: \ x \text{ is in U but not in A}\}.$$

1.1.1. <u>A Set Theory</u>

Now let $\mathcal{T}$ be a family of subsets of U, where $\mathcal{T}$ includes both U and Φ, i.e.

$$\mathcal{T} = \{U, \Phi, A, B, \ldots\}.$$

If A is a member of $\mathcal{T}$, then write $A \in \mathcal{T}$. Note here that $\mathcal{T}$ is a set of sets.

Suppose that $\mathcal{T}$ satisfies the following properties:

i) for any $A \in \mathcal{T}$, $\bar{A} \in \mathcal{T}$
ii) for any A, B in $\mathcal{T}$, $A \cup B$ is in $\mathcal{T}$
iii) for any A, B in $\mathcal{T}$, $A \cap B$ is in $\mathcal{T}$.

In this case we say that T satisfies <u>closure</u> with respect to $(\overline{\ \ },\cup,\cap)$, and call T a <u>set theory</u>.

For example let 2^U be the set of <u>all</u> subsets of U, including both U and Φ. Clearly 2^U satisfies closure with respect to $(\overline{\ \ },\cup,\cap)$.

Since a set theory T satisfies the following axioms we shall call it a <u>Boolean algebra</u>.

<u>Axioms</u>

S1.	Zero element	$A \cup \Phi = A,\ A \cap \Phi = \Phi$
S2.	Identity element	$A \cup U = U,\ A \cap U = A$
S3.	Idempotency	$A \cup A = A,\ A \cap A = A$
S4.	Negative	$A \cup \bar{A} = U,\ A \cap \bar{A} = \Phi$
		$\bar{\bar{A}} = A$
S5.	Commutativity	$A \cup B = B \cup A$
		$A \cap B = B \cap A$
S6.	De Morgan Rule	$\overline{A \cup B} = \bar{A} \cap \bar{B}$
		$\overline{A \cap B} = \bar{A} \cup \bar{B}$
S7.	Associativity	$A \cup (B \cup C) = (A \cup B) \cup C$
		$A \cap (B \cap C) = (A \cap B) \cap C$
S8.	Distributivity	$A \cup (B \cap C) = (A \cup B) \cap (A \cup C)$
		$A \cap (B \cup C) = (A \cap B) \cup (A \cap C)$.

These axioms can be illustrated by Venn diagrams in the following way.

Let the square on the page represent the universal set U. A subset B of points within U can then represent the set B. Given two subsets A, B the union is the hatched area, while the intersection is the double hatched area.

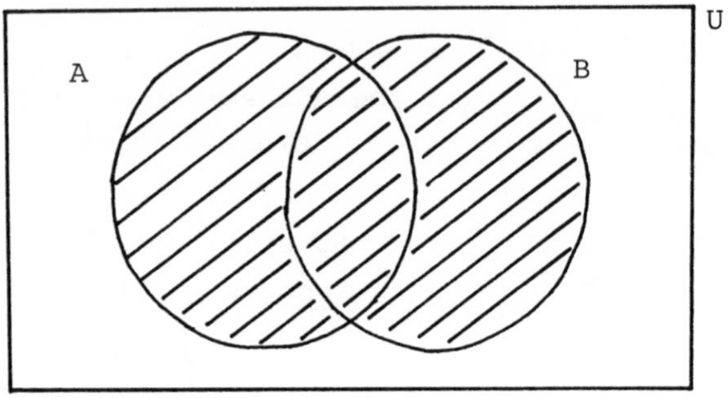

A∪B

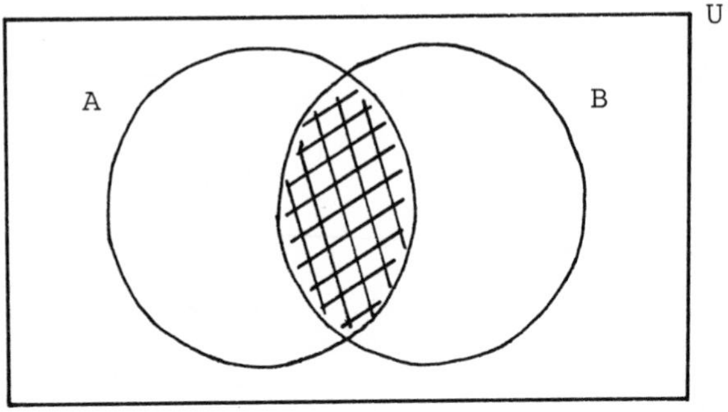

A∩B

Fig.1.1.

We shall use $\subset$ to mean "included in". Thus $A \subset B$ means that every element in A is also an element of B.

Thus:

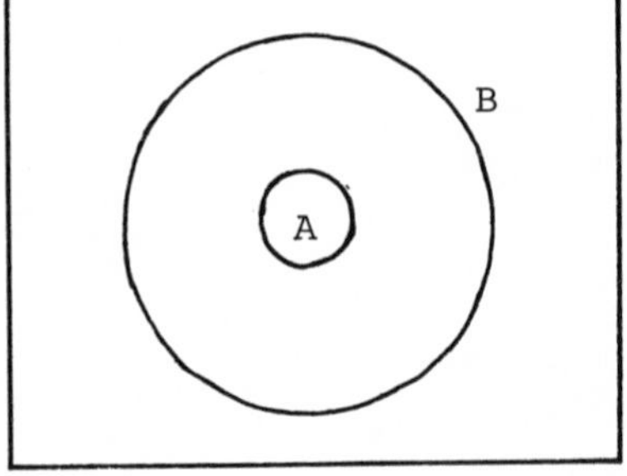

Fig.1.2.

Suppose now that P(A) is the property that characterises A.

Thus A = {x: x satisfies P(A)} .

We use the symbol ≡ to mean "identical to", and so

$[x \in A] \equiv$ "x satisfies P(A)".

Here "x satisfies P(A)" is a proposition. Associated to any set theory is a <u>propositional calculus</u> which satisfies analogous properties, except that we use $\wedge$ and V instead of the symbols $\cap$ and $\cup$ for "and" and "or".

For example:

$A \cup B$ = {x: "x satisfies P(A)" V "x satisfies P(B)"}

$A \cap B$ = {x: "x satisfies P(A)" $\wedge$ "x satisfies P(B)"} .

The analogue of "$\subset$" is "if ... then" or "implies" which is written =>.

Thus

$A \subset B \equiv$ ["x satisfies P(A)" => "x satisfies P(B)"]

The analogue of "=" in set theory is the symbol "<=>" which means "if and only if", generally written "iff".

For example

$[A = B] \equiv$ ["x satisfies P(A)" <=> "x satisfies P(B)"]

Hence

$[A = B] \equiv$ ["$x \in A$" <=> "$x \in B$"]

$\equiv [A \subset B$ and $B \subset A]$

1.1.2. A Propositional Calculus

Let $\{U, \Phi, P_1, \ldots, P_i, \ldots\}$ be a family of simple propositions. U is the universal proposition and always true, whereas Φ is the null proposition and always false. Two propositions P_1, P_2 can be combined to give a proposition $P_1 \wedge P_2$ (i.e. P_1 and P_2) which is true iff both P_1 and P_2 are true, and a proposition $P_1 \vee P_2$ (i.e. P_1 or P_2) which is true if either P_1 or P_2 is true. For a proposition P, the complement $\bar{P}$ in U is true iff P is false, and is false iff P is true.

Now extend the family of simple propositions to a family $\mathcal{P}$,by including in $\mathcal{P}$ any propositional sentence $S(P_1, \ldots, P_i, \ldots)$ which is made up of simple propositions combined under $-, \vee, \wedge$. Then $\mathcal{P}$ satisfies closure with respect to $(-, \vee, \wedge)$ and is called a propositional calculus.

Let T be the truth function, which assigns to any simple proposition, P_i, the value 0 if P_i is false, and 1 if P_i is true. Then T extends to sentences in the obvious way, following the rules of logic, to give a truth function $T: \mathcal{P} \rightarrow \{0,1\}$. If $T(S_1) = T(S_2)$ for all truth values of the constituent simple propositions of the sentences S_1 and S_2, then $S_1 = S_2$ (i.e. S_1 and S_2 are identical propositions).

For example the truth values of the proposition $P_1 \vee P_2$ and $P_2 \vee P_1$ are given by the table:

$T(P_1)$	$T(P_2)$	$T(P_1 \vee P_2)$	$T(P_2 \vee P_1)$
0	0	0	0
0	1	1	1
1	0	1	1
1	1	1	1

Since $T(P_1 \vee P_2) = T(P_2 \vee P_1)$ for all truth values it must be the case that $P_1 \vee P_2 = P_2 \vee P_1$.

On the other hand the truth tables for $P_1 \wedge P_2$ and $P_2 \wedge P_1$ are:

$T(P_1)$	$T(P_2)$	$T(P_1 \wedge P_2)$	$T(P_2 \wedge P_1)$
0	0	0	0
0	1	0	0
1	0	0	0
1	1	1	1

Thus $P_1 \wedge P_2 = P_2 \wedge P_1$.

The propositional calculus satisfies the commutativity of $\wedge$ and V. Using these truth tables the other properties of a Boolean algebra can be shown to be true.

For example:

i) $P \vee \Phi = P, \quad P \wedge \Phi = \Phi.$

$T(P)$	$T(\Phi)$	$T(P \vee \Phi)$	$T(P \wedge \Phi)$
0	0	0	0
1	0	1	0

ii) $P \vee U = U, \quad P \wedge U = P.$

$T(P)$	$T(U)$	$T(P \vee U)$	$T(P \wedge U)$
0	1	1	0
1	1	1	1

iii) Negation is given by reversing the truth value. Hence $\bar{\bar{P}} = P$.

$T(P)$	$T(\bar{P})$	$T(\bar{\bar{P}})$
0	1	0
1	0	1

iv) $P \vee \bar{P} = U, \quad P \wedge \bar{P} = \Phi$.

$T(P)$	$T(\bar{P})$	$T(P \vee \bar{P})$	$T(P \wedge \bar{P})$
0	1	1	0
1	0	1	0

Example 1.1 Truth tables can be used to show that a propositional calculus $\mathcal{P} = (U, \Phi, P_1, P_2 \ldots)$ with the operators $(\bar{\ }, \vee, \wedge)$ is a Boolean algebra.

Suppose now that $S_1(A_1,\ldots,A_n)$ is a set which is made up of the sets $A_1,\ldots A_n$ together with the operators $\{\cup, \cap, \bar{\ }\}$.

For example suppose that

$$S_1(A_1, A_2, A_3) = A_1 \cup (A_2 \cap A_3)$$

Let $P(A_1)$, $P(A_2)$, $P(A_3)$ be the propositions that characterise A_1, A_2, A_3.

Then

$S_1(A_1, A_2, A_3) =$

$\{x$: satisfies "$S_1(P(A_1), P(A_2), P(A_3))$"$\}$

where $S_1(P(A_1), P(A_2), P(A_3))$ has precisely the same form as $S_1(A_1, A_2, A_3)$ except that $P(A_i)$ is substituted for A_i, and $(\wedge, \vee)$ are substituted for $(\cap, \cup)$.

In the example

$$S_1(P(A_1), P(A_2), P(A_3)) = P(A_1) \vee (P(A_2) \wedge P(A_3)).$$

Since $\mathcal{P}$ is a Boolean algebra, we know that

$$P(A_1) \vee (P(A_2) \wedge P(A_3)) =$$
$$(P(A_1) \vee P(A_2)) \wedge (P(A_1) \vee P(A_3))$$
$$= S_2 \ (P(A_1), P(A_2), P(A_3)), \text{ say.}$$

Thus $S_1(P(A_1), P(A_2), P(A_3))$ is identical to the second sentence $S_2(P(A_1), P(A_2), P(A_3))$ and so

$$S_1(A_1, A_2, A_3)$$
$$= \{x: \ x \text{ satisfies } P((A_1) \vee P(A_2)) \wedge (P(A_1) \vee P(A_3))\}$$
$$= (A_1 \cup A_2) \cap (A_1 \cup A_3)$$
$$= S_2(A_1, A_2, A_3).$$

Consequently if $\mathcal{T} = (U, \Phi, A_1, A_2 \ldots)$ is a set theory, then by exactly this procedure $\mathcal{T}$ can be shown to be a Boolean algebra.

Suppose now that $\mathcal{T}$ is a set theory with universal set U, and X is a subset of U. Let $\mathcal{T}_X = (X, \Phi, A_1 \cap X, A_2 \cap X, \ldots)$. Since $\mathcal{T}$ is a set theory on U, $\mathcal{T}_X$ must be a set theory on X.

To see this consider the following:

i) Since $A \in \mathcal{T}$, so must $\bar{A} \in \mathcal{T}$. Now let $A_X = X \cap A$. To define the complement or negation (let us call it $\bar{A}_X$) of A in $\mathcal{T}_X$ we have $\bar{A}_X =$ $\{x{:}x \text{ is in } X \text{ but not in } A\} = X \cap \bar{A}$. This is also often written $X - A$, or $X \setminus A$.
But this must be the same as the complement of $A \cap X$ in X, i.e.

$$\begin{aligned} (\overline{A \cap X}) \cap X &= (\bar{A} \cup \bar{X}) \cap X \\ &= (\bar{A} \cap X) \cup (\bar{X} \cap X) \\ &= X \cap \bar{A}. \end{aligned}$$

ii) If $A, B \in \mathcal{T}$ then $(A \cap B) \cap X = (A \cap X) \cap (B \cap X)$. (The reader should examine the behaviour of union).

A notion that is very close to that of a set theory is that of a topology.

Say that a family $\mathcal{T} = (U, \Phi, A_1, A_2, \ldots)$ is a topology on U iff

T1: If $A_1, A_2 \in \mathcal{T}$ then $A_1 \cap A_2 \in \mathcal{T}$

T2: If $A_j \in \mathcal{T}$ for all j belonging to some index set J (possibly infinite) then

$$\bigcup_{j \in J} A_j \in \mathcal{T}$$

T3: Both U and Φ belong to $\mathcal{T}$.

Axioms T1 and T2 may be interpreted as saying that $\mathcal{T}$ is closed under finite intersection and (infinite) union.

Let X be any subset of U. Then the relative topology $\mathcal{T}_X$ induced from the topology $\mathcal{T}$ on U is defined by

$$\mathcal{T}_X = (X, \Phi, A_1 \cap X, \ldots)$$

where any set of the form $A \cap X$, for $A \in \mathcal{T}$, belongs to $\mathcal{T}_X$.

Example 1.2 We can show that $\mathcal{T}_X$ is a topology. If $U_1, U_2 \in \mathcal{T}_X$ then there must exist sets $A_1, A_2 \in \mathcal{T}$ such that $U_i = A_i \cap X$, for $i = 1, 2$.

But then $U_1 \cap U_2 = (A_1 \cap X) \cap (A_2 \cap X)$
$= (A_1 \cap A_2) \cap X.$

Since $\mathcal{T}$ is a topology, $A_1 \cap A_2 \in \mathcal{T}$.

Thus $U_1 \cap U_2 \in \mathcal{T}_X$. Union follows similarly.

1.1.3. Partitions and Covers

If X is a set, a cover for X is a family $\mathcal{T} = (A_1, A_2, \ldots, A_j \ldots)$ where j belongs to an index set J (possibly infinite) such that

$$X = \cup \{A_j : j \in J\}.$$

A <u>partition</u> for X is a cover which is <u>disjoint</u>, i.e. $A_j \cap A_k = \Phi$ for any distinct j, k $\in$ J.

If T_X is a cover for X, and Y is a subset of X then $T_Y = \{A_j \cap Y: j \in J\}$ is the induced cover on Y.

1.1.4. The Universal and Existential Quantifiers

Two operators which may be used to construct propositions are the universal and existential quantifiers.

For example, "<u>for all</u> x in A it is the case that x satisfies P(A)". The term "for all" is the universal quantifier, and generally written as $\forall$.

On the other hand we may say "there exists some x in A such that x satisfies P(A)". The term "there exists" is the existential quantifier, generally written $\exists$.

Note that these have negations as follows:

not [$\exists$x s.t. x satisfies P] $\equiv$ [$\forall$x: x does not satisfy P]

$\therefore$ not[$\forall$x: x satisfies P] $\equiv$ [$\exists$x s.t. x does not satisfy P]

Here s.t. means "such that".

1.2. RELATIONS, FUNCTIONS AND OPERATIONS

1.2.1. Relations

If X, Y are two sets, the <u>cartesian product set</u> X x Y is the set of <u>ordered pairs</u> (x,y) such that x $\in$ X and y $\in$ Y.

For example if we let $\mathbb{R}$ be the set of real

numbers, then $\mathbb{R} \times \mathbb{R}$ or $\mathbb{R}^2$ is the set

$\{(x,y): x \in \mathbb{R}, y \in \mathbb{R}\}$, namely the plane. Similarly $\mathbb{R}^n = \mathbb{R} \times \ldots \times \mathbb{R}$ (n times) is the set of n-tuples of real numbers, defined by induction i.e. $\mathbb{R}^n = \mathbb{R} \times (\mathbb{R} \times (\mathbb{R} \times \ldots\ldots))$.

A subset of the cartesian product $Y \times X$ is called a <u>relation</u>, P, on YxX. If $(y,x) \in P$ then we sometimes write $y\,P\,x$ and say that y stands in relation P to x. If it is not the case that $(y,x) \in P$ then write $(y, x) \notin P$ or not $(y\,P\,x)$. X is called the <u>set of definition</u> of P and Y is called the target or <u>codomain</u> of P.

If V is a relation on YxX and W is a relation on ZxY then define the relation WoV to be the relation on ZxX given by

$$(z,x) \in W \circ V \text{ iff for some } y \in Y, \quad (z,y) \in W \text{ and } (y,x) \in V.$$

The new relation WoV on ZxX is called the composition of W and V.

The identity relation (or diagonal) e_X on XxX is

$$e_X = \{(x,x): x \in X\}.$$

If P is a relation on YxX, its inverse, P^{-1}, is the relation on XxY defined by

$$P^{-1} = \{(x,y) \in X \times Y: (y,x) \in P\}.$$

Note that:

$$P^{-1} \circ P = \{(z,x) \in X \times X: \exists\, y \in Y \text{ s.t. } (z,y) \in P^{-1} \text{ and } (y,x) \in P\}.$$

Suppose that the <u>domain</u> of P is X, i.e. that for every $x \in X$ there is some $y \in Y$ s.t. $(y,x) \in P$. In this case for every $x \in X$, there exists $y \in Y$ such that $(x,y) \in P^{-1}$ and so $(x,x) \in P^{-1} \circ P$ for any $x \in X$.

Hence $e_X \subset P^{-1} \circ P$.

In the same way

$$P \circ P^{-1} = \{(t, y) \in YxY: \exists x \in X \text{ s.t. } (t, x) \in P \text{ and } (x, y) \in P^{-1}\}$$

and so $e_Y \subset P \circ P^{-1}$.

1.2.2. Mappings

A relation P on YxX defines an assignment <u>or mapping</u> from X to Y, which we call $\emptyset_P$ given by

$$\emptyset_P(x) = \{y: (y,x) \in P\}.$$

In general we write $\emptyset: X \to Y$ for a mapping which assigns to each element of X the <u>set</u>, $\emptyset(x)$, of elements in Y.

The <u>domain</u> of a mapping, $\emptyset$, is the set $\{x \in X: \exists\, y \in Y \text{ s.t. } y \in \emptyset(x)\}$, and the <u>image</u> of $\emptyset$ is

$$\{y \in Y: \exists\, x \in X \text{ s.t. } y \in \emptyset(x)\}.$$

Suppose now that V, W are relations on YxX, ZxY respectively. We have defined the composite relation WoV on ZxX. This defines a mapping $\emptyset_{WoV}: X \to Z$ by $z \in \emptyset_{WoV}(x)$ iff $\exists\, y \in Y$ such that $(y,x) \in V$ and $(z,y) \in W$. This in turn means that $y \in \emptyset_V(x)$ and $z \in \emptyset_W(y)$.

If $\emptyset: X \to Y$ and $\psi: Y \to Z$ are two mappings then define their <u>composition</u> $\psi \circ \emptyset: X \to Z$ by

$$(\psi \circ \emptyset)(x) = \psi\left[\emptyset(x)\right] = \cup\{\psi(y): y \in \emptyset(x)\}.$$

Clearly $z \in \emptyset_{WoV}(x)$ iff

$$z \in \emptyset_W\left[\emptyset_V(x)\right]$$

Thus

$$\emptyset_{WoV}(x) = \emptyset_W\left[\emptyset_V(x)\right] = (\emptyset_W \circ \emptyset_V)(x)$$

for any $x \in X$.

We therefore write $\emptyset_{WoV} = \emptyset_W \circ \emptyset_V$.

For example suppose V and W are given by

V: $\{(2,3), (3,2), (1,2), (4,4), (4,1)\}$ and

W: $\{(1,4), (4,4), (4,1), (2,1), (2,3), (3,2)\}$

with mappings

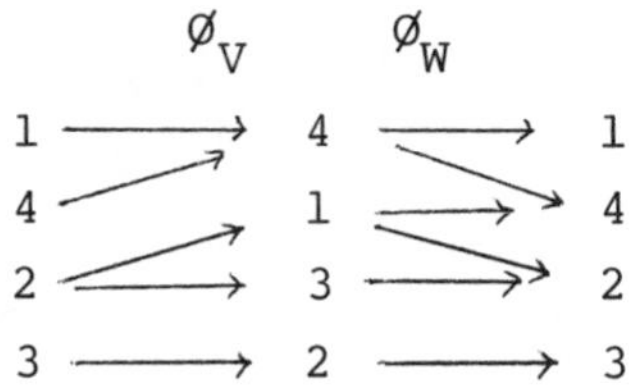

then the composite mapping $\emptyset_W \circ \emptyset_V = \emptyset_{W \circ V}$ is

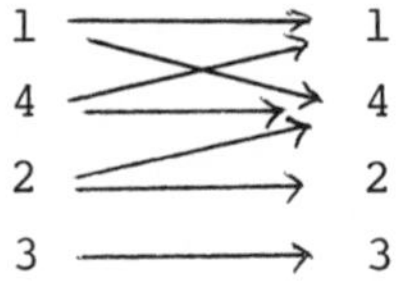

with relation

WoV: $\{(3,3), (2,2), (4,2), (1,4), (4,4), (1,1),$
$(4,1)\}$.

Given a mapping $\emptyset$: $X \to Y$ then the reverse procedure to the above gives a relation, called the graph of $\emptyset$, or graph ($\emptyset$), where

$$\text{graph }(\emptyset) = \bigcup_{x \in X} (\emptyset(x) \times \{x\}) \subset Y \times X.$$

In the obvious way if $\emptyset$: $X \to Y$ and ψ: $Y \to Z$ are mappings, with composition $\psi \circ \emptyset$: $X \to Z$, then graph $(\psi \circ \emptyset)$ = graph (ψ) o graph $(\emptyset)$.

Suppose now that P is a relation on YxX, with inverse P^{-1} on XxY, and let $\emptyset_P$: $X \to Y$ be the mapping defined by P. Then the mapping $\emptyset_{P^{-1}}$: $Y \to X$ is defined as follows:

$$\begin{aligned} \emptyset_{P^{-1}}(y) &= \{x: (x,y) \in P^{-1}\} \\ &= \{x: (y,x) \in P\} \\ &= \{x: y \in \emptyset_P(x)\}\ . \end{aligned}$$

More generally if $\emptyset$: $X \to Y$ is a mapping then the inverse mapping $\emptyset^{-1}$: $Y \to X$ is given by

$$\phi^{-1}(y) = \{x: \ y \in \phi(x)\} .$$

Thus

$$\phi_{P^{-1}} = (\phi_P)^{-1}: \ Y \to X.$$

For example let Z_4 be the first four positive integers and let P be the relation on $Z_4 \times Z_4$ given by

$$P = \{(2,3), (3,2), (1,2), (4,4), (4,1)\}.$$

Then the mapping ϕ_P and inverse $\phi_{P^{-1}}$ are given by:

ϕ_P: 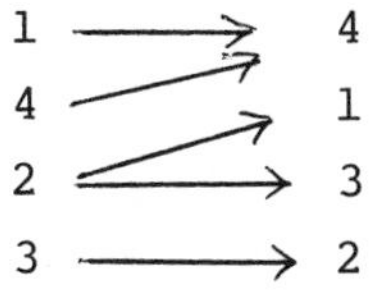

$\phi_P{}^{-1}$: 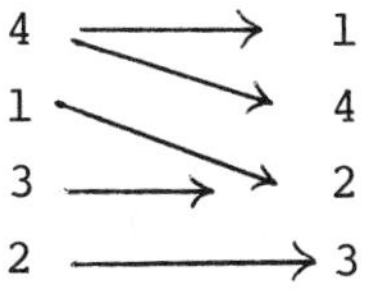

If we compose P^{-1} and P as above then we obtain

$$P^{-1} \circ P = \{(1,1), (1,4), (4,1), (4,4), (2,2), (3,3)\},$$

with mapping

$\phi_{P^{-1}} \circ \phi_P$

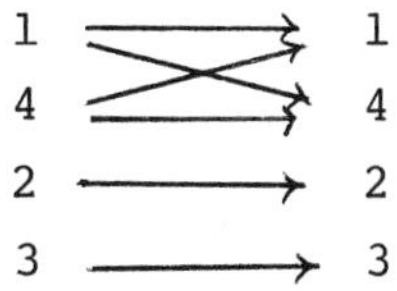

Note that $P^{-1} \circ P$ contains the identity or diagonal relation $e = \{(1,1), (2,2), (3,3), (4,4)\}$ on $Z_4 = \{1, 2, 3, 4\}$. Moreover $\phi_{P^{-1}} \circ \phi_P = \phi_{(P^{-1} \circ P)}$.

The mapping id_X: $X \to X$ defined by $id_X(x) = x$ is called the <u>identity</u> mapping on X. Clearly if e_X is the identity relation, then $\phi_{e_X} = id_X$ and graph $(id_X) = e_X$.

If ϕ, ψ are two mappings $X \to Y$ then write $\psi \subset \phi$ iff for each $x \in X$, $\psi(x) \subset \phi(x)$.

As we have seen $e_X \subset P^{-1} \circ P$

and so $\phi_{e_X} = id_X \subset \phi_{(P^{-1} \circ P)} = \phi_{P^{-1}} \circ \phi_P$

$$= (\phi_P)^{-1} \circ \phi_P.$$

This is only precisely true when X is the domain of P, ie when for every $x \in X$ there exists some $y \in Y$ such that $(y,x) \in P$.

1.2.3 Functions

If for all x in the domain of ϕ, there is exactly one y such that $y \in \phi(x)$ then ϕ is called a <u>function</u>. In this case we generally write $f:X \rightarrow Y$, and sometimes $x \mapsto y$ to indicate that $f(x) = y$. Consider the function f and its inverse f^{-1} given by

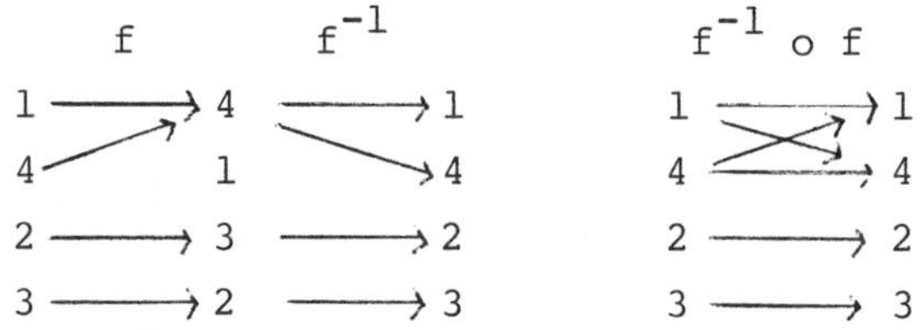

Clearly f^{-1} is not a function since it maps 4 to both 1 and 4 ie the graph of f^{-1} is $\{(1,4),(4,4),(2,3),(3,2)\}$.

In this case id_X is contained in $f^{-1} \circ f$ but is not identical to $f^{-1} \circ f$. Suppose that f^{-1} is in fact a function. Then it is necessary that for each y in the image there be at most one x such that $f(x)=y$. Alternatively if $f(x_1) = f(x_2)$ then it must be the case that $x_1 = x_2$. In this case f is called 1-1 or <u>injective</u>. Then f^{-1} is a function and

$id_X = f^{-1} \circ f$ on the domain X of f

$id_Y = f \circ f^{-1}$ on the image Y of f.

A mapping $\phi:X \rightarrow Y$ is said to be <u>surjective</u> (or called a surjection) iff every $y \in Y$ belongs to the image of ϕ.

A function $f:X \rightarrow Y$ which is both injective and surjective is said to be <u>bijective</u>.

Example 1.3

$$\begin{array}{lccccc} & & \Pi & & \Pi^{-1} & \\ \text{Consider} & 1 & \longrightarrow & 4 & \longrightarrow & 1 \\ & 4 & \longrightarrow & 2 & \longrightarrow & 4 \\ & 2 & \longrightarrow & 3 & \longrightarrow & 2 \\ & 3 & \longrightarrow & 1 & \longrightarrow & 3. \end{array}$$

In this case the domain and image of Π coincide and Π is known as a permutation.

Consider the possibilities where ϕ is a mapping $\mathbb{R} \to \mathbb{R}$, with graph $(\phi) \subset \mathbb{R}^2$. There are three cases:

i) ϕ is a mapping

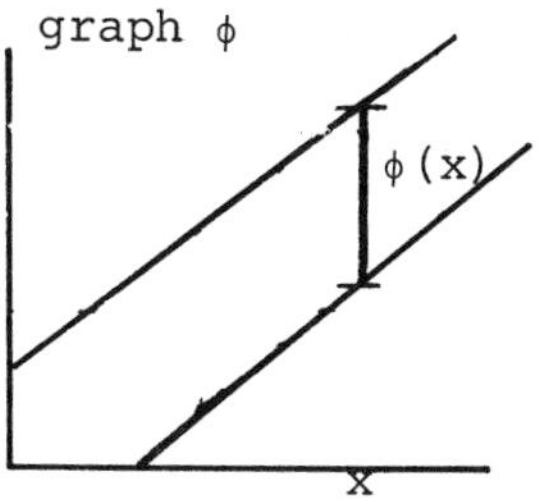

ii) ϕ is a non injective function

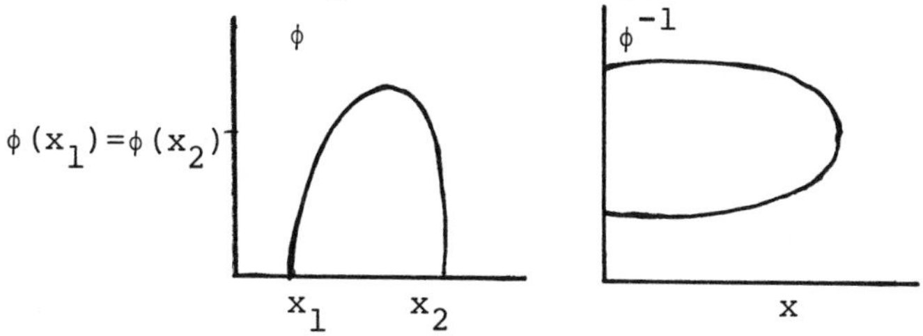

iii) ϕ is an injective function

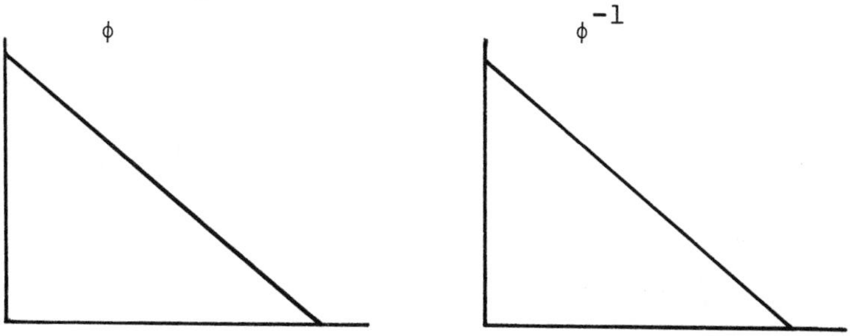

1.3 PREFERENCES

1.3.1. Preference Relations

A binary relation P is a subset of XxX; more simply P is called a relation on X.
For example let X ≡ ℝ (the real line) and let P be ">" meaning strictly greater than. The relation ">" clearly satisfies the following properties:

i) it is never the case that x > x.

ii) it is never the case that x > y and y > x

iii) it is always the case that x > y and y > z implies x > z.

These properties can be considered more abstractly.
A relation P on X is:

i) symmetric iff xPy =>yPx
asymmetric iff xPy =>not (yPx)
antisymmetric iff xPy and yPx =>x = y

ii) reflexive iff (xPx) for ∀x∈X
irreflexive iff not (xPx) ∀x∈X

iii) transitive iff xPy and yPz =>xPz

iv) connected iff for any x,y∈X either xPy or yPx.

By analogy to the relation ">" a relation P which is both irreflexive and asymmetric is called a strict preference relation.
Given a strict preference relation P on X, we can define two new relations called I, for indifference, and R for weak preference as follows.

i) xIy iff not (xPy) and not (yPx)

ii) xRy iff xPy or xIy.

By de Morgans rule xIy iff not (xPy V yPx).
Thus for any x,y∈X either xIy or xPy or yPx.
Since P is asymmetric it cannot be the case that

both xPy,yPx are true. Thus the propositions "xPy", "yPx","xIy" are disjoint, and hence form a partition of the universal proposition, U.

Fig. 1.3 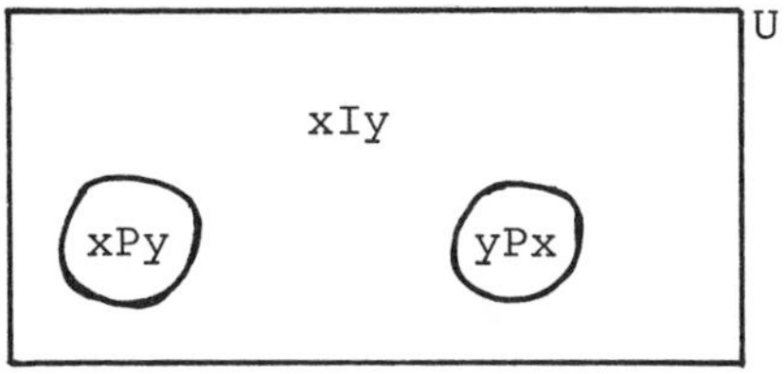

Note that (xPy V xIy) ≡ not (yPx) since these three propositions form a (disjoint) partition.
Thus xRy iff not (yPx).
In the case that P is the strict preference relation ">", it should be clear that indifference is identical to "=" and weak preference to "> or =" usually written "$\geq$".

Lemma 1.1

If P is a strict preference relation then indifference (I) is reflexive and symmetric, while weak preference (R) is reflexive and connected. Moreover if xRy and yRx then xIy.

Proof

i) Since not (xPx) this must imply xIx, so I is reflexive

ii) xIy <=> not (xPy) $\wedge$ not (yPx)
<=> not (yPx) $\wedge$ not (xPy)
<=> yIx.
Hence I is symmetric.

iii) xRy <=> xPy or xIy
Thus xIx =>xRx, so R is reflexive.

iv) xRy <=> xPy or xIy
and yRx <=> yPx or yIx.

Not (xRy V yRx) <=> not (xPy V yPx V xIy)
But xPy V yPx V xIy is always true, since these three propositions form a partition of the universal set. Thus not (xRy V yRx) is always false, and so xRy V yRx is always true. Thus R is connected.

v) Clearly xRy and yRx

$\iff$ (xPy $\wedge$ yPx) V xIy

$\iff$ xIy

since xPy $\wedge$ yPx is always false by asymmetry .

In the case that P corresponds to ">" then $x \geq y$ and $y \geq x \Rightarrow x = y$ so "$\geq$" is antisymmetric.

Suppose that P is a strict preference relation on X, and there exists a function $u: X \to \mathbb{R}$, called a <u>utility function</u>, such that xPy iff $u(x) > u(y)$.

Therefore xRy iff $u(x) \geq u(y)$

xIy iff $u(x) = u(y)$.

The order relation ">" on the real line is transitive (since $x>y>z \Rightarrow x>z$). Therefore P must be transitive when it is representable by a utility function.

We therefore have reason to consider "rationality" properties, such as transitivity, of a strict preference relation.

1.3.2. Rationality

<u>Lemma 1.2</u>

If P is irreflexive and transitive on X then it is asymmetric.

<u>Proof</u> To show that $A \wedge B \Rightarrow C$ we need only show that $B \wedge$ not $(C) \Rightarrow$ not (A)

Therefore suppose that P is transitive but fails asymmetry.
By the latter assumption there exists $x, y \in X$ such that xPy and yPx.
By transitivity this gives xPx, which violates irreflexivity.

Call a strict preference relation, P, on X <u>negatively transitive</u> iff it is the case that, for all $x, y, z \in X$,
not (xPy) $\wedge$ not (yPz) $\Rightarrow$ not (xPz).
Note that xRy $\Leftrightarrow$ not (yPx). Thus the negative transitivity of P is equivalent to the property

$$yRx \wedge zRy \Rightarrow zRx.$$

Hence R must be <u>transitive</u>.

<u>Lemma 1.3</u>

If P is a strict preference relation that is negatively transitive then P,I,R are all transitive.

<u>Proof</u> i) By the above R is transitive.

ii) To prove P is transitive, suppose otherwise, ie that there exist x,y,z such that xPy, yPz but not(xPz).
By definition not (xPz) $\Leftrightarrow$ zRx.
Moreover yPz or yIz $\Leftrightarrow$ yRz.
Thus yPz $\Rightarrow$ yRz.
By transitivity of R,
zRx and yRz gives yRx, or not (xPy).
But we assumed xPy. By contradiction we must have xPz.

iii) To show I is transitive, suppose xIy, yIz but not(xIz).
In particular choose xPz, say.
But then xRz.
Because of the two indifferences we may

write zRy and yRx. But this violates transitivity of R.

In the same way if we choose zPx, and thus zRx, we may also write yRz and xRy, which again violates transitivity of R.

Hence xIz, and so I is transitive.

When P is a negatively transitive strict preference relation on X, then we call it a weak order on X. Let O(X) be the set of weak orders on X. If P is a transitive strict preference relation on X, then we call it a strict partial order. Let T(X) be the set of strict partial orders on X.

By lemma 1.3, $O(X) \subset T(X)$.

Finally call a preference relation acyclic if it is the case that for any finite sequence $x_1, \ldots, x_r$ of points in X if $x_j P x_{j+1}$ for $j = 1, \ldots, r - 1$ then it cannot be the case that $x_r P x_1$.

Let A(X) be the set of acyclic strict preference relations on X. To see that $T(X) \subset A(X)$, suppose that P is transitive, but cyclic, ie that there exists a finite cycle $x_1 P x_2 \ldots P x_r P x_1$.

By transitivity $x_{r-1} P x_r P x_1$ gives $x_{r-1} P x_1$, and by repetition we obtain $x_2 P x_1$. But we also have $x_1 P x_2$, which violates asymmetry.

1.3.3. Choices

If P is a strict preference relation on a set X, then a maximal element, or choice, on X is an element such that for no $y \in X$ is it the case that yPx. We can express this another way. Since $P \subset X \times X$, there is a mapping

$$\phi_P : X \to X \text{ where } \phi_P(x) = \{y: yPx\}.$$

We shall call ϕ_P the <u>preference</u> <u>correspondence</u> of P. The <u>choice</u> of P on X is the set $C_P(X) = \{x:\phi_P(X)=\Phi\}$. Suppose now that P is a strict preference relation on X. For each subset Y of X, let

$$C_P(Y) = \{x\in Y:\phi_P(X) \cap Y = \Phi\}.$$

This defines a <u>choice</u> <u>correspondence</u> $C_P:2^X \rightarrow 2^X$ from 2^X, the set of all subsets of X, into itself.

An important question in social choice and welfare economics concerns the existence of a "social" choice correspondence, C_P, which guarantees the non-emptiness of the social choice $C_P(Y)$ for each <u>feasible</u> <u>set</u>, Y, in X, and an appropriate social preference, P.

<u>Lemma 1.4</u>

If P is an acyclic strict preference relation on a finite set X, then $C_P(Y)$ is non-empty for each subset Y of X.

<u>Proof</u> Suppose that $X = \{x_1,\ldots,x_r\}$. If all elements in X are indifferent then clearly $C_P(X) = X$.

So suppose that x_2Px_1 for some pair x_2,x_1. Now either $x_2 \in C_P(X)$, or there exists a third element x_3 say such that x_3Px_2. If x_1Px_3 then we have a cycle, and so not(x_1Px_3). Hence x_3 belongs to $C_P(\{x_1,x_2,x_3\})$. By induction for each subset Y of X, there exists some element $x\in Y$ such that $x\in C_P(Y)$.

If P is a strict preference relation on X that is representable by a utility function $u:X \rightarrow Y$ then it must be the case that all of P,I,R are transitive. To see this, we note the following:

i) xRy and yRz iff $u(x) \geq u(y) \geq u(z)$

Since "$\geq$" on $\mathbb{R}$ is transitive it follows that $u(x) \geq u(z)$ and so xRz.

ii) xIy and yIz iff $u(x) = u(y) = u(z)$, and thus xIz.

In this case indifference, I, is reflexive, symmetric and transitive. Such a relation on X is called an <u>equivalence relation</u>.

For any point x in X, let [x] be the equivalence class of x in X, ie $[x] = \{y: yIx\}$.

Every point in X belongs to exactly <u>one</u> equivalence class.

To see thus suppose that $x \in [y]$ and $x \in [z]$, then xIy and xIz. By symmetry zIx, and by transitivity zIy. Thus $[y] = [z]$.

The set of equivalence classes in X under an equivalence relation, I, is written $X/_I$.

Clearly if $u: X \to \mathbb{R}$ is a utility function then an equivalence class [x] is of the form

$$[x] = \{y \in X: u(x) = u(y)\}.$$

which we may also write as $u^{-1}[u(x)]$.

If X is a finite set, and P is representable by a utility function then

$$C_P(X) = \{x \in X: u(x) = m\}$$

where m is max $[u(y): y \in X]$, the maximum value of u on X.

Social choice theory is concerned with the existence of a <u>choice</u> under a social preference relation P which in some sense aggregates individual choice.

Typically the social preference relation cannot be representable by a "social" utility function.

For example suppose a society consists of n individuals, each one of whom has a preference relation P_i on the feasible set X.

Define a social preference relation P on X by xPy

iff xP_iy for all $i \in N$ (P is called the <u>strict Pareto rule</u>).
It is clear that if each P_i is transitive, then so must be P. As a result, P must be acyclic. If X is a finite set, then by Lemma 1.4, there exists a choice $C_P(X)$ on X.
The same conclusion follows if we define xQy iff xR_jy $\forall j \in N$, and xP_iy for some $i \in N$.
If we assume that each individual has negatively transitive preferences, then Q will be transitive, and will again have a <u>choice</u>. Q is called the <u>weak Pareto rule</u>. Note that a point x belongs to $C_Q(X)$ iff it is impossible to move to another point y which makes nobody "worse off", but makes some members of the society "better off".
The set $C_Q(X)$ is called the <u>Pareto set</u>.
Although the social preference relation Q has a choice, there is no social utility function which represents Q. To see this suppose the society consists of two individuals 1,2 with transitive preferences xP_1yP_1z and zP_2xP_2y.
By the definition xQy, since both individuals prefer x to y. However conflict of preference between y and z, and between x and z gives yIz and xIz, where I is the social indifference rule associated with Q. Consequently I is not transitive and there is no "social utility function" which represents Q. Moreover the elements of X cannot be partitioned into disjoint indifference equivalence classes.

To see the same phenomenon geometrically define a preference relation P on $\mathbb{R}^2$ by

$$(x_1,x_2)\ P\ (y_1,y_2)$$

iff $x_1 > y_1$ and $x_2 > y_2$.

Fig.1.4.

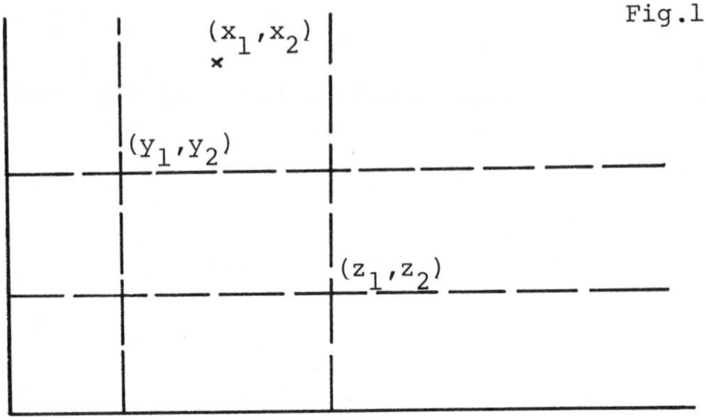

From Figure 1.4 (x_1,x_2) P (y_1,y_2). However (x_1,x_2) I (z_1,z_2) and (y_1,y_2) I (z_1,z_2). Again there is no social utility function representing the preference relation Q. Intuitively it should be clear that when the feasible set is "bounded" in some way in $\mathbb{R}^2$ then the preference relation Q has a choice. We shall show this more generally in a later chapter. (See lemma 3.9).

To provide some further intuition, suppose that X is the unit interval [0,1] in $\mathbb{R}$, and consider the preference relation P with the preference mapping ϕ_P: X → X (note that P is not asymmetric).

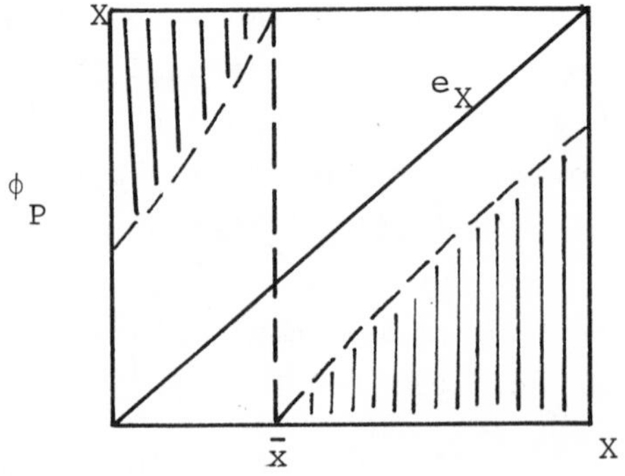

Fig.1.5.

When P is irreflexive the diagonal $e_X = \{(x,x): x \in X\}$ cannot belong to P. From the way Figure 1.5 is drawn it should be clear that $\bar{x}$ is the choice.

1.4 GROUPS AND MORPHISMS

We earlier defined the composition of two mappings ϕ: X —> Y and ψ: Y —> Z to be $\psi o \phi$: X —> Z given by $(\psi o \phi)(x) = \psi[\phi(x)] = \cup\{\psi(y): y \in \phi(x)\}$. In the case of functions f: X → Y and g: Y → Z this translates to

$$(g \circ f)(x) = g[f(x)] = \{g(y): y = f(x)\}.$$

Since both f,g are functions the set on the right is a singleton set, and so g o f is a function. Write F(A,B) for the set of functions from A to B. Thus the composition operator, o, may be regarded as a function

$$\begin{aligned} o: F(X,Y) \times F(Y,Z) &\to F(X,Z) \\ (f,g) &\mapsto g \circ f. \end{aligned}$$

<u>Example 1.4</u>

To illustrate consider the function (or matrix) F given by

$$\begin{pmatrix} a & b \\ c & d \end{pmatrix} \begin{pmatrix} x_1 \\ x_2 \end{pmatrix} = \begin{pmatrix} ax_1 + bx_2 \\ cx_1 + dx_2 \end{pmatrix}$$

This can be regarded as a function $F: \mathbb{R}^2 \to \mathbb{R}^2$ since it maps $(x_1,x_2) \mapsto (ax_1 + bx_2, cx_1 + dx_2) \in \mathbb{R}^2$.

Now let $F = \begin{pmatrix} a & b \\ c & d \end{pmatrix}$, $H = \begin{pmatrix} e & f \\ g & h \end{pmatrix}$.

H o F is represented by

$$\begin{pmatrix} x_1 \\ x_2 \end{pmatrix} \overset{F}{\mapsto} \begin{pmatrix} ax_1 + bx_2 \\ cx_1 + dx_2 \end{pmatrix} \overset{H}{\mapsto} \begin{pmatrix} e(ax_1 + bx_2) + f(cx_1 + dx_2) \\ g(ax_1 + bx_2) + h(cx_1 + dx_2) \end{pmatrix} .$$

Thus $(H \circ F) \begin{pmatrix} x_1 \\ x_2 \end{pmatrix} = \left(\begin{array}{c|c} ea + fc & eb + fd \\ \hline ga + hc & gb + hd \end{array}\right) \begin{pmatrix} x_1 \\ x_2 \end{pmatrix}$

or $(H \circ F) = \begin{pmatrix} e & f \\ g & h \end{pmatrix} \circ \begin{pmatrix} a & b \\ c & d \end{pmatrix} = \left(\begin{array}{c|c} ea + fc & eb + fd \\ \hline ga + hc & gb + hd \end{array}\right) .$

The <u>identity</u> E is the function

$$E \begin{pmatrix} x_1 \\ x_2 \end{pmatrix} = \begin{pmatrix} a & b \\ c & d \end{pmatrix} \begin{pmatrix} x_1 \\ x_2 \end{pmatrix} = \begin{pmatrix} x_1 \\ x_2 \end{pmatrix} .$$

Since this must be true for all x_1, x_2 it follows that $a = d = 1$ and $c = b = 0$.

Thus $E = \begin{pmatrix} 1 & 0 \\ 0 & 1 \end{pmatrix}$.

Suppose that the mapping $F^{-1}: \mathbb{R}^2 \to \mathbb{R}^2$ is actually a matrix. Then it is certainly a function, and by §1.2.3, $F^{-1} \circ F$ must be equal to the identity function on $\mathbb{R}^2$, which here we call E.
To determine F^{-1}, proceed as follows:

Let $F^{-1} = \begin{pmatrix} e & f \\ g & h \end{pmatrix}$. We know $F^{-1} \circ F = \begin{pmatrix} 1 & 0 \\ 0 & 1 \end{pmatrix}$.

Thus
$$\begin{array}{l|l} ea + fc = 1 & eb + fd = 0 \\ ga + hc = 0 & gb + hd = 1 . \end{array}$$

If $a \neq 0$ and $b \neq 0$ then $e = -\frac{fd}{b} = \frac{1-fc}{a}$.

Now let $|F| = (ad-bc)$, where $|F|$ is called the <u>determinant</u> of F. Clearly if $|F| \neq 0$, then $f = -b/|F|$. More generally, if $|F| \neq 0$ then we can solve the equations to obtain:

$$F^{-1} = \begin{pmatrix} e & f \\ g & h \end{pmatrix} = \frac{1}{|F|} \begin{pmatrix} d & -b \\ -c & a \end{pmatrix} .$$

If $|F| = 0$, then what we have called F^{-1} is not defined. This suggests that when $|F| = 0$, the inverse F^{-1} cannot be represented by a matrix, and in particular that F^{-1} is not a function. In this case we shall call F <u>singular</u>. When $|F| \neq 0$ then we shall call F <u>non-singular</u>, and in this case F^{-1} can be represented by a matrix, and thus a function. Let M(2) stand for the set of two by two matrices, and let M*(2) be the subset of M(2) consisting of non-singular matrices.

We have here defined a <u>composition operation</u>

$$\circ: M(2) \times M(2) \to M(2)$$
$$(H,F) \to H \circ F .$$

Suppose we compose E with F then

$$E \circ F = \begin{pmatrix} 1 & 0 \\ 0 & 1 \end{pmatrix} \begin{pmatrix} a & b \\ c & d \end{pmatrix} = \begin{pmatrix} a & b \\ c & d \end{pmatrix} = F.$$

Finally for any $F \in M^*(2)$ it is the case that there exists a <u>unique</u> matrix $F^{-1} \in M(2)$ such that

$$F^{-1} \circ F = E.$$

Indeed if we compute the inverse $(F^{-1})^{-1}$ of F^{-1} then we see that $(F^{-1})^{-1} = F$. Thus F^{-1} itself belongs to M*(2).

M*(2) is an example of what is called a <u>group</u>.

More generally a binary operation, o, on a set G is a function

$$o: G \times G \to G$$
$$(x,y) \mapsto x \circ y \ .$$

Definition 1.1 A group G is a set G together with a binary operation, $o: G \times G \to G$ which

i) is associative: $(x \circ y) \circ z = x \circ (y \circ z)$ for all x,y,z in G;

ii) has an identity $e : e \circ x = x \circ e = x \ \forall \ x \in G$;

iii) has for each $x \in G$ an inverse $x^{-1} \in G$ such that $x \circ x^{-1} = x^{-1} \circ x = e$.

When G is a group with operation, o, write (G,o) to signify this.

Associativity simply means that the order of composition in a sequence of compositions is irrelevant. For example consider the integers, Z, under addition. Clearly $a+(b+c) = (a+b)+c$, where the left hand side means add b to c, and then add a to this, while the right hand side is obtained by adding a to b, and then adding c to this. Under addition, the identity is that element $e \in Z$ such that $a+e = a$. This is usually written 0. Finally the additive inverse of an integer $a \in Z$ is (-a) since $a+(-a) = 0$. Thus (Z,+) is a group.

However consider the integers under multiplication, which we shall write as ".". Again we have associativity since

$$a.(b.c) = (a.b).c.$$

Clearly 1 is the identity since $1.a = a$. However the inverse of a is that object a^{-1} such that $a.a^{-1} = 1$. Of course if a=0, then no such inverse exists. a^{-1} is more commonly written $^1/_a$.

When a is non-zero, and different from ± 1, then $1/a$ is not an integer. Thus $(Z,.)$ is not a group. Consider the set Q of rationals, ie $a \in Q$ iff $a = p/q$ where both p,q are integers. Clearly $1 \in Q$. Moreover if $a = p/q$ then $a^{-1} = q/p$ and so belongs to Q. Although zero does not have an inverse, we can regard $(Q \setminus \{0\},.)$ as a group.

<u>Lemma 1.5</u> If (G,o) is a group, then the identity e is unique and for each $x \in G$ the inverse x^{-1} is unique. By definition $e^{-1} = e$. Also $(x^{-1})^{-1} = x$ for any $x \in G$.

<u>Proof</u> i) Suppose there exists two distinct identities, e, f. The $e \text{ o } x = f \text{ o } x$ for some x.

Thus $(e \text{ o } x) \text{ o } x^{-1} = (f \text{ o } x) \text{o } x^{-1}$.

This is true because the composition operation

$((e \text{ o } x), x^{-1}) \rightarrow (e \text{ o } x) \text{o} x^{-1}$

gives a unique answer.

By associativitiy $(e \text{ o } x) \text{o} x^{-1} = e \text{o} (x \text{ o } x^{-1})$ etc.

Thus $e \text{o} (x \text{ o } x^{-1}) = f \text{o} (x \text{ o } x^{-1})$.

But $x \text{ o } x^{-1} = e$, say.

Since e is an identity, $e \text{ o } e = f \text{ o } e$ and so $e = f$.

Since $e \text{ o } e = e$ it must be the case that $e^{-1} = e$.

ii) In the same way suppose x has two distinct inverses, y, z, so $x \text{ o } y = x \text{ o } z = e$.

$$\begin{aligned} \text{Then } y \text{ o } (x \text{ o } y) &= y \text{ o} (x \text{ o } z) \\ (y \text{ o } x) \text{ o} y &= (y \text{ o } x) \text{ o} z \\ e \text{ o } y &= e \text{ o } z \\ y &= z. \end{aligned}$$

iii) Finally consider the inverse of x^{-1}.
Since $x \circ (x^{-1}) = e$ and by definition $(x^{-1})^{-1} \circ (x^{-1}) = e$ by part (ii), it must be the case that $(x^{-1})^{-1} = x$.

We can now construct some interesting groups.

Lemma 1.6 The set M*(2) of 2 x 2 non-singular matrices form a group under matrix composition, o.

Proof We have already shown that there exists an identity matrix E in M*(2). Clearly $|E| = 1$ and so E has an inverse E.

As we saw in example 1.1, when we solved $H \circ F = E$ we found that $H = F^{-1} = \frac{1}{|F|}\begin{pmatrix} d & -b \\ -c & a \end{pmatrix}$.

By lemma 1.5, $(F^{-1})^{-1} = F$ and so F^{-1} must have an inverse, ie $|F^{-1}| \neq 0$, and so F^{-1} is non-singular.

Suppose now that the two matrices H,F belong to M*(2).

Let $F = \begin{pmatrix} a & b \\ c & d \end{pmatrix}$ and $H = \begin{pmatrix} e & f \\ g & h \end{pmatrix}$.

As in Example 1.1,

$$|H \circ F| = \left|\begin{pmatrix} ea + fc & eb + fd \\ ga + hc & gb + hd \end{pmatrix}\right|$$

$$= (ea + fc)(gb + hd) - (ga + hc)(eb + fd)$$

$$= (eh - gf)(ad - bc)$$

$$= |H|\,|F|.$$

Since both H and F are non-singular, $|H| \neq 0$ and $|F| \neq 0$ and so $|H \circ F| \neq 0$. Thus $H \circ F$ belongs to M*(2), and so matrix composition is a binary operation $M^*(2) \times M^*(2) \to M^*(2)$.

Finally the reader may like to verify that matrix composition on M*(2) is associative. That is to say if F,G,H are non-singular 2x2 matrices then

$$H \circ (G \circ F) = (H \circ G) \circ F.$$

As a consequence (M*(2),o) is a group.

Example 1.5

For a second example consider the addition operation on M(2) defined by

$$\begin{pmatrix} e & f \\ g & h \end{pmatrix} + \begin{pmatrix} a & b \\ c & d \end{pmatrix} = \begin{pmatrix} a+e & f+b \\ g+c & h+d \end{pmatrix}$$

Clearly the identity matrix is $\begin{pmatrix} 0 & 0 \\ 0 & 0 \end{pmatrix}$ and the inverse of F is $-F = -\begin{pmatrix} a & b \\ c & d \end{pmatrix} = \begin{pmatrix} -a & -b \\ -c & -d \end{pmatrix}$.

Thus (M(2),+) is a group.

Finally consider those matrices which represent rotations in $\mathbb{R}^2$.

If we rotate the point (1,0) in the plane through an angle θ in the anticlockwise direction then the result is the point $(\cos\theta, \sin\theta)$, while the point (0,1) is transformed to $(-\sin\theta, \cos\theta)$. As we shall see later this rotation can be represented by the matrix

$$\begin{pmatrix} \cos\theta & -\sin\theta \\ \sin\theta & \cos\theta \end{pmatrix}$$ which we will call $e^{i\theta}$.

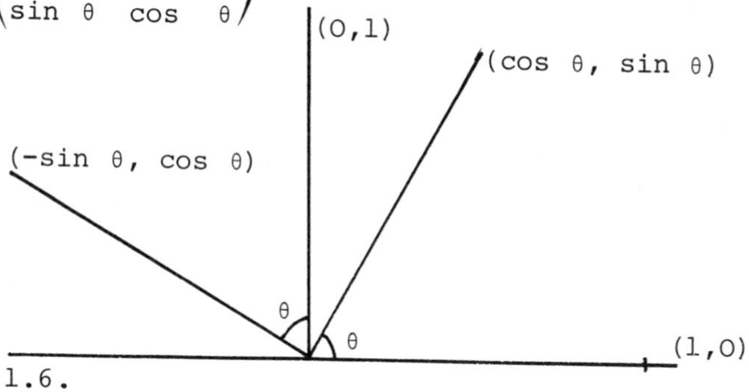

Fig.1.6.

Let Θ be the set of all matrices of this form, where θ can be any angle between 0 and 360°. If

$e^{i\theta}$ and $e^{i\psi}$ are rotations by θ,ψ respectively, and we rotate by θ first and then by ψ, then the result should be identical to a rotation by $\psi+\theta$.

To see this:

$$\begin{pmatrix}\cos\psi & -\sin\psi\\ \sin\psi & \cos\psi\end{pmatrix}\begin{pmatrix}\cos\theta & -\sin\theta\\ \sin\theta & \cos\theta\end{pmatrix}$$

$$= \left(\begin{array}{c|c}\cos\psi\cos\theta-\sin\psi\sin\theta & -\cos\psi\sin\theta - \sin\psi\cos\theta\\ \hline \sin\psi\cos\theta+\cos\psi\sin\theta & -\sin\psi\sin\theta + \cos\psi\cos\theta\end{array}\right)$$

$$= \begin{pmatrix}\cos(\psi+\theta) & -\sin(\psi+\theta)\\ \sin(\psi+\theta) & \cos(\psi+\theta)\end{pmatrix}$$

$$= e^{i(\theta+\psi)}$$

Note that $|e^{i\theta}| = \cos^2\theta + \sin^2\theta = 1.$

Thus $(e^{i\theta})^{-1} = \begin{pmatrix}\cos\theta & \sin\theta\\ -\sin\theta & \cos\theta\end{pmatrix}$

$$= \begin{pmatrix}\cos\theta & -\sin(-\theta)\\ \sin(-\theta) & \cos\theta\end{pmatrix}$$

$$= e^{i(-\theta)}.$$

Hence the inverse to $e^{i\theta}$ is a rotation by $(-\theta)$, that is to say by θ but in the opposite direction. Clearly $E = e^{i0}$, a rotation through a zero angle. Thus (Θ, o) is a group.

Moreover Θ is a subset of $M^*(2)$, since each rotation has non-singular matrix. Thus Θ is a <u>subgroup</u> of $M^*(2)$.

A subset Θ of a group (G,o) is a <u>subgroup</u> of G iff the composition operation, o, restricted to Θ is "closed", and Θ is a group in its own right. That is to say (i) if $x,y \in \Theta$ then $x \circ y \in \Theta$, (ii) the identity e belongs to Θ and (iii) for each x in Θ the inverse, x^{-1}, also belongs to Θ.

Definition 1.2

Let (X,o) and $(Y, .)$ be two sets with binary operations $o, .$, respectively. A function $f: X \to Y$ is called a morphism (with respect to o, .) iff $f(x \, o \, y) = f(x) \, . \, f(y)$, for all $x,y \in X$. If moreover f is bijective as a function, then it is called an isomorphism. If $(X,o),(Y,.)$ are groups then f is called a homomorphism.

A binary operation in a set X is one form of mathematical structure that the set may possess. When an isomorphism exists between two sets X and Y then mathematically speaking their structures are identical.

For example let Rot be the set of all rotations in the plane. If $rot(\theta)$ and $rot(\psi)$ are rotations by θ, ψ respectively then we can combine them to give a rotation $rot(\psi + \theta)$

ie. $rot(\psi) \, o \, rot(\theta) = rot(\psi + \theta)$.

Here o means do one rotation then the other.

To the rotation, $rot(\theta)$ let f assign the 2 x 2 matrix, called $e^{i\theta}$ as above.

Thus $f: (Rot,o) \to (\Theta, o)$

where $f(rot(\theta)) = e^{i\theta}$.

Moreover $f(rot(\psi) \, o \, rot(\theta)) = f(rot(\psi + \theta))$

$$e^{i\psi} o e^{i\theta} = e^{i(\psi+\theta)}$$

Clearly the identity rotation is $rot(0)$ which corresponds to the zero matrix e^{i0}, while the reverse rotation to $rot(\theta)$ is $rot(-\theta)$ corresponding to $e^{-i\theta}$.

Thus f is a morphism.

Here we have a collection of geometric objects, called rotations, with their own structure and we have found another set of "mathematical" objects namely 2 x 2 matrices of a certain type, which has an identical structure.

Lemma 1.7 If $f:(X,o) \to (Y,.)$ is a morphism between groups then

i) $f(e_X) = e_Y$ where e_X, e_Y are the identities in X,Y.

ii) for each x in X, $f(x^{-1}) = [f(x)]^{-1}$.

Proof i) Since f is a morphism

$f(x \text{ o } e_X) = f(x)$. $f(e_X) = f(x)$

By lemma 1.5, e_Y is unique and so $f(e_X) = e_Y$.

ii) $f(x \text{ o } x^{-1}) = f(x).f(x^{-1}) = f(e_X) = e_Y$.

By lemma 1.5, $[f(x)]^{-1}$ is unique, and so $f(x^{-1}) = [f(x)]^{-1}$.

As an example, consider the determinant function $\det: M(2) \to \mathbb{R}$.

From the proof of lemma 1.6, we know that for any 2 x 2 matrices, H and F, it is the case that $|H \text{ o } F| = |H|\,|F|$.

Thus $\det:(M(2),o) \to (\mathbb{R},.)$ is a morphism with respect to matrix composition,o, in M(2) and multiplication,.,in $\mathbb{R}$.

Note also that if F is non-singular then $\det(F) = |F| \neq 0$, and so $\det: M^*(2) \to \mathbb{R} \setminus \{0\}$.

It should be clear that $(\mathbb{R} \setminus \{0\},.)$ is a group. Hence $\det:(M^*(2),o) \to (\mathbb{R} \setminus \{0\},.)$ is a homomorphism between these two groups. This should indicate why those matrices in M(2) which have zero determinant are those without an inverse in M(2).

From example 1.4, the identity in M*(2) is E, while the multiplicative identity in $\mathbb{R}$ is 1.

By lemma 1.7, det(E) = 1.

Moreover $|F|^{-1} = \frac{1}{|F|}$

and so, by lemma 1.7, $|F^{-1}| = \frac{1}{|F|}$.

This is easy to check since

$$|F^{-1}| = \left|\frac{1}{|F|}\begin{pmatrix} d & -b \\ -c & a \end{pmatrix}\right| = \frac{da - bc}{|F|^2} = \frac{1}{|F|^2} = \frac{1}{|F|}.$$

However the determinant det: $M^*(2) \rightarrow \mathbb{R}\backslash 0$ is not injective, since it is clearly possible to find two matrices H,F such that $|H| = |F|$ although H and F are different

Example 1.6

It is clear that the real numbers form a group $(\mathbb{R}, +)$ under addition with identity 0, and inverse (to a) equal to -a. Similarly the reals form a group $(\mathbb{R}\backslash\{0\}, .)$ under multiplication, as long as we exclude 0.

Now let Z_2 be the numbers {0,1} and define "addition modulo 2," written +, on Z_2, by

0 + 0 = 0, 0 + 1 = 1, 1 + 0 = 1, 1 + 1,

and "multiplication modulo 2," written ., on Z_2, by

0 . 0 = 0, 0 . 1 = 1 . 0 = 0, 1 . 1 = 1.

Under "addition modulo 2 " 0 is the identity, and 1 has inverse 1. Associativity is clearly satisfied, and so $(Z_2,+)$ is a group. Under multiplication, 1 is the identity and inverse to itself, but 0 has no inverse. Thus $(Z_2,.)$ is not a group. Note that $(Z_2\backslash\{0\}, .)$ is a group, namely the trivial group containing only one element.

Let Z be the integers, and consider the function

$$f : Z \rightarrow Z_2,$$

defined by $f(x) = 0$ if x is even
1 if x is odd.

We see that this is a morphism $f : (Z,+) \to (Z_2,+)$;

i) if x and y are both even then $f(x) = f(y) = 0$; since $x+y$ is even, $f(x+y) = 0$.

ii) if x is even and y odd, $f(x) = 0$, $f(y) = 1$ and $f(x) + f(y) = 1$. But $x+y$ is odd, so $f(x+y) = 1$.

iii) if x and y are both odd, then $f(x) = f(y) = 1$, and so $f(x) + f(y) = 0$. But $x+y$ is even, so $f(x+y) = 0$.

Since $(Z,+)$ and $(Z_2,+)$ are both groups, f is a homomorphism. Thus $f(-a) = f(a)$.

On the other hand consider

$$f : (Z,.) \to (Z_2,.);$$

i) if x and y are both even then $f(x) = f(y) = 0$ and so $f(x) \,.\, f(y) = 0 = f(xy)$.

ii) if x is even and y odd, then $f(x) = 0$, $f(y) = 1$ and $f(x) \,.\, f(y) = 0$.
But xy is even so $f(xy) = 0$.

iii) if x and y are both odd, $f(x) = f(y) = 1$ and so $f(x)\, f(y) = 1$.
But xy is odd, and $f(xy) = 1$.

Hence f is a morphism. However, neither $(Z,.)$ nor $(Z_2,.)$ is a group, and so f is not a homomorphism.

A computer, since it is essentially a "finite" machine, is able to compute in binary arithmetic, using the two groups $(Z_2,+)$, $(Z_2\backslash\{0\},.)$ rather than with the groups $(\mathbb{R},+)$, $(\mathbb{R}\backslash\{0\},.)$.

This is essentially because the additive and multiplicative groups based on Z_2 form what is called a field.

Definition 1.3

i) A group (G, o) is commutative or abelian iff for all a, b $\in$ G, a o b = b o a.

ii) A field (F, +, ·) is a set together with two operations called addition (+) and multiplication (·) such that (F, +) is an abelian group with zero, or identity 0, and (F \ {0}, ·) is an abelian group with identity 1. For convenience the additive inverse of an element a $\in$ F is written (-a) and the multiplicative inverse of a non zero a $\in$ F is written a^{-1} or $\frac{1}{a}$.

Moreover, multiplication has to be distributive over addition i.e. for all a, b, c in F, a · (b + c) = a · b + a · c.

First of all to give an indication of the notion of abelian group, consider M*(2) again.

As we have seen HoF = $\begin{pmatrix} e & f \\ g & h \end{pmatrix} \circ \begin{pmatrix} a & b \\ c & d \end{pmatrix}$

$$= \begin{pmatrix} ea + fc & eb + fd \\ ga + hc & gb + hd \end{pmatrix}.$$

However, FoH = $\begin{pmatrix} a & b \\ c & d \end{pmatrix} \circ \begin{pmatrix} e & f \\ g & h \end{pmatrix}$

$$= \begin{pmatrix} ea + bg & af + bh \\ ce + dg & cf + dh \end{pmatrix}.$$

Thus HoF $\neq$ FoH in general and so M*(2) is non abelian.

However, if we consider two rotations $e^{i\theta}$, $e^{i\psi}$ then $e^{i\psi} \circ e^{i\theta} = e^{i(\psi+\theta)} = e^{i\theta} \circ e^{i\psi}$. Thus the group (θ ,o) is abelian.

<u>Lemma 1.8</u> Both $(\mathbb{R}, +, .)$ and $(Z_2, +, \cdot)$ are fields.

<u>Proof</u> Consider $(Z_2\ +, .)$ first of all. As we have seen $(Z_2, +)$ and $(Z_2 \setminus \{0\}, \cdot)$ are groups. $(Z_2, +)$ is obviously abelian since $0 + 1 = 1 + 0 = 1$, while $(Z_2 \setminus \{0\}, o)$ is abelian since it only has one element.
To check for distributivity, note that

$$1.(1 + 1) = 1.0 = 0 = 1.1 + 1.1 = 1 + 1.$$

Finally to see that $(\mathbb{R}, +, \cdot)$ is a field, we note that for any real numbers, a, b, c $\mathbb{R}$, $a(b+c)=ab+ac$.

Given a field $(F, +, \cdot)$ we define a new object called F^n where n is a positive integer as follows. Any element $x \in F^n$ is of the form

$$\begin{pmatrix} x_1 \\ \cdot \\ \cdot \\ \cdot \\ x_n \end{pmatrix}$$

where $x_1, \ldots, x_n$ all belong to F.

F1. If $\alpha \in F$, and $x \in F^n$ define $\alpha x \in F^n$ by

$$\alpha \begin{pmatrix} x_1 \\ \cdot \\ \cdot \\ x_n \end{pmatrix} = \begin{pmatrix} \alpha x_1 \\ \cdot \\ \cdot \\ \alpha x_n \end{pmatrix}$$

F2. Define addition in F^n by

$$x+y = \begin{pmatrix} x_1 \\ \cdot \\ \cdot \\ x_n \end{pmatrix} + \begin{pmatrix} y_1 \\ \\ \\ y_n \end{pmatrix} = \begin{pmatrix} x_1 + y_1 \\ \\ \\ x_n + y_n \end{pmatrix}$$

Since F, by definition, is an abelian additive group, it follows that

$$x + y = \begin{pmatrix} x_1 + y_1 \\ \cdot \\ \cdot \\ x_n + y_n \end{pmatrix} = \begin{pmatrix} y_1 + x_1 \\ \cdot \\ \cdot \\ y_n + x_n \end{pmatrix} = y + x$$

Now let $\underline{0} = \begin{pmatrix} 0 \\ \cdot \\ \cdot \\ 0 \end{pmatrix}$

Clearly $x + \underline{0} = \begin{pmatrix} x_1 \\ \cdot \\ \cdot \\ x_n \end{pmatrix} + \begin{pmatrix} 0 \\ \cdot \\ \cdot \\ 0 \end{pmatrix} = x.$

Hence $\underline{0}$ belongs to F^n and is an additive identity in F^n.

Suppose we define $(-x) = -\begin{pmatrix} x_1 \\ \vdots \\ x_n \end{pmatrix} = \begin{pmatrix} -x_1 \\ \vdots \\ -x_n \end{pmatrix}.$

Clearly $x + (-x) = \begin{pmatrix} x_1 \\ \cdot \\ \cdot \\ x_n \end{pmatrix} + \begin{pmatrix} -x_1 \\ \\ -x_n \end{pmatrix} = \begin{pmatrix} x_1 - x_1 \\ \\ x_n - x_n \end{pmatrix} = \underline{0}.$

Thus for each $x \in F^n$ there is an inverse, $(-x)$, in F^n.

Finally, since F is an additive group

$$x + (y+z) = \begin{pmatrix} x_1 \\ \cdot \\ \cdot \\ x_n \end{pmatrix} + \begin{pmatrix} y_1 + z_1 \\ \\ y_n + z_n \end{pmatrix} = \begin{pmatrix} x_1 + y_1 \\ \\ x_n + y_n \end{pmatrix} + \begin{pmatrix} z_1 \\ \\ z_n \end{pmatrix}$$

$$= (x + y) + z.$$

Thus $(F^n, +)$ is an abelian group, with zero $\underline{0}$.

The fact that it is possible to multiply an element $x \in F^n$ by a <u>scalar</u> $\alpha \in F$ endows F^n with further structure. To see this consider the example of $\mathbb{R}^2$.

i) For $\alpha \in \mathbb{R}$ and $x, y \in \mathbb{R}^2$

$$\alpha \left[\begin{pmatrix} x_1 \\ y_2 \end{pmatrix} + \begin{pmatrix} y_1 \\ y_2 \end{pmatrix} \right] = \alpha \begin{pmatrix} x_1 + y_1 \\ x_2 + y_2 \end{pmatrix}$$

$$= \begin{pmatrix} \alpha x_1 + \alpha y_1 \\ \alpha x_2 \quad \alpha y_2 \end{pmatrix} \quad \text{by distribution}$$

$$= \begin{pmatrix} \alpha x_1 \\ \alpha x_2 \end{pmatrix} + \begin{pmatrix} \alpha y_1 \\ \alpha y_2 \end{pmatrix} = \alpha \begin{pmatrix} x_1 \\ x_2 \end{pmatrix} + \alpha \begin{pmatrix} y_1 \\ y_2 \end{pmatrix} \quad \text{by F1.}$$

Thus $\alpha(x + y) = \alpha x + \alpha y$.

ii) $$(\alpha + \beta) \begin{pmatrix} x_1 \\ x_2 \end{pmatrix} = \begin{pmatrix} (\alpha + \beta) x_1 \\ (\alpha + \beta) x_2 \end{pmatrix} \quad \text{by F1}$$

$$= \begin{pmatrix} \alpha x_1 + \beta x_1 \\ \alpha x_2 + \beta x_2 \end{pmatrix}$$

$$= \begin{pmatrix} \alpha x_1 \\ \alpha x_2 \end{pmatrix} + \begin{pmatrix} \beta x_1 \\ \beta x_2 \end{pmatrix} \quad \text{by F2}$$

$$= \alpha \begin{pmatrix} x_1 \\ x_2 \end{pmatrix} + \beta \begin{pmatrix} x_1 \\ x_2 \end{pmatrix} \quad \text{by F1}$$

$\therefore \; (\alpha + \beta) x = \alpha x + \beta x$.

iii) $$(\alpha\beta) \begin{pmatrix} x_1 \\ x_2 \end{pmatrix} = \begin{pmatrix} (\alpha\beta) x_1 \\ (\alpha\beta) x_2 \end{pmatrix} \quad \text{by F1}$$

$$= \alpha \begin{pmatrix} \beta x_1 \\ \beta x_2 \end{pmatrix} \quad \text{by associativity and F1}$$

$$= \alpha (\beta x) \quad \text{by F1 .}$$

Thus $(\alpha\beta) x = \alpha(\beta x)$.

iv) $$1 \begin{pmatrix} x_1 \\ x_2 \end{pmatrix} = \begin{pmatrix} 1 \cdot x_1 \\ 1 \cdot x_2 \end{pmatrix} = \begin{pmatrix} x_1 \\ x_2 \end{pmatrix}$$

$\therefore \; 1 (x) = x$.

These four properties characterise what is known as

a vector space.

Finally, consider the operation of a matrix F on the set of elements in $\mathbb{R}^2$.

By definition F (x + y)

$$= \begin{pmatrix} a & b \\ c & d \end{pmatrix} \left[\begin{pmatrix} x_1 \\ x_2 \end{pmatrix} + \begin{pmatrix} y_1 \\ y_2 \end{pmatrix} \right]$$

$$= \begin{pmatrix} a & b \\ c & d \end{pmatrix} \begin{pmatrix} x_1 + y_1 \\ x_2 + y_2 \end{pmatrix}$$

$$= \begin{pmatrix} a\ (x_1 + y_1) + b\ (x_2 + y_2) \\ c\ (x_1 + y_1) + d\ (x_2 + y_2) \end{pmatrix}$$

$$= \begin{pmatrix} a\ x_1 + b\ x_2 \\ c\ x_1 + d\ x_2 \end{pmatrix} + \begin{pmatrix} a\ y_1 + b\ y_2 \\ c\ y_1 + d\ y_2 \end{pmatrix} \quad \text{by F2}$$

$$= \begin{pmatrix} a & b \\ c & d \end{pmatrix} \begin{pmatrix} x_1 \\ x_2 \end{pmatrix} + \begin{pmatrix} a & b \\ c & d \end{pmatrix} \begin{pmatrix} y_1 \\ y_2 \end{pmatrix}$$

$$= F(x) + F(y).$$

Hence F: $(\mathbb{R}^2, +) \to (\mathbb{R}^2, +)$ is a morphism from the abelian group $(\mathbb{R}^2, +)$ into itself.

By lemma 1.7, we know that $F(\underline{0}) = \underline{0}$, and for any element $x \in \mathbb{R}^2$,

$$F(-x) = F(-1(x))$$
$$= -F(x) = -1\ F(x).$$

A morphism between vector spaces is called a linear transformation. Vector spaces and linear transformations are discussed in the next chapter.

Chapter 2

LINEAR SYSTEMS

2.1 VECTOR SPACES

At the end of chapter 1 we showed that when F was a field, the n-fold product set F^n had an addition operation defined on it, which was induced from addition in F, so that $(F^n,+)$ became an abelian group with zero $\underline{0}$. Moreover we were able to define a product $.:F \times F^n \to F^n$ which took (α,x) to a new element of F^n called (αx). Elements of F^n are known as vectors, and elements of F scalars. The properties that we discovered in F^n characterise a vector space.

Definition 2.1 A vector space (V,+) is an abelian additive group with zero $\underline{0}$, together with a field (F,+,.) with zero 0 and identity 1. An element of V is called a vector and an element of F a scalar. Moreover for any $\alpha \in F, v \in V$ there is a scalar multiplication $(\alpha,v) \to \alpha v \in V$ which satisfies the following properties :

v1 $\alpha(v_1+v_2) = \alpha v_1+\alpha v_2$ for any $\alpha \in F, v_1,v_2 \in V$.

v2 $(\alpha+\beta)v = \alpha v+\beta v$ for any $\alpha,\beta \in F$, $v \in V$.

v3 $(\alpha\beta)v = \alpha(\beta v)$ for any $\alpha,\beta \in F$, $v \in V$.

v4 $1.v = v$ $1 \in F$, and any $v \in V$.

Call V a vector space over the field F.

From the previous discussion the set $\mathbb{R}^n$ becomes an abelian group $(\mathbb{R}^n,+)$ under addition. We shall frequently write $x = \begin{pmatrix} x_1 \\ x_n \end{pmatrix}$ for a vector in $\mathbb{R}^n$,

where $x_1,\ldots x_n$ are called the coordinates of x.

Vector addition is then defined by x+y =

$$\begin{pmatrix} x_1 \\ \cdot \\ \cdot \\ x_n \end{pmatrix} + \begin{pmatrix} y_1 \\ \cdot \\ \cdot \\ y_n \end{pmatrix} = \begin{pmatrix} x_1 + y_1 \\ \cdot \\ \cdot \\ x_n + y_n \end{pmatrix}$$

just as in Figure 2.1, which illustrates addition in $\mathbb{R}^2$.

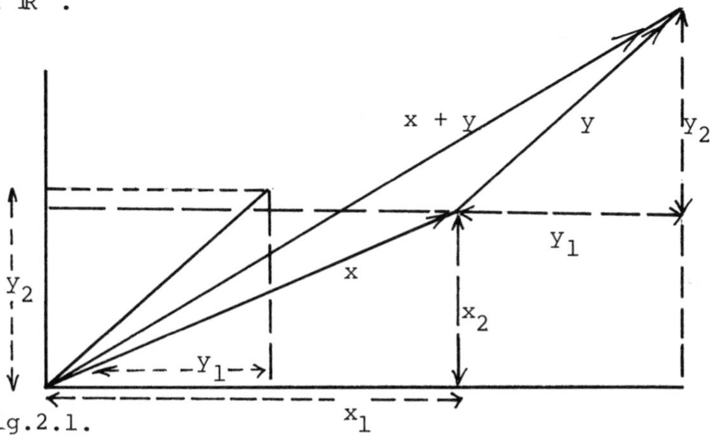

Fig.2.1.

For example $(Z_2,+,.)$ is a field and so $(Z_2)^n$ is a vector space over the field Z_2.

It may not be possible to represent each vector in a vector space by a list of coordinates.

For example consider the set of all functions with domain X and image in $\mathbb{R}$. Call this set $\mathbb{R}^X$. If $f,g \in \mathbb{R}^X$, define f+g to be that function which maps $x \in X$ to f(x)+g(x). Clearly there is a zero function $\underline{0}$ defined by $\underline{0}(x) = 0$, and each f has an inverse (-f) defined by (-f)(x) = -(f(x)).

Finally for $\alpha \in \mathbb{R}, f \in \mathbb{R}^X$ define $\alpha f: X \to \mathbb{R}$ by $(\alpha f)(x) = \alpha(f(x))$. Thus $\mathbb{R}^X$ is a vector space over $\mathbb{R}$.

Definition 2.2 Let $(V,+)$ be a vector space over a field, F. A subset V' of V is called a vector subspace of V if and only if i) $v_1, v_2 \in V' \Rightarrow v_1 + v_2 \in V'$ and ii) if $\alpha \in F$ and $v \in V'$ then $\alpha v' \in V'$.

Lemma 2.1 If $(V,+)$ is a vector space with zero $\underline{0}$ and V' is a vector subspace, then, for each $v \in V'$, the inverse $(-v) \in V'$, and $\underline{0} \in V'$, so $(V',+)$ is a subgroup of $(V,+)$.

Proof Suppose $v \in V'$. Since F is a field, there is an identity 1, with additive inverse -1.

But $(1-1)v = 1.v + (-1)v$ by v2

$= 0.v$ since $1-1 = 0$.

Now $(1+0)v = 1.v + 0.v = 1.v$ and so $0.v = \underline{0}$.

Thus $(-1)v = (-v)$.

Since V' is a vector subspace, $(-1)v \in V'$, and so $(-v) \in V'$.

But then $v + (-v) = \underline{0}$ and so $\underline{0} \in V'$.

From now on we shall write simple V for a vector space, and refer to the field only on occasion.

Definition 2.3 Let $V' = \{v_1, \ldots, v_r\}$ be a set of vectors in the vector space V. A vector v is called a linear combination of the set V' iff v can be written in the form

$$v = \sum_{i=1}^{r} \lambda_i v_i$$

where each $\lambda_i, i=1,\ldots,r$ belongs to the field F.

The span of V', written $\text{Span}(V')$, is the set of vectors which are linear combinations of the set V'. If $V'' = \text{Span}(V')$ then V' is said to span V''.

For example, suppose $V' = \left\{ \begin{pmatrix} 1 \\ 2 \end{pmatrix}, \begin{pmatrix} 2 \\ 1 \end{pmatrix} \right\}$.
Since we can solve the equation

$$\begin{pmatrix} x \\ y \end{pmatrix} = \alpha \begin{pmatrix} 1 \\ 2 \end{pmatrix} + \beta \begin{pmatrix} 2 \\ 1 \end{pmatrix}$$

for any $(x,y) \in \mathbb{R}^2$, by setting $\alpha = \frac{1}{3}(2y-x)$ and $\beta = \frac{1}{3}(2x-y)$, it is clear that V' is a span for $\mathbb{R}^2$.

Lemma 2.2. If V' is a finite set of vectors in the vector space, V, then Span (V') is a vector subspace of V.

Proof. We seek to show that for any $\alpha, \beta \in F$ and any $u, w \in \text{Span}(V')$, then $\alpha u + \beta w \in \text{Span}(V')$.
By definition, if $V' = \{v_1, \ldots, v_r\}$, then

$$u = \sum_{i=1}^{r} \eta_i v_i \text{ and } w = \sum_{i=1}^{r} \mu_i v_i, \text{ where } \eta_i, \mu_i \in F$$

for $i = 1, \ldots, r$.

But then $\alpha u + \beta w = \alpha \sum_{i=1}^{r} \eta_i v_i + \beta \sum_{i=1}^{r} \mu_i v_i = \sum_{i=1}^{r} \lambda_i v_i$,

where $\lambda_i = \alpha\eta_i + \beta\mu_i \in F$, for $i =, \ldots, r$.
Thus $\alpha u + \beta w \in \text{Span}(V')$.

Note that, by this lemma, the zero vector $\underline{0}$ belongs to Span (V').

Definition 2.4. Let $V' = \{v_1, \ldots, v_r\}$ be a set of vectors in V. V' is called a frame iff

$$\sum_{i=1}^{r} \alpha_i v_i = \underline{0} \text{ implies that } \alpha_i = 0 \text{ for } i = 1, \ldots, r.$$

(Here each α_i belongs to the field F).
In this case the set V' is called a linearly independent set. If V' is not a frame, the vectors in V' are said to be linearly dependent.
Say a vector v is linearly dependent on $V' = \{v_1, \ldots, v_r\}$ iff $v \in \text{Span}(V')$.

Note that if V' is a frame, then

i) $\underline{0} \notin V'$ since $\alpha\underline{0} = \underline{0}$ for every non-zero $\alpha \in F$.

ii) If $v \in V'$ then $(-v) \notin V'$, otherwise $1.v + 1(-v) = \underline{0}$ would belong to V', contradicting (i).

Lemma 2.3 i) V' is not a frame iff there is some vector $v \in V'$ which is linearly dependent on $V' \backslash \{v\}$.

ii) If V' is a frame, then any subset of V' is a frame.

iii) If V' spans V'', but V' is not a frame, then there exists some vector $v \in V'$ such that $V''' = V' \backslash \{v\}$ spans V''.

Proof Let $V' = \{v_1, \ldots, v_r\}$ be the set of vectors in the vector space V. i) Suppose V' is not a frame. Then there exists an equation $\sum_{j=1}^{r} \alpha_r v_j = 0$, where, for at least one k, it is the case that $\alpha_k \neq 0$. But then $v_k = -\frac{1}{\alpha_k} (\sum_{j \neq k} \alpha_j v_j)$. Let $v_k = v$. Then v is linearly dependent on $V' \backslash \{v\}$. On the other hand suppose that v_1, say, is linearly dependent on $\{v_2, \ldots, v_r\}$. Then $v_1 = \sum_{j=2}^{r} \alpha_j v_j$, and so $\underline{0} = -v_1 + \sum_{j=2}^{r} \alpha_j v_j = \sum_{j=1}^{r} \alpha_j v_j$ where $\alpha_1 = -1$. Since $\alpha_1 \neq 0$, V' cannot be a frame.

ii) Suppose V'' is a subset of V', but that V'' is not a frame. For convenience let $V'' = \{v_1, \ldots, v_k\}$ where $k \leq r$. Then there is a non-zero solution

$$\underline{0} = \sum_{j=1}^{k} \alpha_j v_j.$$

Since V'' is a subset of V', this implies that V' cannot be a frame. Thus if V' is a frame, so is any subset V''.

iii) Suppose that V' is not a frame, but that it spans V''. By part (i), there exists a vector v_1, say, in V' such that v_1 belongs to Span $(V' \backslash \{v_1\})$.

Thus $v_1 = \sum_{j=2}^{r} \alpha_j v_j$.

Since V' is a span for V", any vector v in V" can be written

$$v = \sum_{j=1}^{r} \beta_j v_j$$

$$= \beta_1\left(\sum_{j=2}^{r} \alpha_j v_j\right) + \sum_{j=2}^{r} \beta_j v_j .$$

Thus v is a linear combination of $V' \setminus \{v_1\}$ and so $V'' = \text{Span}\ (V' \setminus \{v_1\})$.

Let $V''' = V' \setminus \{v_1\}$ to complete the proof.

<u>Definition 2.5</u> A <u>basis</u> for a vector space V is a frame V' which spans V.

For example, we previously considered $V' = \left\{\begin{pmatrix}1\\2\end{pmatrix}, \begin{pmatrix}2\\1\end{pmatrix}\right\}$ and showed that any vector in $\mathbb{R}^2$ could be written as

$$\begin{pmatrix}x\\y\end{pmatrix} = \left(\frac{2y-x}{3}\right)\begin{pmatrix}1\\2\end{pmatrix} + \left(\frac{2x-y}{3}\right)\begin{pmatrix}2\\1\end{pmatrix} = \lambda_1\begin{pmatrix}1\\2\end{pmatrix} + \lambda_2\begin{pmatrix}2\\1\end{pmatrix}.$$

Thus V' is a span for $\mathbb{R}^2$. Moreover if $(x,y)=(0,0)$ then $\lambda_1 = \lambda_2 = 0$ and so V' is a frame. Hence V' is a basis for $\mathbb{R}^2$.

If $V' = \{v_1, \ldots, v_n\}$ is a basis for a vector space V then any vector $v \in V$ be written

$$v = \sum_{j=1}^{n} \alpha_j v_j$$

and the elements $(\alpha_1, \ldots, \alpha_n)$ are known as the <u>coordinates</u> of the vector v, <u>with respect to</u> the basis V'.

For example the <u>natural basis</u> for $\mathbb{R}^n$ is the set $V' = \{e_1, \ldots, e_n\}$ where

$e_i = (0, \ldots, 1, \ldots, 0)$ with a 1 in the ith position.

__Lemma 2.4__ $\{e_1,\ldots,e_n\}$ is a basis for $\mathbb{R}^n$.

__Proof__ We can write any vector x in $\mathbb{R}^n$ as $(x_1,\ldots,x_n)$.

Clearly $x = \begin{pmatrix} x_1 \\ \vdots \\ x_n \end{pmatrix} = x_1 \begin{pmatrix} 1 \\ 0 \\ \vdots \end{pmatrix} + \ldots x_n \begin{pmatrix} 0 \\ \vdots \\ 1 \end{pmatrix}$.

If $x = 0$ then $x_1 = \ldots = x_n = 0$ and so $\{e_1,\ldots,e_n\}$ is a frame, as well as a span, and thus a basis for $\mathbb{R}^n$.

However a single vector x will have different coordinates depending on the basis chosen. For example the vector (x,y) has coordinates (x,y) in the basis $\{e_1,e_2\}$ but coordinates $(\frac{2y-x}{3}, \frac{2x-y}{3})$ with respect to the basis $\left\{\begin{pmatrix} 1 \\ 2 \end{pmatrix}, \begin{pmatrix} 2 \\ 1 \end{pmatrix}\right\}$.

Once the basis is chosen, the coordinates of any vector with respect to that basis are unique.

__Lemma 2.5__ Suppose $V' = \{v_1,\ldots,v_n\}$ is a basis for V.

Let $v = \sum_{i=1}^{n} \alpha_i v_i$. Then the coordinates $(\alpha_1,\ldots,\alpha_n)$, with respect to the basis, are unique.

__Proof__ If the coordinates were not unique then it would be possible to write $v = \sum_{i=1}^{n} \beta_i v_i = \sum_{i=1}^{n} \alpha_i v_i$ with $\beta_i \neq \alpha_i$ for some i.

But $\underline{0} = v - v = \sum_{i=1}^{n} \alpha_i v_i - \sum_{i=1}^{n} \beta_i v_i = \sum_{i=1}^{n} (\alpha_i - \beta_i) v_i$.

Since V' is a frame, $\alpha_i - \beta_i = 0$ for $i=1,\ldots,n$. Thus $\alpha_i = \beta_i$ for all i, and so coordinates are unique.

Note in particular that with respect to __any__ basis

$\{v_1,\ldots,v_n\}$ for V, the unique zero vector $\underline{0}$ always has coordinates $(0,\ldots,0)$.

Definition 2.6 A space V is finitely generated iff there exists a span V', for V, which has a finite number of elements.

Lemma 2.6 If V is a finitely generated vector space, then it has a basis with a finite number of elements.

Proof Since V is finitely generated, there is a finite set $V_1 = \{v_1,\ldots,v_n\}$ which spans V. If V_1 is a frame then it is a basis.

If V_1 is linearly dependent, then by lemma 2.3(iii) there is a vector $v \in V_1$, such that $\text{Span}(V_2) = V$, where $V_2 = V_1 \setminus \{v\}$.

Again if V_2 is a frame then it is a basis.

If there were no subset $V_r = \{v_1,\ldots,v_{n-r+1}\}$ of V_1 which was a frame, then V_1 would have to be the empty set, implying that V was an empty set. But this contradicts $\underline{0} \in V$.

Lemma 2.7 If V is a finitely generated vector space, and V_1 is a frame, then there is a basis V_2 for V which includes V_1.

Proof Let $V_1 = \{v_1,\ldots,v_r\}$.

If $\text{Span}(V_1) = V$ then V_1 is a basis.

So suppose that $\text{Span}(V_1) \neq V$.

Then there exists an element $v_{r+1} \in V$ which does not belong to $\text{Span}(V_1)$.

We seek to show that $V_2 = V_1 \cup \{v_{r+1}\}$ is a frame.

Consider $\underline{0} = \alpha_{r+1} v_{r+1} + \sum_{i=1}^{r} \alpha_i v_i$.

If $\alpha_{r+1} = 0$, then the linear independence of V_1 implies that $\alpha_i = 0$, for $i=1,\ldots,r$. Thus V_2 is a frame.
If $\alpha_{r+1} \neq 0$, then

$$v_{r+1} = -\frac{1}{\alpha_{r+1}} \left(\sum_{i=1}^{r} \alpha_i v_i \right).$$

But this implies that v_{r+1} belongs to $\text{Span}(V_1)$ and therefore that $V = \text{Span}(V_1)$.
Thus V_2 is a frame. If V_2 is a span for V, then it is a basis. If V_2 is not a span, reiterate this process. Since V is finitely generated, there must be some frame $V_{n-r+1} = \{v_1,\ldots v_r, v_{r+1},\ldots v_n\}$ which is a span, and thus a basis for V.

These two lemmas show that if V is a finitely generated vector space, and $\{v_1,\ldots v_m\}$ is a span then some subset $\{v_1,\ldots,v_n\}$, with $n \leq m$, is a basis. A basis is a minimal span.

On the other hand if $X = \{v_1,\ldots,v_r\}$ is a frame, but not a span, then elements may be added to X in such a way as to preserve linear independence, until this "superset" of X becomes a basis. Consequently a basis is a maximal frame.
These two results can be combined into one theorem.

Exchange Theorem Suppose that V is a finitely generated vector space. Let $X = \{x_1,\ldots,x_m\}$ be a frame and $Y = \{y_1,\ldots,y_n\}$ a span. Then there is some subset Y' of Y such that X union Y' is a basis for V.
Proof By induction.

Let $X_s = \{x_1,\ldots,x_s\}$, for each $s=1,\ldots,m$, and let $X_0 = \Phi$.
We know already from lemma 2.6 that there is some

subset Y_0 of Y such $X_0 \cup Y_0$ is a basis for V.
Suppose for some s < m, there is a subset Y_s of Y such that $X_s \cup Y_s$ is a basis.
Let $Y_s = \{y_1,\ldots,y_t\}$.
Now $x_{s+1} \in \text{Span}(X_s \cup Y_s)$ since $X_s \cup Y_s$ is a basis.

Thus: $x_{s+1} = \sum_1^s \alpha_i x_i + \sum_1^t \beta_i y_i$.

But $X_{s+1} = \{x_1,\ldots,x_{s+1}\}$ is a frame, since it is a subset of X.
Thus at least one $\beta_j \neq 0$. Let $Y_{s+1} = Y_s \setminus \{y_j\}$,
so $y_j \in \text{Span}(X_{s+1} \cup Y_{s+1})$
and so $X_{s+1} \cup Y_{s+1} = \{x_1,\ldots,x_{s+1}\} \cup \{y_1,\ldots,y_{j-1}, y_{j+1},\ldots,y_t\}$ is a basis for V.
Thus if there is some subset Y_s of Y such that $X_s \cup Y_s$ is a basis, there is a subset Y_{s+1} of Y such that $X_{s+1} \cup Y_{s+1}$ is a basis.
By induction, there is a subset $Y_m = Y'$ of Y such that $X_m \cup Y_m = X \cup Y'$ is a basis.

Corollary 2.8 If $X = \{x_1,\ldots,x_m\}$ is a frame in a vector space V, and $Y = \{y_1,\ldots,y_n\}$ is a span for V, then $m \leq n$.

Lemma 2.9 If V is a finitely generated vector space, then any two bases have the same number of vectors, where this number is called the dimension of V, and written dim(V).

Proof Let X,Y be two bases with m,n number of elements.
Consider X as a frame and Y as a span. Thus $m \leq n$.
However Y is also a frame and X a span. Thus $n \leq m$.
Hence m = n.

If V' is a vector subspace of a finitely generated

vector space V, then any basis for V' can be extended to give a basis for V. To see this, there must exist some finite set $V'' = \{v_1,\ldots,v_r\}$ of vectors all belonging to V' such that Span (V") = V'. Otherwise V could not be finitely generated. As before eliminate members of V" until a frame is obtained. This gives a basis for V'. Clearly $\dim(V') \leq \dim(V)$. Moreover if V' has a basis $V''' = \{v_1,\ldots,v_r\}$ then further linear independent vectors belonging to $V \setminus V'$ can be added to V''' to give a basis for V.

As we showed in lemma 2.3, the vector space $\mathbb{R}^n$ has a basis $\{e_1,\ldots,e_n\}$ consisting of n elements. Thus $\dim(\mathbb{R}^n) = n$.

If V^m is a vector subspace of $\mathbb{R}^n$ of dimension m, where of course $m \leq n$, then in a certain sense V^m is identical to a copy of $\mathbb{R}^m$ through the origin $\underline{0}$. We make this more explicit below.

2.2. LINEAR TRANSFORMATIONS

At the end of chapter 1 we considered a morphism from the abelian group $(\mathbb{R}^2,+)$ to itself. A morphism between vector spaces is called a linear tranformation.

Definition 2.7 Let V,U be two vector spaces of dimension n,m respectively, over the same field F. Then a linear transformation $T: V \to U$ is a function from V to U with domain V, such that

i) for any $\alpha \in F$, any $v \in V$, $T(\alpha v) = \alpha(T(v))$

ii) for any $v_1, v_2 \in V$, $T(v_1 + v_2) = T(v_1) + T(v_2)$.

Note that a linear transformation is simply a

morphism between (V,+) and (U,+) which respects the operation of the field F. We shall show that any linear transformation T can be represented by an array of the form

$$M(T) = \begin{pmatrix} a_{11} & \cdot & \cdot & a_{1n} \\ \cdot & \cdot & \cdot & \cdot \\ \cdot & \cdot & \cdot & \cdot \\ a_{m1} & \cdot & \cdot & a_{mn} \end{pmatrix}$$

consisting of n x m elements in F. An array such as this is called an n by m (or n x m) matrix. The set of n x m matrices we shall write as M(n,m).

2.2.1 Matrices

For convenience we shall consider finitely generated vector spaces over $\mathbb{R}$, so that we restrict attention to linear transformations between $\mathbb{R}^n$ and $\mathbb{R}^m$, for any integers n and m.
Now let $V = \{v_1,\ldots,v_n\}$ be a basis for $\mathbb{R}^n$ and $U = \{u_1,\ldots,u_m\}$ a basis for $\mathbb{R}^m$.
Since V is a basis for $\mathbb{R}^n$, any vector $x \in \mathbb{R}^n$ can be written as $x = \sum_{j=1}^{n} x_j v_j$, with coordinates $(x_1,\ldots,x_n)$.
If T is a linear transformation, then
$T(\alpha v_1+\beta v_2) = T(\alpha v_1) + T(\beta v_2) = \alpha T(v_1) + \beta T(v_2)$.

$$\text{Therefore } T(x) = T\left(\sum_{j=1}^{n} x_j v_j\right)$$

$$= \sum_{j=1}^{n} x_j \; T(v_j) \, .$$

Since each $T(v_j)$ lies in $\mathbb{R}^m$ we can write

$$T(v_j) = \sum_{i=1}^{m} a_{ij} u_i$$

where $(a_{1j}, a_{2j}, \ldots a_{mj})$ are the coordinates of $T(v_j)$ with respect to the basis U for $\mathbb{R}^m$.

Thus $T(x) = \sum_{j=1}^{n} x_j \sum_{i=1}^{m} a_{ij} u_i = \sum_{i=1}^{m} y_i u_i$

where the ith coordinate, y_i, of T(x) is equal to $\sum_{j=1}^{n} a_{ij} x_j$.

We obtain a set of linear equations:

$$y_1 = a_{11}x_1 + a_{12}x_2 + .. + a_{1j}x_j + .. a_{1n}x_n$$
$$\cdot$$
$$\cdot$$
$$y_i = a_{i1}x_1 + a_{i2}x_2 + .. + a_{ij}x_j + .. a_{in}x_n$$
$$\cdot$$
$$\cdot$$
$$y_m = a_{m1}x_1 + a_{m2}x_2 + .. \quad a_{mj}x_j + .. a_{mn}x_n.$$

This set of equations is more conveniently written

$$\text{row } i \begin{pmatrix} a_{11} & \cdots & a_{1j} & \cdots & a_{1n} \\ \vdots & & & & \vdots \\ a_{i1} & & a_{ij} & & a_{in} \\ \vdots & & & & \vdots \\ a_{m1} & \cdots & a_{mj} & \cdots & a_{mn} \end{pmatrix} \begin{pmatrix} x_1 \\ \vdots \\ x_j \\ \vdots \\ x_n \end{pmatrix} = \begin{pmatrix} y_1 \\ \vdots \\ y_i \\ \vdots \\ y_m \end{pmatrix}$$

j^{th} column

or as $M(T)x = y$, where M(T) is the n x m array whose i^{th} row is $(a_{i1}, \ldots a_{in})$ and whose j^{th} column is $(a_{1j}, \ldots a_{mj})$. This matrix is commonly written as (a_{ij}) where it is understood that $i=1,\ldots m$ and $j=1,\ldots,n$.

Note that the operation of M(T) on x is as follows: to obtain the ith coordinate, y_i, take the ith row vector $(a_{11},\ldots,a_{1n})$ and form the <u>scalar product</u> of this with the column vector $(x_1,\ldots,x_n)$, where this scalar product is defined to be $\sum_{j=1}^{n} a_{ij}x_j$.

The coefficients of $T(v_j)$ with respect to the basis $(u_1,\ldots,u_m)$ are $(a_{1j},\ldots,a_{mj})$ and these turn up as the jth column of the matrix.

Thus we could write the matrix as

$$M(T) = (T(v_1) \;..\; T(v_j) \;..\; T(v_n))$$

where $T(v_j)$ is the column of coordinates in $\mathbb{R}^m$.

Suppose now that $W = \{w_1,\ldots,w_p\}$ is a basis for $\mathbb{R}^p$ and $S\colon \mathbb{R}^m \to \mathbb{R}^p$ is a linear transformation. Then to represent S as a matrix with respect to the two sets of bases, U and W, for each $i = 1,\ldots,m$, we need to know

$$S(u_i) = \sum_{k=1}^{p} b_{ki}w_k .$$

Then as before S is represented by the matrix

$$M(S) = \begin{pmatrix} b_{11} & .. & b_{1i} & .. & b_{1m} \\ \vdots & & b_{ki} & & \vdots \\ b_{p1} & .. & b_{pi} & .. & b_{pm} \end{pmatrix}$$

where the ith column is the column of coordinates of $S(u_i)$ in $\mathbb{R}^p$.

We can compute the composition

$$(S \circ T) : \mathbb{R}^n \xrightarrow{T} \mathbb{R}^m \xrightarrow{S} \mathbb{R}^p.$$

The question is how should we compose the two matrices M(S) and M(T) so that the result "corresponds" to the matrix M(S o T) which represents S o T.

First of all we show that $S \circ T\colon \mathbb{R}^n \to \mathbb{R}^p$ is a linear transformation, so that we know that it can be represented by an (n x p) matrix.

<u>Lemma 2.10</u> If $T:\mathbb{R}^n \to \mathbb{R}^m$ and $S:\mathbb{R}^m \to \mathbb{R}^p$ are linear transformations, then $S \circ T:\mathbb{R}^n \to \mathbb{R}^p$ is a linear transformation.

<u>Proof</u> Consider $\alpha, \beta \in \mathbb{R}$, $v_1, v_2 \in \mathbb{R}^n$

Then $(S \circ T)(\alpha v_1 + \beta v_2)$

$$= S[T(\alpha v_1 + \beta v_2)]$$

$$= S(\alpha T(v_1) + \beta T(v_2)) \text{ since } T \text{ is linear}$$

$$= \alpha S(T(v_1)) + \beta S(T(v_2)) \text{ since } S \text{ is linear}$$

$$= \alpha(S \circ T)(v_1) + \beta(S \circ T)(v_2).$$

Thus $S \circ T$ is linear.

By the previous analysis, $(S \circ T)$ can be represented by an $(n \times p)$ matrix whose j^{th} column is $(S \circ T)(v_j)$.

$$\text{Thus } (S \circ T)(v_j) = S\left(\sum_{i=1}^{m} a_{ij}u_i\right)$$

$$= \sum_{i=1}^{m} a_{ij}S(u_i)$$

$$= \sum_{i=1}^{m} a_{ij} \sum_{k=1}^{p} b_{ki}w_k$$

$$= \sum_{k=1}^{p} \left(\sum_{i=1}^{m} a_{ij}b_{ki}\right)w_k.$$

Thus the kth entry in the jth column of $M(S \circ T)$ is $\sum_{i=1}^{m} b_{ki}a_{ij}$.

Thus $(S \circ T)$ can be represented by the matrix

$$M(S \circ T) = \quad k^{th} \text{ row} \overset{\longleftarrow n \longrightarrow}{\left(\cdots \sum_{i=1}^{m} b_{ki}a_{ij} \cdots \right)} \updownarrow p$$

$$\qquad\qquad\qquad j^{th} \text{ column}$$

The jth column in this matrix can be obtained more simply by operating the matrix $M(S)$ on the jth column vector $T(v_j)$ in the matrix $M(T)$.

Thus $M(S \circ T) = (M(S)(T(v_1)) \; \dots \; M(S)(T(v_n))) =$

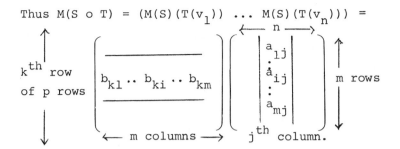

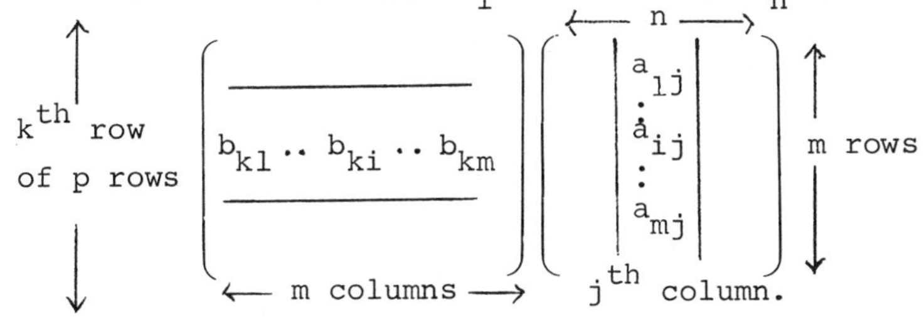

$= M(S) \circ M(T)$.

Thus the "natural" method of matrix composition corresponds to the composition of linear transformations.

Now let $L(\mathbb{R}^n, \mathbb{R}^n)$ stand for the set of linear transformations from $\mathbb{R}^n$ to $\mathbb{R}^n$. As we have shown, if S,T belong to this set then $S \circ T$ is also a linear transformation from $\mathbb{R}^n$ to $\mathbb{R}^n$. Thus composition of functions (o) is a binary operation $L(\mathbb{R}^n, \mathbb{R}^n) \times L(\mathbb{R}^n, \mathbb{R}^n) \to L(\mathbb{R}^n, \mathbb{R}^n)$.

Let $M: L(\mathbb{R}^n, \mathbb{R}^n) \to M(n,n)$ be the mapping which assigns to any linear transformation $T: \mathbb{R}^n \to \mathbb{R}^n$ the matrix M(T) as above. Note that M is dependent on the choice of bases $\{v_1, \dots, v_n\}$ and $\{u_1, \dots, u_n\}$ for the domain and codomain , $\mathbb{R}^n$. There is in general no reason why these two bases should be the same.

Now let o be the method of matrix composition which we have just defined.

Thus the mapping M satisfies

$$M(S \circ T) = M(S) \circ M(T)$$

for any two linear transformations, S and T.

Suppose now that we are given a linear transformation, $T \in L(\mathbb{R}^n, \mathbb{R}^n)$. Clearly the matrix M(T) which represents T with respect to the two bases is unique, and so M is a function.

On the other hand suppose that T,S are both represented by the same matrix $A = (a_{ij})$.

By definition $T(v_j) = S(v_j) = \sum_{i=1}^{m} a_{ij}u_i$

for each $j=1,\ldots,n$.

But then $T(x) = S(x)$ for any $x \in \mathbb{R}^n$, and so $T = S$.

Thus M is injective.

Moreover if A is any matrix then it represents a linear transformation, and so M is surjective.

Thus we have a bijective morphism

$$M: (L(\mathbb{R}^n, \mathbb{R}^n), o) \to (M(n,n), o) .$$

As we saw in the case of 2 x 2 matrices, the subset of non-singular matrices in M(n,n) forms a group. We repeat the procedure for the more general case.

2.2.2. <u>The Dimension Theorem</u>

Let $T: V \to U$ be a linear transformation between the vector spaces V,U of dimension n,m respectively over a field F. The transformation is characterised by two subspaces, of V and U.

<u>Definition 2.8</u> i) The <u>kernel</u> of a transformation $T: V \to U$ is the set $\text{Ker}(T) = \{x \in V : T(x) = \underline{0}\}$ in V.

ii) The <u>image</u> of the transformation is the set $\text{Im}(T) = \{y \in U : \exists x \in V \text{ st. } T(x) = y\}$.

Both these sets are vector subspaces of U,V respectively.

To see this suppose $v_1, v_2 \in \text{Ker}(T)$, and $\alpha, \beta \in F$.

Then $T(\alpha v_1 + \beta v_2) = \alpha T(v_1) + \beta T(v_2) = \underline{0}+\underline{0} = \underline{0}$.

Hence $\alpha v_1 + \beta v_2 \in \text{Ker}(T)$.

If $u_1, u_2 \in \text{Im}(T)$ then there exist $v_1, v_2 \in V$ such that

$T(v_1) = u_1$, $T(v_2) = u_2$.

But then $\alpha u_1 + \beta u_2 = \alpha T(v_1) + \beta T(v_2)$

$= T(\alpha v_1 + \beta v_2)$.

Since V is a vector space, $\alpha v_1 + \beta v_2 \in V$ and so $\alpha u_1 + \beta u_2 \in \text{Im}(T)$.

By the exchange theorem there exists a basis $k_1, \ldots, k_p$ for Ker(T), where p = dim Ker(T) and a basis $u_1, \ldots, u_s$ for Im(T) where s = dim(Im(T)) Here p is called the kernel rank of T, often written kr(T), and s is the rank of T, or rk(T).

The Dimension Theorem

If $T:V \to U$ is a linear transformation between vector spaces over a field F, where dimension (V) = n, then the dimension of the kernal and image of T satisfy the relation

$$\dim(\text{Im}(T)) + \dim(\text{Ker}(T)) = n.$$

Proof Let $\{u_1, \ldots, u_s\}$ be a basis for Im(T) and for each $i=1, \ldots, s$, let v_i be the vector in V^n such that $T(v_i) = u_i$.

Let v be any vector in V.

Then $T(v) = \sum_{i=1}^{s} \alpha_i u_i$, for $T(v) \in \text{Im}(T)$.

$$\text{So } T(v) = \sum_{i=1}^{s} \alpha_i T(v_i)$$

$$= T\left(\sum_{i=1}^{s} \alpha_i v_i\right)$$

and $T\left(v - \sum_{i=1}^{s} \alpha_i v_i\right) = \underline{0}$ the zero vector in U.

i.e. $v - \sum_{i=1}^{s} \alpha_i v_i \in$ kernel T. Let $\{k_1, \ldots, k_p\}$ be the basis for Ker(T).

Then $v - \sum_{i=1}^{s} \alpha_i v_i = \sum_{j=1}^{p} \beta_j k_j$

or $v = \sum_{i=1}^{s} \alpha_i v_i + \sum_{j=1}^{p} \beta_j k_j$.

Thus $\{v_1,\ldots,v_s,k_1,\ldots,k_p\}$ is a span for V.

Suppose we consider $\sum_{i=1}^{s} \alpha_i v_i + \sum_{j=1}^{p} \beta_j k_j = \underline{O}$. (*)

Then $T(\sum_{i=1}^{s} \alpha_i v_i + \sum_{j=1}^{p} \beta_j k_j) = \sum_{i=1}^{s} \alpha_i T(v_i) + \sum_{j=1}^{p} \beta_j T(k_j)$

(since $T(k_j)=0$ for $j=1,\ldots,p$). $= \sum_{i=1}^{s} \alpha_i T(v_i)$

$= \sum_{i=1}^{s} \alpha_i u_i = \underline{O}$.

Now $\{u_i,\ldots,u_s\}$ is a basis for Im(T), and hence these vectors are linearly independent. So $\alpha_i = 0, i=1,\ldots,s$.

Therefore (*) gives $\sum_{j=1}^{p} \beta_j k_j = \underline{O}$.

However $\{k_1,\ldots,k_p\}$ is a basis for Ker(T) and therefore a frame, so $\beta_j = 0$ for $j=1,\ldots,p$. Hence $\{v_1,\ldots,v_s,k_1,\ldots,k_p\}$ is a frame, and therefore a basis for V. By the exchange theorem the dimension of V is the unique number of vectors in a basis. Therefore $s+p = n$.

Note that this theorem is true for general vector spaces. We specialise now to vector spaces $\mathbb{R}^n$ and $\mathbb{R}^m$.

Suppose $\{v_1,\ldots,v_n\}$ is a basis for $\mathbb{R}^n$. The coordinates of v_j with respect to this basis are $(0,\ldots,1,\ldots0)$ with 1 in the jth place. As we have noted the image of v_j under the transformation T can be represented by the jth column

$(a_{ij},\ldots,a_{mj})$ in the matrix M(T), with respect to the original basis $(e_1,\ldots,e_m)$, say, for $\mathbb{R}^m$.
Call the n different column vectors of this matrix $a_1,..a_j,..,a_n$.
Then the equation M(T)(x) = y is identical to the equation

$$\sum_{j=1}^{n} x_j a_j = y \quad \text{where } x = (x_1,\ldots,x_n).$$

Clearly any vector y in the image of M(T) can be written as a linear combination of the columns $A = \{a_1,\ldots,a_n\}$. Thus Span(A) = Im(M(T)).
Suppose now that A is not a frame. In this case a_n, say, can be written as a linear combination of $\{a_1,\ldots,a_{n-1}\}$, i.e. $\sum_{j=1}^{n} k_{1j}a_j = \underline{0}$ and $k_{1n} \neq 0$. Then the vector $k_1 = (k_{11},\ldots,k_{1n})$ satisfies $M(T)(k_1) = \underline{0}$.
Thus k_1 belongs to Ker(M(T)).
Eliminate a_n, say, and proceed in this way. After p iterations we will have obtained p kernel vectors $\{k_1,\ldots,k_p\}$ and the remaining column vectors $\{a_1,\ldots,a_{n-p}\}$ will form a frame, and thus a basis for the image of M(T).
Consequently dim(Im(M(T)) = n-p = n-dim(Ker(M(T)).
The number of linearly independent columns in the matrix M(T) is called the <u>rank</u> of M(T), and is clearly the dimension of the image of M(T).
In particular if $M_1(T)$ and $M_2(T)$ are two matrix representations with respect to different bases, of the linear transformation T, then rank $M_1(T)$ = rank $M_2(T)$ = rank(T).
Thus rank(T) is an invariant, in the sense of being independent of the particular bases chosen for $\mathbb{R}^n$ and $\mathbb{R}^m$.
In the same way the kernel rank of T is an invariant, in that for any matrix representation

ker rank(M(T)) = ker rank(T).

In general if $y \in \text{Im}(T)$, x_o satisfies $T(x_o) = y$, and k belongs to the kernel, then

$T(x_o+k) = T(x_o) + T(k) = y + \underline{0} = y$.

Thus if x_o is a solution to the equation $T(x_o) = y$, the point x_o+k is also a solution. More generally $x_o+\text{Ker}(T) = \{x_o+k : k \in \text{Ker}(T)\}$ will also be the set of solutions. Thus for a particular $y \in \text{Im}(T)$,

$T^{-1}(y) = \{x: T(x) = y\} = x_o+\text{Ker}(T)$.

By the dimension theorem dimKer(T) = n-rank(T). Thus $T^{-1}(y)$ is a geometric object of "dimension" dimKer(T) = n-rank(T).

We defined T to be <u>injective</u> iff $T(x_o) = T(x)$ implies $x_o = x$. Thus T is injective iff Ker(T) = $\{\underline{0}\}$. In this case if there is a solution to the equation $T(x_o) = y$, then this solution is unique.

Suppose that $n \leq m$, and that the n different column vectors of the matrix are linearly independent. In this case rank(T) = n and so dimKer(T) = 0. Thus T must be <u>injective</u>. In particular if $n < m$ then not every $y \in \mathbb{R}^m$ belongs to the image of T, and so not every equation $T(x) = y$ has a solution.

Suppose on the other hand that $n > m$. In this case the maximum possible rank is m (since n vectors cannot be linearly independent in $\mathbb{R}^m$ when $n > m$). If rank(T) = m, then there must exist a kernel of dimension (n-m).

Moreover $\text{Im}(T) = \mathbb{R}^m$, and so for every $y \in \mathbb{R}^m$ there exists a solution to this equation $T(x) = y$. Thus T is <u>surjective</u>. However the solution is not unique, since $T^{-1}(y) = x+\text{Ker}(T)$ is of dimension (n-m) as before.

Suppose now that n=m, and that $T: \mathbb{R}^n \to \mathbb{R}^n$ has maximal rank n. Then T is both injective and surjective and thus an isomorphism. Indeed T will have an inverse function $T^{-1} : \mathbb{R}^n \to \mathbb{R}^n$. Moreover T^{-1} is linear. To see this note that if $x_1 = T^{-1}(y_1)$ and $x_2 = T^{-1}(y_2)$ then $T(x_1) = y_1$ and $T(x_2) = y_2$ so $T(x_1 + x_2) = y_1 + y_2$. Thus $T^{-1}(y_1 + y_2) = x_1 + x_2 = T^{-1}(y_1) + T^{-1}(y_2)$. Moreover if $x = T^{-1}(\alpha y)$ then $T(x) = \alpha y$. If $\alpha \neq 0$, then $\frac{1}{\alpha} T(x) = T(\frac{1}{\alpha} x) = y$ or $\frac{1}{\alpha} x = T^{-1}(y)$ hence $x = \alpha T^{-1}(y)$. Thus $T^{-1}(\alpha y) = \alpha T^{-1}(y)$. Since T^{-1} is linear it can be represented by a matrix $M(T^{-1})$. As we know $M : (L(\mathbb{R}^n, \mathbb{R}^n), o) \to (M(n,n), o)$ is a bijective morphism, so M maps the identity linear transformation, Id, to the identity matrix

$$M(Id) = I = \begin{pmatrix} 1 & .. & 0 \\ \vdots & & \vdots \\ 0 & .. & 1 \end{pmatrix}.$$

When T is an isomorphism with inverse T^{-1}, then the representation $M(T^{-1})$ of T^{-1} is $[M(T)]^{-1}$. We now show how to compute the inverse matrix $[M(T)]^{-1}$ of an isomorphism.

2.2.3 The General Linear Group

To compute the inverse of an n x n matrix A, we define, by induction, the determinant of A. For a 1 x 1 matrix (a_{11}) define $\det(A_{11}) = a_{11}$, and for a 2 x 2 matrix $A = \begin{pmatrix} a_{11} & a_{12} \\ a_{21} & a_{22} \end{pmatrix}$ define

$\det A = a_{11}a_{22} - a_{21}a_{12}$.

For an nxn matrix A define the $(i,j)^{th}$ cofactor to be the determinant of the $(n-1) \times (n-1)$ matrix $A(i,j)$ obtained from A by removing the ith

row and j^{th} column, then multiplying by $(-1)^{i+j}$.
Write this cofactor as A_{ij}.
For example in the 3 x 3 matrix, the cofactor in the (1,1) position is

$$A_{11} = \det \begin{pmatrix} a_{22} & a_{23} \\ a_{32} & a_{33} \end{pmatrix} = a_{22}a_{33} - a_{32}a_{23}.$$

The n x n matrix (A_{ij}) is called the <u>cofactor matrix</u>.
The determinant of the n x n matrix A is then $\sum_{j=1}^{n} a_{1j}A_{1j}$. The determinant is also often written as $|A|$.
This procedure allows us to define the determinant of any n x n matrix. For example if $A = (a_{ij})$ is a 3 x 3 matrix, then

$$|A| = a_{11}\begin{vmatrix} a_{22} & a_{23} \\ a_{32} & a_{33} \end{vmatrix} - a_{12}\begin{vmatrix} a_{21} & a_{23} \\ a_{31} & a_{33} \end{vmatrix} + a_{13}\begin{vmatrix} a_{21} & a_{22} \\ a_{31} & a_{32} \end{vmatrix}$$

$$= a_{11}(a_{22}a_{33}-a_{32}a_{23})-a_{12}(a_{21}a_{33}-a_{31}a_{23})+a_{13}(a_{21}a_{32}-a_{31}a_{22}).$$

An alternative way of defining the determinant is as follows. A permutation of n is a bijection $s:\{1,\ldots,n\} \to \{1,\ldots,n\}$, with degree $d(s)$ the number of exchanges needed to give the permutation.

Then $|A| = \sum_{s} (-1)^{d(s)} \prod_{i=1}^{n} a_{is(i)} = a_{11}a_{22}a_{33}\ldots + \ldots$
where the summation is over all permutations.
The two definitions are equivalent, and it can be shown that

$$|A| = \sum_{j=1}^{n} a_{ij}A_{ij} \quad \text{(for any } i=1,\ldots,n)$$

$$= \sum_{i=1}^{n} a_{ij}A_{ij} \text{ (for any } j=1,\ldots,n) \text{ while}$$

$$0 = \sum_{i=1}^{n} a_{ij}A_{ik} \text{ if } j \neq k$$

$$= \sum_{j=1}^{n} a_{ij}A_{kj} \text{ if } i \neq k.$$

$$\text{Thus } \left(a_{ij}\right)\left(A_{jk}\right)^t = \left(\sum_{j=1}^{n} a_{ij}A_{kj}\right)$$

$$= \begin{pmatrix} |A| & \cdots & 0 \\ \vdots & \ddots & \vdots \\ 0 & \cdots & |A| \end{pmatrix}$$

$$= |A| \quad I.$$

Here $(A_{jk})^t$ is the n x n matrix obtained by transposing the rows and columns of (A_{jk}).

Now the matrix A^{-1} satisfies $A \circ A^{-1} = I$, and if A^{-1} exists then it is unique.

Thus $A^{-1} = \frac{1}{|A|}\left(A_{ij}\right)^t$.

Suppose that the matrix A is non-singular, so $|A| \neq 0$. Then we can construct an inverse matrix A^{-1}.

Moreover if $A(x) = y$ then $y = A^{-1}(x)$ which implies that A is both injective and surjective. Thus rank(A) = n and the column vectors of A must be linearly independent.

As we have noted, however, if A is not injective, with $\text{Ker}(A) \neq \{0\}$, then $\text{rank}(A) < n$, and the column vectors of A must be linearly dependent. In this case the inverse A^{-1} is not a function and cannot therefore be represented by a matrix and so we would expect $|A|$ to be zero.

<u>Lemma 2.11</u> If A is an n x n matrix with rank(A)<n then $|A| = 0$.

<u>Proof</u> Let A' be the matrix obtained from A by adding a multiple (α) of the kth column of A to the jth column of A. The jth column of A' is therefore $a_j + \alpha a_k$. This operation leaves the jth column of the cofactor matrix unchanged.

$$
\begin{aligned}
\text{Thus } |A'| &= \sum_{i=1}^{n} a'_{ij}A_{ij} \\
&= \sum_{i=1}^{n} (a_{ij} + \alpha a_{ik})A_{ij} \\
&= \sum_{i=1}^{n} a_{ij}A_{ij} + \alpha\sum_{i=1}^{n} a_{ik}A_{ij} \\
&= |A| + 0 = |A|.
\end{aligned}
$$

Suppose now that the columns of A are linearly dependent, and that $a_j = \sum_{k\neq j} \alpha_k a_k$ for example.

Let A' be the matrix obtained from A by substituting $a'_j = 0 = a_j - \sum_{k\neq j} \alpha_k a_k$ for the jth column.

By the above $|A'| = \sum_{i=1}^{n} a_{ij}' A_{ij} = 0 = |A|$.

Supose now that A,B are two non-singular matrices $(a_{ij}),(b_{ki})$. The composition is then

$$B \circ A = \left(\sum_{i=1}^{m} b_{ki}a_{ij}\right)$$

with determinant $|B \circ A| = \sum_s (-1)^{d(s)} \prod_{k=1}^{n} . \left(\sum_{i=1}^{m} b_{ki}a_{is(k)}\right)$.

This expression can be shown to be equal to

$$\left(\sum_s (-1)^{d(s)} \prod_{i=1}^{n} a_{is(i)}\right)\left(\sum_s (-1)^{d(s)} \prod_{i=1}^{n} b_{ks(k)}\right)$$

$= |B|\ |A| \neq 0.$

Hence the composition (B o A) has an inverse $(B \circ A)^{-1}$ given by $A^{-1} \circ B^{-1}$.

Now let $(GL(\mathbb{R}^n, \mathbb{R}^n), o)$ be the set of invertible linear transformations, with o composition of functions, and let $M^*(n,n)$ be the set of non-singular n x n matrices. Choice of bases $\{v_1, \ldots, v_n\}$, $\{u_1, \ldots, u_n\}$ for the domain and codomain defines a morphism

$$M : (GL(\mathbb{R}^n, \mathbb{R}^n), o) \rightarrow (M^*(n,n), o).$$

Suppose now that T belongs to $GL(\mathbb{R}^n, \mathbb{R}^n)$. As we have seen this is equivalent to $|M(T)| \neq 0$, so the image of M is precisely $M^*(n,n)$.

Moreover if $|M(T)| \neq 0$ then $|M(T^{-1})| = \frac{1}{|M(T)|}$ and $M(T^{-1})$ belongs to $M^*(n,n)$.

On the other hand if $S, T \in GL(\mathbb{R}^n, \mathbb{R}^n)$ then S o T also has rank n, and has inverse $T^{-1} \circ S^{-1}$ with rank n.

The matrix M(S o T) representing **T** o S has inverse $M(T^{-1} \circ S^{-1}) = M(T^{-1}) \circ M(S^{-1})$

$$= [M(T)]^{-1} \circ [M(S)]^{-1}.$$

Thus M is an <u>isomorphism</u> between the two groups $(GL(\mathbb{R}^n, \mathbb{R}^n, o)$ and $(M^*(n,n), o)$.

The group of invertible linear transformations is also called the <u>general linear group</u>.

2.2.4 Change of Basis

Let $L(\mathbb{R}^n, \mathbb{R}^m)$ stand for the set of linear transformations from $\mathbb{R}^n$ to $\mathbb{R}^m$, and let M(n,m) stand for the set of n x m matrices.

We have seen that choice of bases for $\mathbb{R}^n, \mathbb{R}^m$ defines a <u>function</u>

$$M : L(\mathbb{R}^n, \mathbb{R}^m) \to M(n,m)$$

which takes a linear transformation T to its representation M(T). We now examine the relationship between two representations $M_1(T), M_2(T)$ of a single linear transformation.

Basis Change Theorem

Let $\{v_1, \ldots, v_n\}$ and $\{u_1, \ldots, u_m\}$ be bases for $\mathbb{R}^n, \mathbb{R}^m$ respectively.

Let T be a linear transformation which is represented by a matrix $A = (a_{ij})$ with respect to these bases. If $V' = \{v'_1, \ldots, v'_n\}$, $U' = \{u'_1, \ldots, u'_m\}$ are new bases for $\mathbb{R}^n, \mathbb{R}^m$ then T is represented by the matrix $B = Q^{-1} \circ A \circ P$,

where P,Q are respectively $(n \times n)$ and $(m \times m)$ invertible matrices.

Proof For each $v'_k \in V' = \{v'_1, \ldots, v'_n\}$ let $v'_k = \sum_{i=1}^{n} b_{ik} v_i$ and $b_k = (b_{1k}, \ldots, b_{nk})$.

Let $P = (b_1, \ldots, b_n)$ where the kth column of P is the column of coordinates of b_k.

With respect to the new basis V', v'_k has coordinates $e_k = (0, \ldots, 1, \ldots, 0)$ with a 1 in the kth place.

But then $P(e_k) = b_k$ the coordinates of v'_k with respect to V.

Thus P is the matrix that transforms coordinates with respect to V' into coordinates with respect to V. Since V is a basis, the columns of P are linearly independent, and so rankP = n, and P is invertible.

In the same way let $u'_k = \sum_{i=1}^{m} c_{ik} u_i$,

$c_k = (c_{1k}, \ldots, c_{mk})$ and $Q = (c_1, \ldots, c_m)$ the matrix with columns these coordinates.

Hence Q represents change of basis from U' to U. Since Q is an invertible m x m matrix it has inverse Q^{-1} which represents change of basis from U to U'.

Thus we have the diagram

$$\begin{array}{ccc} \{v_1,\ldots,v_n\} & \xrightarrow{\ A\ } & \{u_1,\ldots,u_m\} \\ P \uparrow & & Q^{-1} \downarrow \ \uparrow Q \\ \{v_1',\ldots,v_n'\} & \xrightarrow[\ B\ ]{} & \{u_1',\ldots,u_m'\} \end{array}$$

from which we see that the matrix B, representing the linear transformation $T:\mathbb{R}^n \to \mathbb{R}^m$ with respect to the new bases is given by $B = Q^{-1} \circ A \circ P$.

<u>Isomorphism Theorem</u>

Any linear transformation $T:\mathbb{R}^n \to \mathbb{R}^m$ of rank r can, by suitable choice of bases for $\mathbb{R}^n$ and $\mathbb{R}^m$ represented by an n x m matrix

$$\begin{pmatrix} I_r & 0 \\ 0 & 0 \end{pmatrix}$$

where $I_r = \begin{pmatrix} 1 & & 0 \\ & \ddots & \\ 0 & & 1 \end{pmatrix}$ is the (r x r) identity matrix.

In particular

i) if n < m and T is <u>injective</u> then there is an isomorphism $S:\mathbb{R}^m \to \mathbb{R}^m$ such that

$S \circ T(x_1,\ldots,x_n) = (x_1,\ldots,x_n,0,\ldots 0)$

with (n-m) zero entries, for any vector $(x_1,\ldots,x_n)$ in $\mathbb{R}^n$

ii) if $n \geq m$ and T is <u>surjective</u> then there are isomorphisms $R:\mathbb{R}^n \to \mathbb{R}^n$, $S:\mathbb{R}^m \to \mathbb{R}^m$ such that

$S \circ T \circ R\ (x_1,\ldots,x_n) = (x_1,\ldots,x_m)$.

If n=m, then $S \circ T \circ R$ is the identity isomorphism.

Proof Of necessity $\text{rank}(T) = r \leq \min(n,m)$.
If $r < n$, let $p = n-r$ and choose a basis $k_1,\ldots,k_p$ for $\text{Ker}(T)$. Let $V = \{v_1,\ldots,v_n\}$ be the original basis for $\mathbb{R}^n$. By the exchange theorem there exists $r = (n-p)$ different members $\{v_1,\ldots,v_r\}$ say of V such that $V' = \{v_1,\ldots,v_r,k_1,\ldots k_p\}$ is a basis for $\mathbb{R}^n$.
Choose V' as the new basis for $\mathbb{R}^n$, and let P be the basis change matrix whose columns are the column vectors in V'. As in the proof of the dimension theorem the image of the vectors $v_1,\ldots,v_{n-p}$ under T provide a basis for the image of T. Let $U = \{u_1,\ldots,u_m\}$ be the original basis of $\mathbb{R}^m$. By the exchange theorem there exists some subset $U' = \{u_1,\ldots,u_{m-r}\}$ of U such that $U'' = \{T(v_1),\ldots T(v_r), u_1,\ldots,u_{m-r}\}$ form a basis for $\mathbb{R}^m$. Note that $T(v_1),\ldots T(v_r)$ are represented by the r linearly independent columns of the original matrix A representing T. Now let Q be the matrix whose columns are the members of U''. By the basis change theorem, $B = Q^{-1} \circ A \circ P$, where B is the matrix representing T with respect to these new bases. Thus we obtain

$$\begin{array}{ccc} \{v_1,\ldots v_n\} & \xrightarrow{\;A\;} & \{u_1,\ldots,u_m\} \\ P \uparrow & & \downarrow Q^{-1} \\ \{v_1,\ldots v_r,k_1,\ldots\} & \xrightarrow{\;B\;} & \{T(v_1)\ldots T(v_r),u_1,\ldots,u_{m-r}\}. \end{array}$$

With respect to these new bases, the matrix B representing T has the required form:

$$\begin{pmatrix} I_r & 0 \\ 0 & 0 \end{pmatrix}.$$

i) If $n < m$ and T is injective then $r = n$. Hence P is the identity matrix, and so $B = Q^{-1} \circ A$.

But Q^{-1} is an m x m invertible matrix, and thus represent an isomorphism $\mathbb{R}^n \to \mathbb{R}^n$, while

$$B\begin{pmatrix} x_1 \\ \\ x_n \end{pmatrix} = \begin{pmatrix} I_n \\ \\ 0 \end{pmatrix} \begin{pmatrix} x_1 \\ \\ x_n \end{pmatrix} = \begin{pmatrix} x_1 \\ \\ x_n \\ \vdots \\ 0 \end{pmatrix}.$$

Write a vector $x = \sum_{i=1}^{n} x_i v_i$ as $(x_1,\ldots,x_n)$, and let S be the linear transformation $\mathbb{R}^m \to \mathbb{R}^m$ represented by the matrix Q^{-1}.

Then $S \circ T(x_1,\ldots,x_n) = (x_1,\ldots,x_n,0,\ldots0)$.

ii) If $n \geq m$ and T is surjective then $\text{rank}(T) = m$, and $\dim \text{Ker}(T) = n-m$.

Thus $B = (I_m \quad 0) = Q^{-1} \circ A \circ P$.

Let S,R be the linear transformations represented by Q^{-1} and P respectively.

Then $S \circ T \circ R(x_1,\ldots,x_n) = (x_1,\ldots,x_m)$.

If n=m then $S \circ T \circ R$ is the identity transformation.

Suppose now that V,U are the two bases for $\mathbb{R}^n, \mathbb{R}^m$ as in the basis theorem. A linear transformation $T:\mathbb{R} \to \mathbb{R}^m$ is represented by a matrix $M_1(T)$ with respect to these bases. If V',U' are two new bases, then T will be represented by the matrix $M_2(T)$, and by the basis theorem

$$M_2(T) = Q^{-1} \circ M_1(T) \circ P$$

where Q,P are non-singular (m x m) and (n x n) matrices respectively. Since $M_1(T)$ and $M_2(T)$ represent the same linear transformation, they are in some sense equivalent. We show this more formally.

Say that two matrices $A,B \in M(n,m)$ are <u>similar</u> iff there exist non singular square matrices $P\in M^*(n,n)$ and $Q\in M^*(m,m)$ such that $B = Q^{-1} \circ A \circ P$, and in this case write $B \sim A$.

Lemma 2.12 The similarity relation ($\sim$) on $M(n,m)$ is an equivalence relation.

Proof i) to show that $\sim$ is reflexive note that

$A = I_m^{-1} \circ A \circ I_n$

where I_m, I_n are respectively the $(m \times m)$ and $(n \times n)$ identity matrices.

ii) to show that $\sim$ is symmetric we need to show that $B \sim A$ implies that $A \sim B$. Suppose therefore that

$$B = Q^{-1} \circ A \circ P .$$

Since $Q \in M^*(m,m)$ it has inverse $Q^{-1} \in M^*(m,m)$. Moreover $(Q^{-1})^{-1} \circ Q^{-1} = I_m$, and thus $Q = (Q^{-1})^{-1}$.

$$\begin{aligned} \text{Thus } Q \circ B \circ P^{-1} &= (Q \circ Q^{-1}) \circ A \circ (P \circ P^{-1}) \\ &= A \\ &= (Q^{-1})^{-1} \circ B \circ (P^{-1}) . \end{aligned}$$

Thus $A \sim B$.

iii) to show $\sim$ is transitive, we seek to show that $C \sim B \sim A$ implies $C \sim A$.

Suppose therefore that $C = R^{-1} \circ B \circ S$ and $B = Q^{-1} \circ A \circ P$ where $R,Q \in M^*(m,m)$ and $S,P \in M^*(n,n)$.

$$\begin{aligned} \text{Then } C &= R^{-1} \circ Q^{-1} \circ A \circ P \circ S \\ &= (Q \circ R)^{-1} \circ A \circ (P \circ S). \end{aligned}$$

Now $(M^*(m,m),\circ)$, $(M^*(n,n),\circ)$ are both groups and so $Q \circ R \in M^*(m,m)$, $P \circ S \in M^*(n,n)$.

Thus $C \sim A$.

The isomorphism theorem shows that if $T:\mathbb{R}^n \to \mathbb{R}^m$ is a linear transformation of rank r, then the $(n \times m)$ matrix $M_1(T)$ which represents T, with respect to some pair of bases, is similar to an n x m matrix $B = \begin{pmatrix} I_r & 0 \\ 0 & 0 \end{pmatrix}$ i.e. $M(T) \sim B$.

If S is a second linear transformation of rank r then $M_1(S) \sim B$.

By lemma 2.12, $M_1(S) \sim M_1(T)$.

Suppose now that U',V' are a second pair of bases for $\mathbb{R}^n, \mathbb{R}^m$ and let $M_2(S), M_2(T)$ represent S and T. Clearly $M_2(S) \sim M_2(T)$.

Thus if S,T are linear transformations $\mathbb{R}^m \to \mathbb{R}^n$ we may say that S,T are equivalent iff for any choice of bases the matrices M(S),M(T) which represent S,T are similar.

For any linear transformation $T \in L(\mathbb{R}^n, \mathbb{R}^m)$ let [T] be the equivalence class $\{S \in L(\mathbb{R}^n, \mathbb{R}^m) : S \sim T\}$. Alternatively a linear transformation S belongs to [T] iff rank (S) = rank (T). Consequently the equivalence relation partitions $L(\mathbb{R}^n, \mathbb{R}^m)$ into a finite number of distinct equivalence classes where each class is classified by its rank, and the rank runs from 0 to min(n,m).

2.2.5 Examples

Example 2.1. To illustrate the use of these procedures in the solution of linear equations, consider the case with n < m and the equation A(x) = y

where $A = \begin{pmatrix} 1 & -1 & 2 \\ 5 & 0 & 3 \\ -1 & -4 & 5 \\ 3 & 2 & -1 \end{pmatrix}$ and $y_1 = \begin{pmatrix} -1 \\ 1 \\ -1 \\ 1 \end{pmatrix}, y_2 = \begin{pmatrix} 0 \\ 5 \\ -5 \\ 5 \end{pmatrix}$.

To find Im(A), we first of all find Ker(A).

The equation $A(x) = \underline{0}$ gives four equations

$x_1 - x_2 + 2x_3 = 0$ with solution
$5x_1 + 0 + 3x_3 = 0$ $k = (x_1, x_2, x_3) = (-3, 7, 5)$.
$-x_1 - 4x_2 + 5x_3 = 0$
$3x_1 + 2x_2 - x_3 = 0$

Thus $\text{Ker}(A) \supset \{\lambda k \in \mathbb{R}^3 : \lambda \in \mathbb{R}\}$.
Hence dim Im(A) ≤ 2. Clearly the first two columns (a_1, a_2) of A are linearly independent and so dim Im(A) = 2. However $y_2 = a_1 + a_2$. Thus a particular solution to the equation $A(x) = y_2$ is $x_0 = (1,1,0)$.
The full set of solutions to the equation is
$x_0 + \text{Ker}(A) = \{(1,1,0) + \lambda(-3,7,5) : \lambda \in \mathbb{R}\}$.
To see whether $y_1 \in \text{Im}(A)$ we need only attempt to solve the equation $y_1 = \alpha a_1 + \beta a_2$.
This gives
$$-1 = \alpha - \beta$$
$$1 = 5\alpha$$
$$-1 = -\alpha - 4\beta$$
$$1 = 3\alpha + 2\beta.$$
From the first two equations $\alpha = 1/5$, $\beta = 6/5$, which is incompatible with the fourth equation. Thus y_1 cannot belong to Im(A).

<u>Example 2.2</u> Consider now an example of the case $n > m$
where $A = \begin{pmatrix} 2 & 1 & 1 & 1 & 1 \\ 1 & 2 & -1 & 1 & 1 \end{pmatrix} : \mathbb{R}^5 \to \mathbb{R}^2$.
Obviously the first two columns are linearly independent and so dim Im(A) ≥ 2. Let $\{a_i : i=1,..,5\}$ be the five column vectors of the matrix and consider the equation $\begin{pmatrix} 2 \\ 1 \end{pmatrix} - \begin{pmatrix} 1 \\ 2 \end{pmatrix} - \begin{pmatrix} 1 \\ -1 \end{pmatrix} = \begin{pmatrix} 0 \\ 0 \end{pmatrix}$.
Thus $k_1 = (1,-1,-1,0,0)$ belongs to Ker(A).
On the other hand
$$\begin{pmatrix} 2 \\ 1 \end{pmatrix} + \begin{pmatrix} 1 \\ 2 \end{pmatrix} - 3\begin{pmatrix} 1 \\ 1 \end{pmatrix} = \begin{pmatrix} 0 \\ 0 \end{pmatrix}.$$

Thus $k_2 = (1,1,0,-3,0)$ and $k_3 = (1,1,0,0,-3)$ both belong to Ker(A).

Consequently the rank of A has its maximal value of 2, while the kernel is three-dimensional. Hence for any $y \in \mathbb{R}^2$ there is a set of solutions of the form $x_0 + \text{Span}\{k_1, k_2, k_3\}$ to the equation $A(x) = y$.

Change the bases of $\mathbb{R}^5$ and $\mathbb{R}^2$ to

$$\begin{pmatrix}1\\0\\0\\0\\0\end{pmatrix}, \begin{pmatrix}0\\1\\0\\0\\0\end{pmatrix}, \begin{pmatrix}1\\-1\\-1\\0\\0\end{pmatrix}, \begin{pmatrix}1\\1\\0\\-3\\0\end{pmatrix}, \begin{pmatrix}1\\1\\0\\0\\-3\end{pmatrix}$$

and $\begin{pmatrix}2\\1\end{pmatrix}, \begin{pmatrix}1\\2\end{pmatrix}$ respectively.

then $$B = \begin{pmatrix}2 & 1\\1 & 2\end{pmatrix}^{-1} \begin{pmatrix}2 & 1 & 1 & 1 & 1\\1 & 2 & -1 & 1 & 1\end{pmatrix} \begin{pmatrix}1 & 0 & 1 & 1 & 1\\0 & 1 & -1 & 1 & 1\\0 & 0 & -1 & 0 & 0\\0 & 0 & 0 & -3 & 0\\0 & 0 & 0 & 0 & -3\end{pmatrix}$$

$$= \frac{1}{3}\begin{pmatrix}2 & -1\\-1 & 2\end{pmatrix} \begin{pmatrix}2 & 1 & 0 & 0 & 0\\1 & 2 & 0 & 0 & 0\end{pmatrix}$$

$$= \begin{pmatrix}1 & 0 & 0 & 0 & 0\\0 & 1 & 0 & 0 & 0\end{pmatrix}.$$

Example 2.3 Consider the matrix

$$Q = \begin{pmatrix}1 & -1 & 0 & 0\\5 & 0 & 0 & 0\\-1 & -4 & 1 & 0\\3 & 2 & 0 & 1\end{pmatrix}.$$

Since $|Q| = 5$ we can compute its inverse.

The cofactor matrix (Q_{ij}) of Q

is
$$\begin{pmatrix} 0 & -5 & -20 & 10 \\ 1 & 1 & 5 & -5 \\ 0 & 0 & 5 & 0 \\ 0 & 0 & 0 & 5 \end{pmatrix}$$

and thus $Q^{-1} = \frac{1}{|Q|} (Q_{ij})^t$

$$= \begin{pmatrix} 0 & 1/5 & 0 & 0 \\ -1 & 1/5 & 0 & 0 \\ -4 & 1 & 1 & 0 \\ 2 & -1 & 0 & 1 \end{pmatrix}$$

<u>Example 2.4</u> Let $T: \mathbb{R}^3 \to \mathbb{R}^4$ be the linear transformation represented by the matrix A of Example 2.1, with respect to the standard bases for $\mathbb{R}^3, \mathbb{R}^4$. We seek to change the bases so as to represent T by a diagonal matrix $B = \begin{pmatrix} I_r & \\ & 0 \end{pmatrix}$.

By example 2.1, the kernel is spanned by $(-3,7,5)$, and so we choose a new basis

$$e_1 = \begin{pmatrix} 1 \\ 0 \\ 0 \end{pmatrix}, \quad e_2 = \begin{pmatrix} 0 \\ 1 \\ 0 \end{pmatrix}, \quad k = \begin{pmatrix} -3 \\ 7 \\ 5 \end{pmatrix}$$

with basis change matrix $P = (e_1, e_2, k)$. Note that $|P| = 5$ and P is non-singular. Thus $\{e_1, e_2, k\}$ form a basis for $\mathbb{R}^3$.

Now Im(A) is spanned by the first two columns a_1, a_2 of A.

Moreover $A(e_1) = a_1$ and $A(e_2) = a_2$.

Thus choose

$$a_1 = \begin{pmatrix} 1 \\ 5 \\ -1 \\ 3 \end{pmatrix}, \quad a_2 = \begin{pmatrix} -1 \\ 0 \\ -4 \\ 2 \end{pmatrix}, \quad e_3' = \begin{pmatrix} 0 \\ 0 \\ 1 \\ 0 \end{pmatrix}, \quad e_4' = \begin{pmatrix} 0 \\ 0 \\ 0 \\ 1 \end{pmatrix}$$

as the new basis for $\mathbb{R}^4$.

Let $Q = (a_1, a_2, e_3', e_4')$ be the basis change matrix.

The inverse Q^{-1} is computed in Example 2.3.

Thus we have $(B) = Q^{-1} \circ A \circ P$.

To check that this is indeed the case we compute:

$$Q^{-1} \circ A \circ P = \begin{pmatrix} 0 & 1/5 & 0 & 0 \\ -1 & 1/5 & 0 & 0 \\ -4 & 1 & 1 & 0 \\ 2 & -1 & 0 & 1 \end{pmatrix} \begin{pmatrix} 1 & 1 & 2 \\ 5 & 0 & 3 \\ -1 & -4 & 5 \\ 3 & 2 & -1 \end{pmatrix} \begin{pmatrix} 1 & 0 & -3 \\ 0 & 1 & 7 \\ 0 & 0 & 5 \end{pmatrix}$$

$$= \begin{pmatrix} 1 & 0 & 0 \\ 0 & 1 & 0 \\ 0 & 0 & 0 \\ 0 & 0 & 0 \end{pmatrix} \quad \text{as required.}$$

2.3. CANONICAL REPRESENTATION

When considering a linear transformation $T: \mathbb{R}^n \to \mathbb{R}^n$ it is frequently convenient to change the basis of $\mathbb{R}^n$ to a new basis $V = \{v_1, \ldots, v_n\}$ such that T is now represented by a matrix

$$M_2(T) = P^{-1} \circ M_1(T) \circ P \text{ .}$$

In this case it is generally not possible to obtain $M_2(T)$ in the form $\begin{pmatrix} I_r & 0 \\ 0 & 0 \end{pmatrix}$ as before.

Under certain conditions however $M_2(T)$ can be written in a diagonal form $= \begin{pmatrix} \lambda_1 & & 0 \\ & \cdot & \\ 0 & & \lambda_n \end{pmatrix}$

where $\lambda_1, \ldots, \lambda_n$ are known as the <u>eigenvalues</u>. More explicitly, a vector x is called an <u>eigenvector</u> of the matrix A iff there is a solution to the equation $A(x) = \lambda x$ where λ is a real number. In this case λ is called the <u>eigenvalue</u> associated with the eigenvector x. (Note that we assume $x \neq \underline{0}$).

2.3.1 Eigenvectors and eigenvalues

Suppose that it is possible to find n linearly independent eigenvectors $\{x_1,\ldots,x_n\}$ for A, where (for each i=1,...,n) λ_i is the eigenvalue associated with x_i. Clearly the eigenvector x_i belongs to Ker(A) iff $\lambda_i = 0$. If rank(A) = r then there would be a subset $\{x_1,\ldots,x_r\}$ of eigenvectors which form a basis for Im(A), while $\{x_1,\ldots,x_n\}$ form a basis for $\mathbb{R}^n$. Now let Q be the (n x n) matrix representing a basis change from the new basis to the original basis. That is to say the ith column, v_i, of Q is the coordinate of x_i with respect to the original basis.

After transforming, the original becomes

$$= Q^{-1} \circ A \circ Q = \begin{pmatrix} \lambda_1 & \cdot\cdot & 0 \\ \vdots & \cdot\lambda_r & \vdots \\ 0 & & \cdot 0 \end{pmatrix}$$

where rank Λ = rankA = r.

In general we can perform this diagonalisation only if there are enough eignevectors, as the following lemma indicates.

<u>Lemma 2.13</u> If A is an n x n matrix, then there exists a non-singular matrix Q, and a diagonal matrix Λ such that $\Lambda = Q^{-1}AQ$ iff the eigenvectors of A form a basis for $\mathbb{R}^n$.

<u>Proof</u> i) Suppose the eigenvectors form a basis, and let Q be the eigenvector matrix. By definition, if v_i is the ith column of Q, then $A(v_i) = \lambda_i v_i$, where λ_i is real.

Thus $AQ = Q\Lambda$.

But since $\{v_1,\ldots,v_n\}$is a basis, Q^{-1} exists and so $\Lambda = Q^{-1}AQ$.

ii) On the other hand if $\Lambda = Q^{-1}AQ$, where Q is non-singular then $AQ = Q\Lambda$. But this is equivalent to $A(v_1) = \lambda_i v_i$ for i=1,...,n where λ_i is the ith diagonal entry in Λ, and v_i is the ith column of Q.

Since Q is non-singular, the columns $\{v_1,\dots,v_n\}$ are linearly independent, and thus the eigenvectors form a basis for $\mathbb{R}^n$.

If there are n distinct (real) eigenvalues then this gives a basis, and thus a diagonalisation.

<u>Lemma 2.14</u> If $\{v_1,\dots,v_m\}$ are eigenvectors corresponding to distinct eigenvalues $\{\lambda_1,\dots,\lambda_m\}$, of a linear transformation $T:\mathbb{R}^n \to \mathbb{R}^n$, then $\{v_1,\dots,v_m\}$ are linearly independent.

<u>Proof</u> Since v_1 is assumed to be an eigenvector, it is non-zero, and thus $\{v_1\}$ is a linearly independent set.

Proceed by induction.

Suppose $V_k = \{v_1,\dots,v_k\}$, with $k < m$, are linearly independent.

Let v_{k+1} be another eigenvector and suppose

$$v = \sum_{r=1}^{k+1} a_r v_r = \underline{0}. \quad \text{Then } \underline{0} = T(v) = \sum_{r=1}^{k+1} a_r T(v_r)$$

$$= \sum_{r=1}^{k+1} a_r \lambda_r v_r.$$

If $\lambda_{k+1} = 0$, then $\lambda_i \neq 0$ for i=1,...,k and by the linear independence of $V_k, a_r\lambda_r = 0$, and thus $a_r = 0$ for r=1,...,k.

Suppose $\lambda_{k+1} \neq 0$. Then

$$\lambda_{k+1} v = \sum_{r=1}^{k+1} \lambda_{k+1} a_r v_r = \sum_{r=1}^{k+1} a_r \lambda_r v_r = \underline{0}.$$

Thus $\sum_{r=1}^{k} (\lambda_{k+1} - \lambda_r) a_r v_r = \underline{0}$.

By the linear independence of V_k,

$$(\lambda_{k+1} - \lambda_r)a_r = 0 \text{ for } r=1,\ldots,k.$$

But the eigenvalues are distinct and so $a_r = 0$, for $r = 1,\ldots k$.

Thus $a_{k+1}v_{k+1} = \underline{0}$ and so $a_r = 0$, $r = 1,\ldots,k+1$.

Hence $V_{k+1} = \{v_1,\ldots,v_{k+1}\}, k < m$, is linearly independent.

By induction V_m is a linearly independent set.

Having shown how the determination of the eigenvectors gives a diagonalisation, we proceed to compute eigenvalues.

Consider again the equation $A(x) = \lambda x$.

This is equivalent to the equation $A'(x) = 0$

$$\text{where } A' = \begin{pmatrix} a_{11}-\lambda & a_{12} & \cdot & \cdot & a_{1n} \\ a_{21} & a_{22}-\lambda & & & \cdot \\ \cdot & & & \cdot & \cdot \\ \cdot & & & \cdot & \\ a_{n1} & \cdot & & \cdot & a_{nn}-\lambda \end{pmatrix}.$$

For this equation to have a non zero solution it is necessary and sufficient that $|A'| = 0$.

Thus we obtain a polynomial equation (called the characteristic equation) of degree n in λ, with n roots $\lambda_1,\ldots,\lambda_n$ not necessarily all real.

In the 2 x 2 case for example this equation is

$$\lambda^2 - \lambda(a_{11} + a_{22}) + (a_{11}a_{22} - a_{21}a_{12}) = 0.$$

If the roots of this equation are λ_1,λ_2 then we obtain

$$(\lambda-\lambda_1)(\lambda-\lambda_2) = \lambda^2 - \lambda(\lambda_1 + \lambda_2) + \lambda_1\lambda_2.$$

Hence $\lambda_1\lambda_2 = (a_{11}a_{22} - a_{21}a_{22}) = |A|$

$$\lambda_1 + \lambda_2 = a_{11} + a_{22}.$$

The sum of the diagonal elements of a matrix is called the <u>trace</u> of A.

In the 2 x 2 case therefore

$$\lambda_1\lambda_2 = |A| , \quad \lambda_1 + \lambda_2 = a_{11} + a_{22} = \text{trace } (A).$$

In the 3 x 3 case we find

$$(\lambda-\lambda_1)(\lambda-\lambda_2)(\lambda-\lambda_3) = \lambda^3 - \lambda^2(\lambda_1+\lambda_2+\lambda_3)$$

$$+ \lambda(\lambda_1\lambda_2 + \lambda_1\lambda_3 + \lambda_2\lambda_3) - \lambda_1\lambda_2\lambda_3$$

$$= \lambda^3 - \lambda^2 (\text{trace } A) + \lambda(A_{11} + A_{22} + A_{33}) - |A| = 0,$$

where A_{ii} is the ith diagonal cofactor of A.

Suppose all the roots are non-zero (this is equivalent to the non-singularity of the matrix A).

Let $\Lambda = \begin{pmatrix} \lambda_1 & 0 & 0 \\ 0 & \lambda_2 & 0 \\ 0 & 0 & \lambda_3 \end{pmatrix}$

be the diagonal eigenvalue matrix, with

$|\Lambda| = \lambda_1\lambda_2\lambda_3$.

The cofactor matrix of Λ is then $\begin{pmatrix} \lambda_2\lambda_3 & 0 & 0 \\ 0 & \lambda_1\lambda_3 & 0 \\ 0 & 0 & \lambda_1\lambda_2 \end{pmatrix}$.

Thus we see that the sum of the diagonal cofactors of A and Λ are identical. Moreover trace (A) = trace (Λ) and $|\Lambda| = |A|$.

Now let $\sim$ be the equivalence relation defined on $L(\mathbb{R}^n, \mathbb{R}^n)$ by $B \sim A$ iff there exist basis change matrices P,Q and a diagonal matrix Λ such that

$$\Lambda = P^{-1}AP = Q^{-1}BQ.$$

On the set of matrices which can be diagonalised, $\sim$ is an equivalence relation, and each class is characterised by n invariants, namely the trace, the determinant, and (n-2) other numbers involving the cofactors.

2.3.2. Examples

Example 2.5. Let $A = \begin{pmatrix} 2 & 1 & -1 \\ 0 & 1 & 1 \\ 2 & 0 & -2 \end{pmatrix}$.

The characteristic equation is

$$(2-\lambda)\left[(1-\lambda)\ (-2-\lambda)\right] \quad -1(-2) \quad -1(-2(1-\lambda)$$

$$= -\lambda\ (\lambda^2 - \lambda-2) \quad = \quad -\lambda(\lambda-2)(\lambda+1) \quad = \quad 0 .$$

Hence $(\lambda_1, \lambda_2, \lambda_3) = (0, 2, -1)$.

Note that $\lambda_1 + \lambda_2 + \lambda_3 = \text{trace } A = 1$ and

$\lambda_2\ \lambda_3 = -2 = A_{11} + A_{22} + A_{33}$.

Eigenvectors corresponding to these eigenvalues are

$$x_1 = \begin{pmatrix} 1 \\ -1 \\ 1 \end{pmatrix}, \quad x_2 = \begin{pmatrix} 2 \\ 1 \\ 1 \end{pmatrix}, \quad x_3 = \begin{pmatrix} 1 \\ -1 \\ 2 \end{pmatrix}.$$

Let P be the basis change matrix given by these three column vectors. The inverse can be readily computed, to give

$$P^{-1}\ A\ P = \begin{pmatrix} 1 & -1 & -1 \\ \frac{1}{3} & \frac{1}{3} & 0 \\ -\frac{2}{3} & \frac{1}{3} & 1 \end{pmatrix} \begin{pmatrix} 2 & 1 & -1 \\ 0 & 1 & 1 \\ 2 & 0 & 2 \end{pmatrix} \begin{pmatrix} 1 & 2 & 1 \\ -1 & 1 & -1 \\ 1 & 1 & 2 \end{pmatrix}$$

$$= \begin{pmatrix} 0 & 0 & 0 \\ 0 & 2 & 0 \\ 0 & 0 & -1 \end{pmatrix}.$$

Suppose we now compute $A^2 = A \circ A: \mathbb{R}^3 \to \mathbb{R}^3$.

This can easily be seen to be $\begin{pmatrix} 2 & 3 & 1 \\ 2 & 1 & -1 \\ 0 & 2 & 2 \end{pmatrix}$.

The characteristic function of A^2 is $\lambda^3 - 5\lambda^2 + 4\lambda$ with roots $\mu_1 = 0, \mu_2 = 4, \mu_3 = 1$.

In fact the eigenvectors of A^2 are x_1, x_2, x_3, the same as A, but with eigenvalues $\lambda_1^2, \lambda_2^2, \lambda_3^2$. In this case $\text{Im}(a) = \text{Im}(A^2)$ is spanned by $\{x_2, x_3\}$ and $\text{Ker}(A) = \text{Ker}(A^2)$ has basis $\{x_1\}$.

More generally consider a linear transformation $A: \mathbb{R}^n \to \mathbb{R}^n$. Then if x is an eigenvector with a non-zero eigenvalue λ, $A^2(x) = A \circ A(x) = A[\lambda x] = \lambda A(x) = \lambda^2 x$, and so $x \in \text{Im}(A) \cap \text{Im}(A^2)$.

If there exist n <u>distinct</u> real roots to the characteristic equation of A, then a basis consisting of eigenvectors can be found. Then A can be diagonalised, and $\text{Im}(A) = \text{Im}(A^2)$, $\text{Ker}(A) = \text{Ker}(A^2)$.

<u>Example 2.6</u> Let $A = \begin{pmatrix} 3 & -1 & -1 \\ 1 & 3 & -7 \\ 5 & -3 & 1 \end{pmatrix}$

Then Ker(A) has basis $\{(1,2,1)\}$, and Im(A) has basis $\{(3,1,5), (-1,3,-3)\}$.

The eigenvalues of A are 0,0,7. Since we cannot find three linearly independent eigenvectors, A cannot be diagonalised.

Now $A^2 = \begin{pmatrix} +3 & -3 & 3 \\ -29 & 29 & -29 \\ 17 & -17 & 17 \end{pmatrix}$

and thus $\text{Im}(A^2)$ has basis $\{(3,-29,17)\}$.

Note that $\begin{pmatrix} 3 \\ -29 \\ 17 \end{pmatrix} = -2 \begin{pmatrix} 3 \\ 1 \\ 5 \end{pmatrix} - 9 \begin{pmatrix} -1 \\ 3 \\ -3 \end{pmatrix} \in \text{Im}(A)$

and so $\text{Im}(A^2)$ is a <u>subspace</u> of Im(A).

Moreover $Ker(A^2)$ has basis $\{(1, 2, 1), (1, -1, 0)\}$ and so Ker(A) is a subspace of $Ker(A^2)$.

This can be seen more generally. Suppose $f: \mathbb{R}^n \to \mathbb{R}^n$ is linear, and $x \in Ker(f)$. Then $f^2(x) = f(f(x)) = \underset{\sim}{0}$, and so $x \in Ker(f^2)$. Thus $Ker(f) \subset Ker(f^2)$. On the other hand if $v \in Im(f^2)$ then there exists $w \in \mathbb{R}^n$ such that $f^2(w) = v$. But $f(w) \in \mathbb{R}^n$ and so $f(f(w)) = v \in Im(f)$. Thus $Im(f^2) \subset Im(f)$.

2.3.3. Symmetric Matrices and Quadratic Forms

Given two vectors $x = (x_1,\ldots,x_n)$ and $y = (y_1,\ldots,y_n)$ in $\mathbb{R}^n$, let $(x,y) = \sum_{i=1}^{n} x_i y_i \in \mathbb{R}$ be the scalar product of x and y. Note that $(\lambda x,y) = \lambda(x,y) = (x,\lambda y)$ for any real λ.

An nxn matrix $A = (a_{ij})$ may be regarded as a map $A^*: \mathbb{R}^n \times \mathbb{R}^n \to \mathbb{R}$

where $A^*(x,y) = (x, A(y))$.

A^* is linear in both x and y and is called <u>bilinear</u>.

By definition $(x, A(y)) = \sum_{i=1}^{n} \sum_{j=1}^{n} x_i a_{ij} y_j$.

Call an nxn matrix A <u>symmetric</u> iff $A = A^t$ where $A^t = (a_{ji})$ is obtained from A by exchanging rows and columns.

In this case $(A(x),y) = \sum_{i=1}^{n} (\sum_{j=1}^{n} a_{ji} x_i) y_j$

$$= \sum_{i=1}^{n} \sum_{j=1}^{n} x_i a_{ij} y_j,$$

since $a_{ij} = a_{ji}$ for all i,j.

Hence $(A(x),y) = (x,A(y))$ for any $x,y \in \mathbb{R}^n$ whenever A is symmetric

Lemma 2.15. If A is a symmetric $n \times n$ matrix, and x,y are eigenvectors of A corresponding to distinct eigenvalues then $(x,y) = 0$, i.e. x and y are orthogonal.

Proof. Let $\lambda_1 \neq \lambda_2$ be the eigenvalues corresponding to the distinct eigenvectors x,y.

$$\begin{aligned} \text{Now} \quad (A(x),y) &= (x,A(y)) \\ = (\lambda_1 x,y) &= (x,\lambda_2 y) \\ = \lambda_1(x,y) &= \lambda_2(x,y). \end{aligned}$$

Here $(A(x),y) = (x,A(y))$ since A is symmetric.

Moreover $\quad (x,\lambda y) = \sum_{i=1}^{n} x_i(\lambda y_i) = \lambda(x,y).$

Thus $(\lambda_1 - \lambda_2)\ (x,y) = 0$. If $\lambda_1 \neq \lambda_2$ then $(x,y) = 0$.

Lemma 2.16. If there exist n distinct eigenvalues to a symmetric $n \times n$ matrix A, then the eigenvectors $X = \{x_1,\ldots,x_n\}$ form an orthogonal basis for $\mathbb{R}^n$.

Proof. Directly by lemmas 2.14 and 2.15.

We may also give a brief direct proof of lemma 2.16 by supposing that $\sum_{i=1}^{n} \alpha_i x_i = 0$. But then for each $j = 1,\ldots,n$,

$0 = (x_j,\underline{0}) = \sum_{i=1}^{n} \alpha_i(x_j,x_i) = \alpha_j(x_j,x_j)$. But since $x_j \neq 0$, $(x_j,x_j) > 0$ and so $\alpha_j = 0$ for each j. Thus X is a frame. Since the vectors in X are mutually orthogonal, X is an orthogonal basis for $\mathbb{R}^n$.

For a symmetric matrix the roots of the

characteristic equation will all be real. To see this in the 2 x 2 case, consider the characteristic equation

$$(\lambda - \lambda_1)(\lambda - \lambda_2) = \lambda^2 - \lambda(a_{11} + a_{22}) = (a_{11}a_{22} - a_{21}a_{22}).$$

The roots of this equation are $\dfrac{-b \pm \sqrt{b^2 - 4c}}{2}$ with real roots iff $b^2 - 4c \geq 0$.

But this is equivalent to

$$(a_{11} + a_{22})^2 - 4(a_{11}a_{22} - a_{21}a_{12})$$
$$= (a_{11} - a_{22})^2 + 4(a_{12})^2 \geq 0, \text{ since } a_{12} = a_{21}.$$

Both terms in this expression are non-negative, and so λ_1, λ_2 are real.

In this case of a symmetric matrix, A, let E_λ be the set of eigenvectors association with a particular eigenvalue, λ, of A together with the zero vector. Suppose x_1, x_2 belong to E_λ. Clearly $A(x_1 + x_2) = A(x_1) + A(x_2) = \lambda(x_1 + x_2)$ and so $x_1 + x_2 \varepsilon E_\lambda$. If $x \varepsilon E_\lambda$, then $A(\alpha x) = \alpha A(x) = \alpha(\lambda x) = \lambda(\alpha x)$ and $\alpha x \varepsilon E_\lambda$ for each non-zero real number, α.

Since we also now suppose that for each eigenvalue, λ, the <u>eigenspace</u> E_λ contains $\underline{0}$, then E_λ will be a vector subspace of $\mathbb{R}^n$. If $\lambda = \lambda_1 = \ldots = \lambda_r$ are repeated roots of the characteristic equation, then, in fact, the eigenspace, E_λ, will be of dimension r, and we can find r mutually orthogonal vectors in E_λ, forming a basis for E_λ.

Suppose now that A is a symmetric n x n matrix. As we shall show we may write $\Lambda = P^{-1} A P$ where P is the n x n basis change matrix whose columns are the n linearly independent eigenvectors of A.

Now <u>normalise</u> each eigenvector x_j by defining

$$z_j = \frac{1}{\|x_j\|}(x_{1j},\ldots,x_{nj}) \text{ where}$$

$\|x_j\| = \sqrt{\sum(x_{kj})^2} = \sqrt{(x_j, x_j)}$ is called the <u>norm</u> of x_j.

Let $Q = (z_1,\ldots,z_n)$ be the nxn matrix whose columns consist of $z_1,\ldots,z_n$.

$$\text{Now } Q^tQ = \begin{pmatrix} z_{11} & z_{21} & z_{n1} \\ & & \\ z_{1j} & & z_{nj} \\ z_{1n} & & z_{nn} \end{pmatrix} \begin{pmatrix} z_{11} & z_{1j} & z_{1n} \\ z_{21} & z_{2j} & z_{2n} \\ & & \\ z_{n1} & z_{nj} & z_{nn} \end{pmatrix}$$

$$= \begin{pmatrix} (z_1,z_1) & (z_1,z_2) & \cdots & (z_{11}z_n) \\ (z_2,z_1) & & & \\ \vdots & & & \\ & \cdots & & (z_n,z_n) \end{pmatrix}$$

since the $(i,k)^{th}$ entry in Q^tQ is $\sum_{r=1}^{n} z_{ri}\, z_{rk} = (z_i, z_k)$.

But $(z_i,z_k) = \left(\frac{x_i}{\|x_i\|}, \frac{x_k}{\|x_k\|}\right) = \frac{1}{\|x_i\|\|x_k\|}(x_i,x_k) = 0$ if $i \neq k$.

On the other hand $(z_i,z_i) = \frac{1}{\|x_i\|^2}(x_i,x_i) = 1.$

This $Q^tQ = I_n$, the n x n identity matrix.

Thus $Q^t = Q^{-1}$.

Since $\{z_1,\ldots,z_n\}$ are eigenvectors of A with real eigenvalues $\{\lambda_1,\ldots,\lambda_n\}$ we obtain

$$\Lambda = \begin{pmatrix} \lambda_1 & & 0 \\ & \lambda_r & \\ 0 & & 0 \end{pmatrix} = Q^tAQ$$

where the last (n-r) columns of Q correspond to the kernel vectors of A.

When A is a symmetric $n \times n$ matrix the function

$$A^*: \mathbb{R}^n \times \mathbb{R}^n \to \mathbb{R} \text{ given by } A^*(x,y) = (x,A(y))$$

is called a <u>quadratic form</u>, and in matrix notation is given by

$$(x_1,\ldots,x_n) \begin{pmatrix} & & \\ & a_{ij} & \\ & & \end{pmatrix} \begin{pmatrix} y_1 \\ \\ y_n \end{pmatrix}$$

Consider $A^*(x,x) = (x,A(x))$

$$= (x, Q\Lambda A^t\ (x))$$

$$= (Q^t(x), \Lambda Q^t(x)).$$

Now $Q^t(x) = (x_1',\ldots,x_n')$ is the coordinate representation of the vector x with respect to the new basis $\{z_1,\ldots,z_n\}$ for $\mathbb{R}^n$.

Thus $A^*(x,x) = (x_1',\ldots,x_n') \begin{pmatrix} \lambda_1 & & & & \\ & \ddots & & & \\ & & \lambda_r & & \\ & & & \ddots & \\ & & & & 0 \end{pmatrix} \begin{pmatrix} x_1' \\ \\ \\ x_n' \end{pmatrix}$

$$= \sum_{i=1}^{r} \lambda_i (x_i')^2.$$

Suppose that rank $A = r$ and all eigenvalues of A are non-negative.

In this case $A^*(x,x) = \sum_{i=1}^{n} |\lambda_i|\ (x_i')^2 \geq 0.$

Moreover if x is a non-zero vector then $Q^t(x) \neq 0$, since Q^t must have rank n.

Define the nullity of A^* to be $\{x : A^*(x,x) = 0\}$. Clearly if x is a non-zero vector in Ker(A) then it is an eigenvector with eigenvalue 0. Thus the nullity of A^* is a vector subspace of $\mathbb{R}^n$ of dimension at least n-r, where $r = \text{rank}(A)$. If the nullity of A^* is $\{\underline{0}\}$ then call A^* <u>non-degenerate</u>.

If all eigenvalues of A are strictly positive (so that A^* is non-degenerate) then $A^*(x,x) > 0$ for all non-zero $x \in \mathbb{R}^n$. In this case A^* is called positive definite. If all eigenvalues of A are non-negative but some are zero, then A^* is called positive semi-definite, and in this case $A^*(x,x)>0$, for all x in a subspace of dimension r in $\mathbb{R}^n$. Conversely if A^* is non-degenerate and all eigenvalues are strictly negative, then A^* is called negative definite. If the eigenvalues are non-positive, but some are zero, then A^* is called negative semi-definite.

The index of the quadratic form A^* is the maximal dimension of the subspace on which A^* is negative definite. Therefore index(A^*) is the number of strictly negative eigenvalues of A.

When A has some eigenvalues which are strictly positive and some which are strictly negative, then we call A^* a saddle.

We have not as yet shown that a symmetric $n \times n$ matrix has n real roots to its characteristic equation.

We can show however that any (symmetric) quadratic form can be diagonalised.

Let $A = (a_{ij})$ and $(x,A(x)) = \sum_{i=1}^{n} \sum_{j=1}^{n} a_{ij}x_i x_j$.

If $a_{ii} = 0$ for all $i = 1,\ldots,n$ then it is possible to make a linear transformation of coordinates such that $a_{jj} \neq 0$ for some j. After relabelling coordinates we can take $a_{11} \neq 0$. In this case the quadratic form can be written

$$(x,A(x)) = a_{11} x_1^2 + 2a_{12}x_1x_2 \ldots$$

$$= a_{11}(x_1 + \frac{a_{12}}{a_{11}} x_2 \ldots)^2$$

$$+\left(a_{22} - \frac{a_{12}{}^2}{a_{11}}\right)(x_2 + \ldots)^2 + \ldots$$

$$= \sum_{i=1}^{n} \alpha_i y_i{}^2 .$$

Here each y_i is a linear combination of $\{x_i,\ldots,x_n\}$. Thus the transformation $x \to P(x) = y$ is non-singular and has inverse Q say.

Letting $x = Q(y)$ we see the quadratic form becomes

$$\begin{aligned}(x,A(x)) &= (Q(y),A \circ Q(y)) \\ &= (y,Q^tAQ(y)) \\ &= (y,D(y)),\end{aligned}$$

where D is a diagonal matrix with real diagonal entries $(\alpha_1,\ldots,\alpha_n)$. Note that $D = Q^tAQ$ and so rank(D) = rank(A) = r, say. Thus only r of the diagonal entries may be non zero.

Since the symmetric matrix,A, can be diagonalised, not only are all its eigenvalues real, but its eigenvectors form a basis for $\mathbb{R}^n$. Consequently $\Lambda = P^{-1}AP$ where P is the nxn basis change matrix whose columns are these eigenvectors. Moreover, if λ is an eigenvalue with multiplicity r (ie λ occurs as a root of the characterstic equation r times) then the eigenspace,E_λ,has dimension r.

2.3.4. Examples

Example 2.7 To give an illustration of this procedure consider a matrix $A = \begin{pmatrix} 0 & 0 & 1 \\ 0 & 1 & 0 \\ 1 & 0 & 0 \end{pmatrix}$

representing the quadratic form $x_2^2 + 2x_1x_3$.

Let $P_1(x) = \begin{pmatrix} 0 & 1 & 0 \\ 1 & 0 & 0 \\ 1 & 0 & 1 \end{pmatrix} \begin{pmatrix} x_1 \\ x_2 \\ x_3 \end{pmatrix} = \begin{pmatrix} z_1 \\ z_2 \\ z_3 \end{pmatrix}$

giving the quadratic form $z_1^2 - 2(z_2 - \frac{1}{2}z_3)^2 + \frac{1}{2}z_3^2$

and $P_2(z) = \begin{pmatrix} 1 & 0 & 0 \\ 0 & 1 & -\frac{1}{2} \\ 0 & 0 & 1 \end{pmatrix} \begin{pmatrix} z_1 \\ z_2 \\ z_3 \end{pmatrix} = \begin{pmatrix} y_1 \\ y_2 \\ y_3 \end{pmatrix}$.

Then $(x,A(x)) = (y,D(y))$

where $D = \begin{pmatrix} 1 & 0 & 0 \\ 0 & -2 & 0 \\ 0 & 0 & \frac{1}{2} \end{pmatrix} = \begin{pmatrix} \alpha_1 & 0 & 0 \\ 0 & \alpha_2 & 0 \\ 0 & 0 & \alpha_3 \end{pmatrix}$

and $A = P_1^t P_2^t D P_2 P_1$.

Consequently the matrix A can be diagonalised.

A has characteristic equation $(1-\lambda)(\lambda^2-1)$

with eigenvalues 1,1,-1.

Then normalized eigenvectors of A are

$\frac{1}{\sqrt{2}} \begin{pmatrix} 1 \\ 0 \\ 1 \end{pmatrix}, \begin{pmatrix} 0 \\ 1 \\ 0 \end{pmatrix}, \frac{1}{\sqrt{2}} \begin{pmatrix} 1 \\ 0 \\ -1 \end{pmatrix},$

corresponding to the eigenvalues 1,1,-1.

Thus A* is a non-degenerate saddle of index 1.

Let Q be the basis change matrix $\frac{1}{\sqrt{2}} \begin{pmatrix} 1 & 0 & 1 \\ 0 & 2 & 0 \\ 1 & 0 & -1 \end{pmatrix}$.

$$Q^tAQ = \frac{1}{2} \begin{pmatrix} 1 & 0 & 1 \\ 0 & 2 & 0 \\ 1 & 0 & -1 \end{pmatrix} \begin{pmatrix} 0 & 0 & 1 \\ 0 & 1 & 0 \\ 1 & 0 & 0 \end{pmatrix} \begin{pmatrix} 1 & 0 & 1 \\ 0 & 2 & 0 \\ 1 & 0 & -1 \end{pmatrix}$$

$$= \begin{pmatrix} 1 & 0 & 0 \\ 0 & 1 & 0 \\ 0 & 0 & -1 \end{pmatrix}.$$

As a quadratic form

$$(x_1,x_2,x_3)\ A \begin{pmatrix} x_1 \\ x_2 \\ x_3 \end{pmatrix} = (x_1,x_2,x_3) \begin{pmatrix} x_3 \\ x_2 \\ x_1 \end{pmatrix} = x_1x_3+x_2^2 .$$

We can also write this as

$$(x_1,x_2,x_3)\ \frac{1}{2}\begin{pmatrix} 1 & 0 & 1 \\ 0 & \sqrt{2} & 0 \\ 1 & 0 & -1 \end{pmatrix}\begin{pmatrix} 1 & 0 & 0 \\ 0 & 1 & 0 \\ 0 & 0 & -1 \end{pmatrix}\begin{pmatrix} 1 & 0 & 1 \\ 0 & \sqrt{2} & 0 \\ 1 & 0 & -1 \end{pmatrix}\begin{pmatrix} x_1 \\ x_2 \\ x_3 \end{pmatrix}$$

$$= \frac{1}{2}(x_1+x_3, \sqrt{2}x_2, x_1-x_3) \begin{pmatrix} 1 & 0 & 0 \\ 0 & 1 & 0 \\ 0 & 0 & -1 \end{pmatrix}\begin{pmatrix} x_1 + x_3 \\ \sqrt{2}x_2 \\ x_1 - x_3 \end{pmatrix}$$

$$= \frac{1}{2}((x_1+x_3)^2 + 2x_2^2 - (x_1 - x_3)^2) .$$

Note that A is positive definite on the subspace $\{(x_1,x_2,x_3)\in\mathbb{R}^3 : (x_1 = x_3)\}$ spanned by the first two eigenvectors.

We can give a geometric interpretation of the behaviour of a matrix A with both positive and negative eigenvalues.

For example $A = \begin{pmatrix} 1 & 2 \\ 2 & 1 \end{pmatrix}$

has eigenvectors $z_1 = \begin{pmatrix} 1 \\ 1 \end{pmatrix}$ $z_2 = \begin{pmatrix} 1 \\ -1 \end{pmatrix}$ corresponding to

the eignevalues 3,-1 respectively.

Thus A maps the vector z_1 to $3z_1$ and z_2 to $-z_2$.

The second operation can be regarded as a reflection of the vector z_2 in the line $\{(x,y): x-y = 0\}$, associated with the first eigenvalue. The first operation $z_1 \to 3z_1$ is a translation of z_1 to $3z_1$.

Consider now any point $x\in\mathbb{R}^2$. We can write

$x = \alpha z_1 + \beta z_2$.

Thus $A(x) = 3\alpha z_1 - \beta z_2$.

In other words A may be decomposed into two operations: a translation in the direction z_1, followed by a reflection about z_1.

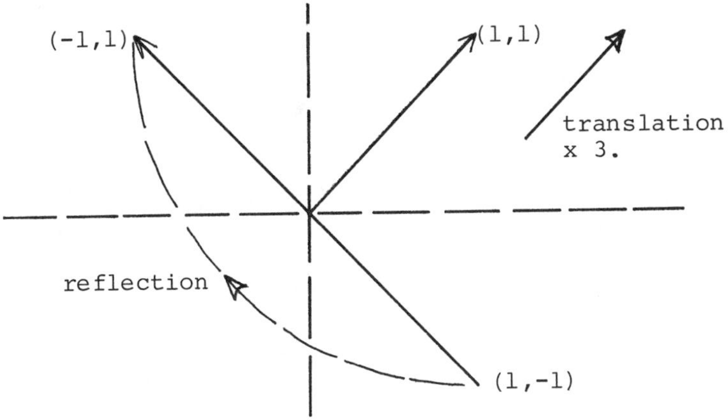

Fig.2.2.

2.4 GEOMETRIC INTERPRETATION OF A LINEAR TRANSFORMATION

More generally suppose A has real roots to the characteristic equation and has eigenvectors $\{x_1,\ldots,x_s,z_1,\ldots z_t,k_1,\ldots k_p\}$.

The first s vectors correspond to positive eigenvalues, the next t vectors to negative eigenvalues, and the final p vectors belong to the kernel, with zero eigenvalues.

Then A may be described in the following way:

i) collapse the kernel vectors on to the image spanned by $\{x_1,\ldots,x_s,z_1,\ldots,z_t\}$.

ii) translate each x_i to $\lambda_i x_i$.

iii) reflect each z_j to $-z_j$, and then translate to $-|\mu_j|z_j$ (where μ_j is the negative eigenvalue associated with z_j).

These operations completely describe a symmetric matrix or a matrix, A, which is diagonalisable. When A is non-symmetric then it is possible for A to have complex roots.

For example consider the matrix

$$\begin{pmatrix} \cos\theta & -\sin\theta \\ \sin\theta & \cos\theta \end{pmatrix}.$$

As we have seen this corresponds to a rotation by θ in an anticlockwise direction in the plane $\mathbb{R}^2$.

To determine the eigenvalues, the characteristic equation is $(\cos\theta - \lambda)^2 + \sin^2\theta =$

$$\lambda^2 - 2\lambda\cos\theta + (\cos^2\theta + \sin^2\theta) = 0.$$

But $\cos^2\theta + \sin^2\theta = 1.$

Thus $\lambda = \dfrac{2\cos\theta \pm 2\sqrt{\cos^2\theta - 1}}{2} = \cos\theta \pm i\sin\theta.$

More generally a 2 x 2 matrix with complex roots may be regarded as a transformation $\lambda e^{i\theta}$ where λ corresponds to a translation by λ and $e^{i\theta}$ corresponds to a rotation by θ.

<u>Example 2.8</u>

Consider $A = \begin{pmatrix} 2 & -2 \\ 2 & 2 \end{pmatrix}$ with trace (A) = tr(A) = 4 and $|A| = 8$.

As we have seen the characteristic equation for A is $\lambda^2 - (\text{trace } A) + |A| = 0$, with roots

$$\frac{\text{trace }(A) \pm \sqrt{(\text{trace } A)^2 - 4|A|}}{2}.$$

Thus the roots are $2 \pm \frac{1}{2}\sqrt{16-32} = 2 \pm 2i$

$$= 2\sqrt{2}\left[\frac{1}{\sqrt{2}} \pm \frac{i}{\sqrt{2}}\right]$$

where $\cos\theta = \sin\theta = \dfrac{1}{\sqrt{2}}$ and so $\theta = 45^\circ$.

Thus A: $\begin{pmatrix} x \\ y \end{pmatrix} \rightarrow 2\sqrt{2}\begin{pmatrix} x\cos 45 & - y\sin 45 \\ x\sin 45 & + y\cos 45 \end{pmatrix}$.

Consequently A first sends (x,y) by a translation to $(2\sqrt{2}\,x, 2\sqrt{2}\,y)$ and then rotates this vector through an angle 45°.

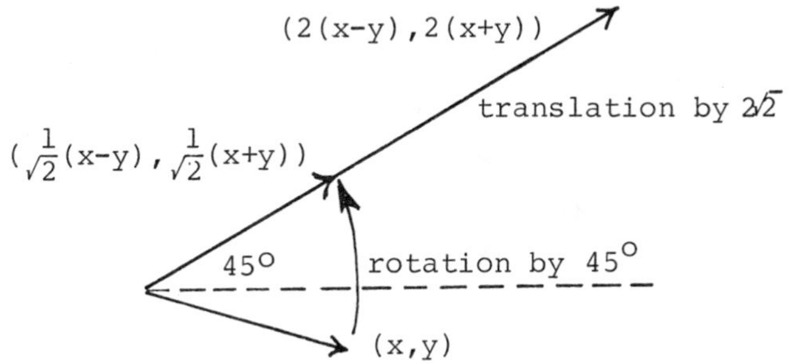

Fig.2.3

More abstractly if A is a n x n matrix with two complex conjugate eigenvalues $(\cos\theta + i\sin\theta)$, $(\cos\theta - i\sin\theta)$, then there exists a two dimensional eigenspace E^{θ} such that

$$A(x) = \lambda e^{i\theta}(x) \qquad \text{for all } x \in E_{\theta},$$

where $\lambda e^{i\theta}(x)$ means rotate x by θ within E_{θ} and then translate by λ.

In some cases a linear transformation, A, can be given a canonical form in terms of rotations, translations and reflections, together with a collapse onto the kernel. What this means is that there exists a number of distinct eigenspaces

$$\{E_1,\ldots,E_p,X_1,\ldots,X_s,K\}$$

where A maps i) E_j to E_j by rotating any vector in E_j through an angle θ_j

ii) X_j to X_j by translating a vector x in X_j to $\lambda_j x$, for some non zero real number λ_j.

iii) the kernel K to {O}.

In the case that the dimensions of these eigenspaces sum to n, then the canonical form of the matrix A is

$$\begin{pmatrix} e^{i\Theta} & 0 & 0 \\ 0 & \Lambda & 0 \\ 0 & 0 & 0 \end{pmatrix}$$

where $e^{i\Theta}$ consists of p different 2x2 matrices on the diagonal, and Λ is a diagonal sxs matrix, while O is an (n-r)x(n-r) zero matrix, where $r = \text{rank}(A) = 2p + s$.

However, even when all the roots of the characteristic equation are real, it need not be possible to obtain a diagonal, canonical form of the matrix.

To illustrate, in Example 2.6 (page 87) it is easy to show that the eigenvalue $\lambda = 0$ occurs twice as a root of the characteristic equation for the non-symmetric matrix A, even though the kernel is of dimension 1. The eigenvalue $\lambda = 7$ occurs once. Moreover the vector (3,-29,17) clearly must be an eigenvector for $\lambda = 7$,and thus span the image of A^2. However it is also clear that the vector (3,-29,17) does not span the image of A. Thus the eigenspace E_7 does not provide a basis for the image of A, and so the matrix A cannot be diagonalised.

However, as we have shown, for any symmetric matrix the dimensions of the eigenspaces sum to n, and the matrix can be expressed in canonical, diagonal, form.

In chapter 4 below we consider smooth functions and show that "locally" such a function can be analysed in terms of the canonical form of a particular symmetric matrix.

Chapter 3

TOPOLOGY AND CONVEX OPTIMISATION

3.1 A TOPOLOGICAL SPACE

In the previous chapter we introduced the notion of the scalar product of two vectors in $\mathbb{R}^n$. More generally if a scalar product is defined on some space, then this permits the definition of a norm, or length, associated with a vector, and this in turn allows us to define the distance between two vectors. A distance function or metric may be defined on a space, X, even when X admits no norm. For example let X be the surface of the earth. Clearly it is possible to say what the shortest distance, d(x,y), between two points on the earth's surface is, although it is not meaningful to talk of the "length" of a point on the surface. More general than the notion of a metric is that of a topology. Essentially a topology on a space is a mathematical notion for making more precise the idea of "nearness". The notion of topology can then be used to define what we mean by continuity.

3.1.1 Scalar Product and norms

In §2.3.3 we defined the scalar product of two

vectors $x = \sum_{i=1}^{n} x_i e_i$, $y = \sum_{i=1}^{n} y_i e_i$ in $\mathbb{R}^n$ where $\{e_1,\ldots,e_n\}$ is the standard basis, to be

$$(x,y) = \sum_{i=1}^{n} x_i y_i .$$

More generally suppose that $\{v_1,\ldots,v_n\}$ is a basis for $\mathbb{R}^n$, and $(x_1,\ldots,x_n),(y_1,\ldots,y_n)$ are the coordinates of x,y with respect to this basis. Then $(x,y) = \sum_{i=1}^{n} \sum_{j=1}^{n} x_i y_j (v_i,v_j)$ where (v_i,v_j) is the scalar product of v_i and v_j.

Thus $(x,y) = (x_1,\ldots,x_n)\begin{pmatrix} & & \\ & a_{ij} & \\ & & \end{pmatrix}\begin{pmatrix} y_1 \\ \\ y_n \end{pmatrix}$

where $A = (a_{ij}) = ((v_i,v_j))_{i=1,\ldots n;j=1,\ldots,n}$.

If we let $v_i = \sum_{k=1}^{n} v_{ik} e_k$, then clearly

$(v_i,v_i) = \sum_{k=1}^{n} (v_{ik})^2 > 0$. Moreover $(v_i,v_j)=(v_j,v_i)$.

Thus the matrix A is symmetric. Since A must be of rank n, it can be diagonalized to give a matrix $\Lambda = Q^t A Q$ all of whose diagonal entries are positive. Here Q is the orthogonal basis change matrix and $Q^t(x_1,\ldots,x_n) = (x'_1,\ldots,x'_n)$ gives the coordinates of x with respect to the basis of eigenvectors of A.

Hence $(x,y) = (x,A(y)) = (x,Q\Lambda Q^t(y))$

$$= (Q^t(x),\Lambda Q^t(y)).$$

$$= \sum_{i=1}^{n} \lambda_i x'_i y'_i .$$

Thus a scalar product is a non-degenerate positive definite quadratic form. Note that the scalar product is <u>bilinear</u> since $(x_1 + x_2,y) = (x_1,y)+(x_2,y)$ and $(x,y_1 + y_2) = (x,y_1)+(x,y_2)$, and <u>symmetric</u> since $(x,y) = (x,A(y)) = (y,A(x))=(y,x)$.

The scalar product given by $(x,y) = \sum_{i=1}^{n} x_i y_i$ we shall call the <u>Euclidean</u> scalar product. Define the

Euclidean norm, $\| \ \|_E$,

by $\| x \|_E = \sqrt{(x,x)} = \sqrt{\sum_{i=1}^{n} x_i^2}$.

Note that $\| x \|_E \geq 0$ for any $x \in \mathbb{R}^n$, and that $\| x \|_E = 0$ if and only if $x = (0,\ldots,0)$.

Moreover, if $a \in \mathbb{R}$, then $\| ax \|_E = \sqrt{\sum_{i=1}^{n} a^2 x_i^2} = |a| \ \| x \|_E$.

Lemma 3.1 If $x, y \in \mathbb{R}^n$, then $\| x+y \|_E \leq \| x \|_E + \| y \|_E$.

Proof. For convenience write $\| x \|_E$ as $\| x \|$.

Now $\| x+y \|^2 = (x+y, x+y) = (x,x) + (x,y) + (y,x) + (y,y)$.

But the scalar product is symmetric.

Therefore $\| x+y \|^2 = \| x \|^2 + \| y \|^2 + 2(x,y)$.

Furthermore $(\| x \| + \| y \|)^2 = \| x \|^2 + \| y \|^2 + 2 \| x \| \ \| y \|$.

Thus $\| x+y \| \leq \| x \| + \| y \|$ iff $(x,y) \leq \| x \| \ \| y \|$.

To show this note that $\sum_{i<j} (x_i y_j - x_j y_i)^2 \geq 0$.

Thus $\sum_{i<j} (x_i^2 y_j^2 + x_j^2 y_i^2) \geq 2 \sum_{i<j} x_i y_i x_j y_j$.

Add $\sum_{i=1}^{n} x_i^2 y_i^2$ to both sides.

This gives $\left(\sum_{i=1}^{n} x_i^2 \right) \left(\sum_{i=1}^{n} y_i^2 \right) \geq \left(\sum_{i=1}^{n} x_i y_i \right)^2$.

Therefore $\| x \|^2 \ \| y \|^2 \geq (x,y)^2$

and so $\dfrac{(x,y)}{\| x \| \ \| y \|} \leq 1$,

or $\| x+y \| \leq \| x \| + \| y \|$.

In this lemma we have shown that

$$-1 \leq \frac{(x,y)}{\| x \| \| y \|} \leq 1.$$

This ratio can be identified with $\cos \theta$, where θ is the angle between the two vectors x, y. In the case of unit vectors (x,y) can be identified with the perpendicular projection of y onto x as in Figure 3.1.

Fig.3.1.

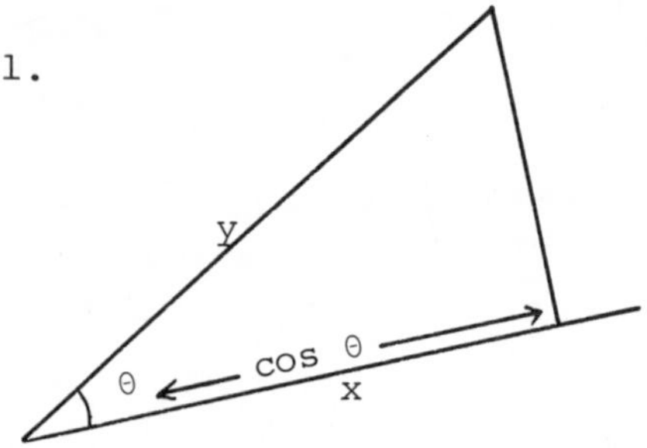

The property $\| x+y \| \leq \|x\| + \|y\|$ is known as the <u>triangle inequality</u> (see Figure 3.2)

Fig 3.2.

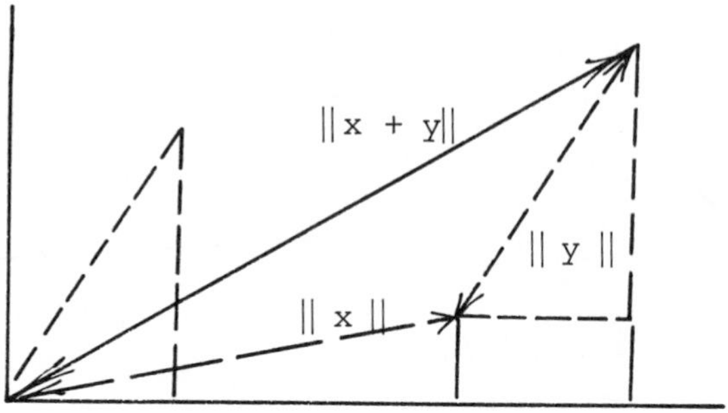

<u>Definition 3.1</u> Let X be a vector space over the field $\mathbb{R}$. A <u>norm</u>, $\| \ \|$, on X is a mapping $\| \ \|: X \to \mathbb{R}$ which satisfies the following three properties:

N1 : $\|x\| \geq 0$ for all $x \in X$, and $\|x\| = 0$ iff $x = \underline{0}$

N2 : $\|ax\| = |a| \, \|x\|$ for all $x \in X$, and $a \in \mathbb{R}$.

N3 : $\|x+y\| \leq \|x\| + \|y\|$ for all $x, y \in X$.

There are many different norms on a vector space. For example if A is a non-degenerate positive definite symmetric matrix, we could define $\| \ \|_A$

by $\|x\|_A = \sqrt{(x,Ax)}$.

The cartesian norm is $\|x\|_C = \|(x_1,\ldots,x_n)\|_C$
$= \max\{|x_1|,\ldots,|x_n|\}$.

Clearly $\|x\|_C \geq 0$ and $\|x\|_C = 0$ iff $x_i = 0$ for all $i=1,\ldots,n$.

Moreover $\|ax\|_C = \max\{|ax_1|,\ldots,|ax_n|\}$
$= \max\{|a||x_1|,\ldots,|a||x_n|\}$
$= |a||x_i|$, for some i
$= |a|(\max\{|x_1|,\ldots,|x_n|\})$
$= |a| \;\|x\|_C$.

Finally $\|x+y\|_C = |x_i + y_i|$ for some i
$\leq |x_i| + |y_i|$
$\leq \max\{|x_1|,\ldots,|x_n|\}$
$+ \max\{|y_1|,\ldots,|y_n|\}$
$= \|x\|_C + \|y\|_C$.

There is also the city block norm $\|x\|_B$ given by

$$\|x\|_B = \sum_{i=1}^{n}|x_i|.$$

Clearly $\|x+y\|_B = \sum_{i=1}^{n}|x_i+y_i| \leq \sum_{i=1}^{n}\left(|x_i| + |y_i|\right)$
$= \|x\|_B + \|y\|_B$.

If $\|\;\|$ is a norm on the vector space X, the distance function or metric d on X induced by $\|\;\|$ is the function

$$d: X \times X \to \mathbb{R} : d(x,y) = \|x-y\|.$$

Note that $d(x,y) \geq 0$ for all $x,y \in X$ and that $d(x,y)=0$ iff $x-y = 0$ i.e. $x=y$.

Moreover $d(x,y) + d(y,z) = \|x-y\| + \|y-z\|$
$\geq \|(x-y) + (y-z)\|$
$= \|x-z\| = d(x,z)$.

Hence $d(x,z) \leq d(x,y) + d(y,z)$.

Definition 3.2

A metric on a set X is a function $d: X \times X \to \mathbb{R}$ such that

D1 $d(x,y) \geq 0$ for all $x,y \in X$ and

$d(x,y) = 0$ iff $x = y$

D2 $d(x,z) \leq d(x,y) + d(y,z)$ for all $x,y,z \in X$.

Note that a metric d may be defined on a set X even when X is not a vector space. In other words d may be defined without reference to a particular norm. At the beginning of the chapter for example we mentioned that the surface of the earth, S^2, admits a metric d, where the distance between two points x,y on the surface is measured along a great circle through x,y. A second metric on S^2 is obtained by defining d(x,y) to be the angle ,θ, subtended at the centre of the earth by the two radii to x,y (see Figure 3.3)

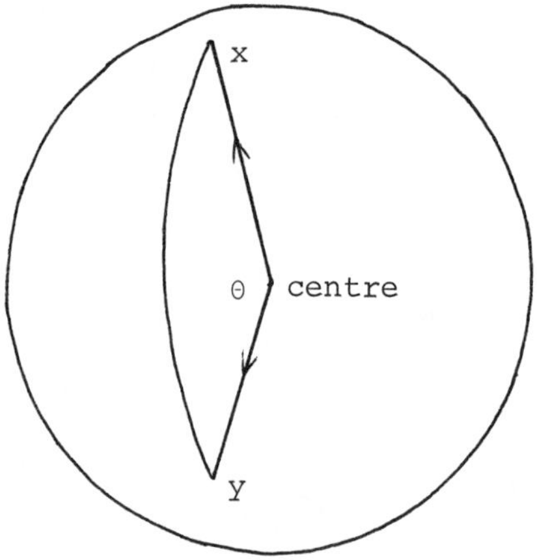

Fig.3.3.

Any set X which admits a metric,d, we shall call <u>metrisable</u>, or a <u>metric space</u>. To draw attention to the metric,d, we shall sometimes write (X,d) for a metric space.

In a metric space (X,d) the <u>open ball</u> at x of radius r in X is

$$B_d(x,r) = \{y \in X : d(x,y) < r\},$$

and the closed ball centre x of radius r is

$$\overline{B_d(x,r)} = \{y \in X : d(x,y) \leq r\}.$$

The <u>sphere</u> of radius r at x is

$$S_d(x,r) = \{y \in X : d(x,y) = r\}.$$

In $\mathbb{R}^n$, the Euclidean sphere of radius r is therefore

$$S_e(x,r) = \{y : \sum_{i=1}^{n} (x_i - y_i)^2 = r^2\}.$$

For convenience a sphere in $\mathbb{R}^n$ is often written as S^{n-1}. Here the superfix is n-1 because as we shall see the sphere in $\mathbb{R}^n$ is (n-1)-dimensional, even though it is not a vector space.

If (X,d) is a metric space, say a set V in X is d-<u>open</u> iff for any $x \in V$ there is some radius r_x (dependent on x) such that

$$B_d(x, r_x) \subset V.$$

<u>Lemma 3.2</u>

Let $\mathcal{T}_d$ be the set of all sets in X which are d-open. Then $\mathcal{T}_d$ satisfies the following properties :

T1 If $U, V \in \mathcal{T}_d$, then $U \cap V \in \mathcal{T}_d$.

T2 If $U_j \in \mathcal{T}_d$ for all j belonging to an index set J (which is possibly infinite) then $\bigcup_{j \in J} U_j \in \mathcal{T}_d$.

T3 Both X and the empty set, Φ, belong to $\mathcal{T}_d$.

<u>Proof</u> Clearly X and Φ are d-open.

If U and $V \in \mathcal{T}_d$, but $U \cap V = \Phi$ then $U \cap V$ is d-open. Suppose on the other hand that $x \in U \cap V$. Since both U and V are open, there exist r_1, r_2 such that

$$B_d(x, r_1) \subset U \text{ and } B_d(x, r_2) \subset V.$$

Let $r = \min(r_1, r_2)$. By definition

$$B_d(x,r) = B_d(x,r_1) \cap B_d(x,r_2) \subset U \cap V.$$

Thus there is an open ball, centre x, of radius r contained in $U \cap V$.

Finally suppose $x \in \bigcup_{j \in J} U_j = U$. Since x belongs to at least one U_j, say U_1, there is an open ball $B = B(x, r_1)$ contained in U_1. Thus U_1 and so U are open.

Note that by T1 the finite intersection of open sets is an open set, but infinite intersection of open sets need not be open.
To see this consider a set of the form

$$I = (a,b) = \{x \in \mathbb{R} : a < x < b\}.$$

For any $x \in I$ it is possible to find an ε such that $a + \varepsilon < x < b - \varepsilon$. Hence the open ball $B(x,\varepsilon) = \{y : x - \varepsilon < y < x + \varepsilon\}$ belongs to I, and so I is open.
Now consider the family $\{U_r : r = 1, \ldots, \infty\}$ of sets of the form $U_r = (-\frac{1}{r}, \frac{1}{r})$.
Clearly the origin, 0, belongs to each U_r, and so $0 \in \bigcap U_r = U$. Suppose that U is open. Since $0 \in U$, there must be some open ball $B(0,\varepsilon)$ belonging to U.
Let r_o be an integer such that $r_o > \frac{1}{\varepsilon}$, so $\frac{1}{r_o} < \varepsilon$.
But then $U_{r_o} = (-\frac{1}{r_o}, \frac{1}{r_o})$ is strictly contained in $(-\varepsilon, \varepsilon)$.
Therefore the ball $B(0,\varepsilon) = \{y \in \mathbb{R} : |y| < \varepsilon\} = (-\varepsilon,\varepsilon)$ is not contained in U_{r_o}, and so cannot be contained in U. Hence U is not open.

3.1.2. A Topology on a Set

We may define a topology on a set X to be any collection of sets in X which satisfies the three properties T1, T2, T3.

Definition 3.3

A topology $\mathcal{T}$ on a set X is a collection of sets in X which satisfies the following properties:

T1 If $U,V \in \mathcal{T}$ then $U \cap V \in \mathcal{T}$.

T2 If J is any index set and $U_j \in \mathcal{T}$ for each $j \in J$, then $\bigcup_J U_j \in \mathcal{T}$.

T3 Both X and the empty set belong to $\mathcal{T}$.

A set X which has a topology $\mathcal{T}$ is called topological space, and written $(X,\mathcal{T})$. The sets in $\mathcal{T}$ are called $\mathcal{T}$-open, or simply open. An open set, in $\mathcal{T}$, which contains a point x is called a neighbourhood (or nbd) of x.

A base $\mathcal{B}$ for a topology $\mathcal{T}$ is a collection of $\mathcal{T}$-open sets such that any member U of $\mathcal{T}$ can be written as a union of members of $\mathcal{B}$. Equivalently if x belongs to an $\mathcal{T}$-open set U, then there is a member V of the base such that $x \in V \subset U$.

By lemma 3.2, the collection $\mathcal{T}_d$ of sets which are open with respect to the metric d form a topology called the metric topology $\mathcal{T}_d$ on X. We also said that a set U belonged to $\mathcal{T}_d$ iff each point $x \in U$ had a neighbourhood $B_d(x,r)$ which belonged to U. Thus the family of sets $\mathcal{B} = \{B_d(x,r) : x \in X, r > 0\}$ forms a base for the metric topology $\mathcal{T}_d$ on X.

Consider again the metric topology on $\mathbb{R}$. As we have shown any set of the form (a,b) is open. Indeed a set of the form $(-\infty,a)$ or (b,∞) is also open.

In general if U is an open set (in the topology $\mathcal{T}$ for the topological space X) then the complement $\overline{U}_X = X \backslash U$ of U in X is called closed.

Thus in $\mathbb{R}$, the set $[a,b] = \{x \in \mathbb{R} : a \leq x \leq b\}$ is closed since it is the complement of the open set $(-\infty,a) \cup (b,\infty)$. Note that the sets $(-\infty,a]$ and $[b,\infty)$ are also closed since they are complements of the open sets (a,∞) and $(-\infty,b)$ respectively.

If A is any set in a topological space, $(X,\mathcal{J})$, then define the open set, Int(A), or the interior of A by $x \in \text{Int}(A)$ iff x is in A and there exists an open set G containing x such that $G \subset A$.

Conversely, define the closed set, Clos(A), or closure of A, by $x \in \text{Clos}(A)$ iff x is in X and for any open set G containing x, $G \cap A$ is non empty.

Clearly $\text{Int}(A) \subset A \subset \text{Clos}(A)$. See Ex.3.1(p.276). The boundary of A, written δA, is $\text{Clos}(A) \cap \text{Clos}(\bar{A}_X)$.

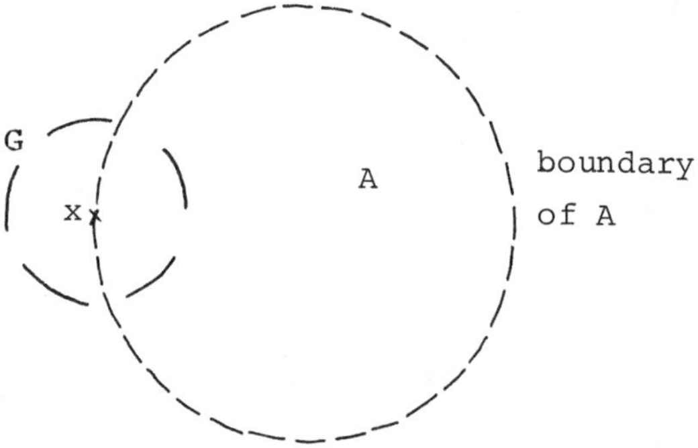

Fig 3.4

For example, if A is an open set, the complement $\overline{A_X}$ of A in X is a closed set containing δA (ie $\text{Clos}\overline{A_X} = \bar{A}_X$). The closure, Clos(A), on the other hand is the closed set which intersects $\overline{A_X}$ precisely in δA. Clearly if x belongs to the boundary of A, then any neighbourhood of x intersects both A and its complement.

A point x is an accumulation or limit point of a set A if any open set U containing x also contains points of A different from x. If A is closed then it contains its limit points. If A is a subset of X and Clos(A) = X then call A dense in X. Note that this means that any point $x \in X$ either belongs to A or, if it belongs to $X \setminus A$, has the property that for any nbd. U of x, $U \cap A \neq \Phi$. Thus if $x \in X \setminus A$ it is an accumulation point of A. If A is dense in X a point outside A may be 'approximated arbitrarily closely' by points inside A.

For example the set of non-integer real numbers is dense (as well as open) in $\mathbb{R}$. The set of rational numbers $\mathbb{Q} = \{{}^{p}/_{q} : p, q \in Z\}$ is also dense in $\mathbb{R}$, but not open, since any neighbourhood of a rational number must contain irrational numbers. For each rational $q \in Q$, note that $\mathbb{R} \setminus \{q\}$ is open, and dense.

Thus $\mathbb{R} \setminus \mathbb{Q} = \bigcap_{q \in Q} \{\mathbb{R} \setminus \{q\}\}$:

the set of irrationals is the "countable" intersection of open dense sets. Moreover $\mathbb{R} \setminus \mathbb{Q}$ is itself dense. Such a set is called a <u>residual</u> set, and is in a certain sense "more dense" than a dense set.

We now consider different topologies on a set X.

<u>Definition 3.4</u>

i) If $(X, \mathcal{T})$ is a topological space, and Y is a subset of X, the <u>relative topology</u> $\mathcal{T}_Y$ on Y is the topology whose open sets are $\{U \cap Y : U \in \mathcal{T}\}$.

ii) If $(X, \mathcal{T})$ and $(Y, \mathcal{S})$ are topological spaces the <u>product topology</u> $\mathcal{T} \times \mathcal{S}$ on the set X x Y is the topology whose base consists of all sets of the form $\{U \times V : U \in \mathcal{T}, V \in \mathcal{S}\}$.

We already introduced the relative topology in §1.1.2, and showed that this formed a topology. To show that $\mathcal{T} \times \mathcal{S}$ is a topology for X x Y we need to show that the union and intersection properties are satisfied.

Suppose that $W_i = U_i \times V_i$ for $i=1,2$, where $U_i \in \mathcal{T}, V_i \in \mathcal{S}$.

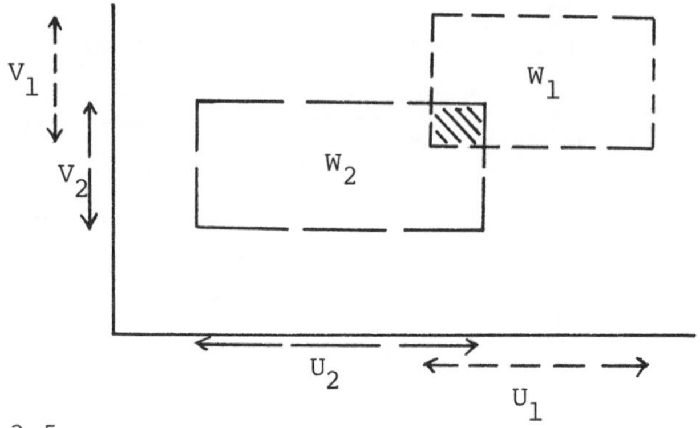

Fig. 3.5

Now $W_1 \cap W_2 = (U_1 \times V_1) \cap (U_2 \times V_2)$
$= (U_1 \cap U_2) \times (V_1 \cap V_2)$.

But $U_1 \cap U_2 \in \mathcal{T}$, $V_1 \cap V_2 \in \mathcal{S}$, since $\mathcal{S}$ and $\mathcal{T}$ are topologies.

Thus $W_1 \cap W_2 \in \mathcal{T} \times \mathcal{S}$.

Suppose now that $x \in W_1 \cup W_2$. Then x belongs either to $U_1 \times V_1$ or $U_2 \times V_2$ (or both). In either case x belongs to a member of the base for $\mathcal{T} \times \mathcal{S}$.

Another way of expressing the product topology is that W is open in the product topology iff for any $x \in W$ there exist open sets, $U \in \mathcal{T}$ and $V \in \mathcal{S}$, such that $x \in U \times V$ and $U \times V \subset W$.

For example consider the metric topology $\mathcal{T}$ induced by the norm $| \ |$ on $\mathbb{R}$. This gives the product topology $\mathcal{T}^n$ on $\mathbb{R}^n$, where U is open in $\mathcal{T}^n$ iff for each $x = (x_1, \ldots, x_n) \in U$ there exists an open interval $B(x_i, r_i)$ of radius r_i about the ith coordinate x_i such that

$$B(x_1, r_1) \times \ldots \times B(x_n, r_n) \subset U.$$

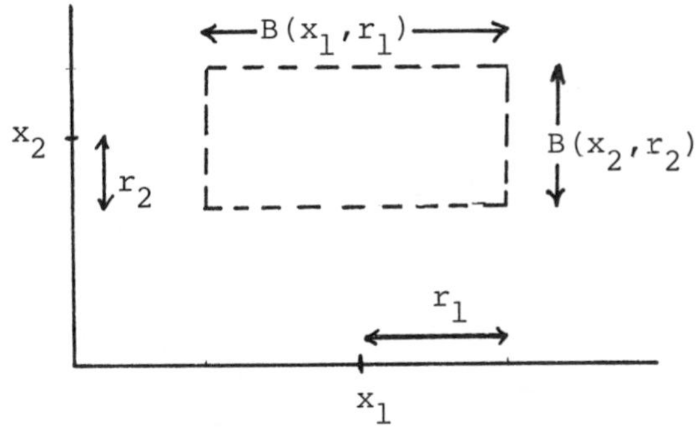

Fig. 3.6 The product topology in $\mathbb{R}^2$.

Consider now the cartesian norm on $\mathbb{R}^n$, where

$$\| x \|_c = \max\{|x_1|,\ldots,|x_n|\}.$$

This induces a cartesian metric

$$d_c(x,y) = \max\{|x_1-y_1|,\ldots,|x_n-y_n|\}.$$

A cartesian open ball of radius r about x is then the set $B_c(x,r) = \{y\in\mathbb{R}^n: |y_i-x_i| < r \ \forall_i=1,\ldots,n\}$.

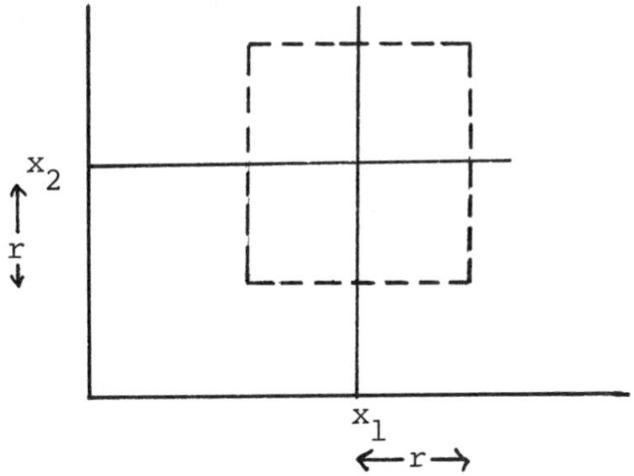

Fig. 3.7 A cartesian open ball of radius r in $\mathbb{R}^2$.

A set U is open in the cartesian topology $\mathcal{T}_c$ for $\mathbb{R}^n$ iff for every $x\in U$ there exists some $r > 0$ such that the ball $B_c(x,r) \subset U$.

Suppose now that U is an open set in the product topology $\mathcal{T}^n$ for $\mathbb{R}^n$. At any point $x \in U$, there exist $r_1, \ldots, r_n$ all > 0 such that
$B = B(x_1, r_1) \times \ldots \times B(x_n, r_n) \subset U$.
Now let $r = \min(r_1, \ldots, r_n)$. Then clearly the cartesian ball $B_c(x,r)$ belongs to the product ball B, and hence to U. Thus U is open in the cartesian topology.

On the other hand if U is open in the cartesian topology, for each point x in U, the cartesian ball $B_c(x,r)$ belongs to U. But this means the product ball

$$B(x_1, r) \times \ldots \times B(x_n, r) \text{ also belongs to U.}$$

Hence U is open in the product topology.

We have therefore shown that a set U is open in the product topology $\mathcal{T}^n$ on $\mathbb{R}^n$ iff it is open in the cartesian topology $\mathcal{T}_c$ on $\mathbb{R}^n$. Thus the two topologies are identical.

We have also introduced the <u>Euclidean</u> and <u>city block metrics</u> on $\mathbb{R}^n$. These induce the <u>Euclidean topology</u> $\mathcal{T}_E$ and <u>city block topology</u> $\mathcal{T}_B$ on $\mathbb{R}^n$. As before a set U is open in $\mathcal{T}_E$ (resp. $\mathcal{T}_B$) iff for any point $x \in U$, there is an open neighbourhood

$$B_E(x,r) = \{y \in \mathbb{R}^n: \sum_{i=1}^{n} (y_i - x_i)^2 < r^2\}$$

$$(\text{resp } B_B(x,r) = \{y \in \mathbb{R}^n: \Sigma |y_i - x_i| < r\})$$

of x which belongs to U.
(The reason we called d_B the city block metric should be obvious from the nature of a city block ball in $\mathbb{R}^2$).

In fact these three topologies $\mathcal{T}_c, \mathcal{T}_E$ and $\mathcal{T}_B$ on $\mathbb{R}^n$ are all identical. We shall show this in the case $n = 2$.

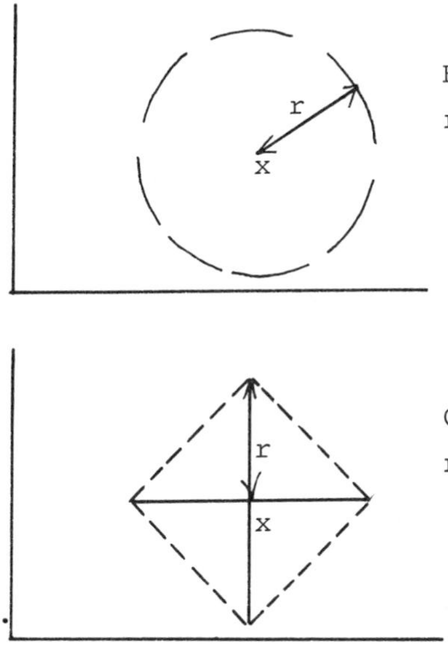

Euclidean ball of radius r at x.

City Block of radius r at x.

Fig.3.8.

Lemma 3.3

The cartesian, Euclidean and city block topologies on $\mathbb{R}^2$ are identical.

Proof

Suppose that U is an open set in the Euclidean topology $\mathcal{T}_E$ for $\mathbb{R}^2$.
Thus at $x \in U$, there is an $r > 0$, such that the set $B_E(x,r) = \{y \in \mathbb{R}^2 : \sum_{i=1}^{2} (y_i - x_i)^2 < r^2\} \subset U$.
From Figure 3.9, it is obvious that the city block ball $B_B(x,r)$ also belongs to $B_E(x,r)$ and thus U.
Thus U is open in $\mathcal{T}_B$.
On the other hand the cartesian ball $B_c(x,{}^r/_2)$ belongs to $B_B(x,r)$ and thus to U.
Hence U is open in $\mathcal{T}_c$.
Finally the Euclidean ball $B_E(x,{}^r/_2)$ belongs to $B_c(x,{}^r/_2)$. Hence if U is open in $\mathcal{T}_c$ it is open in $\mathcal{T}_E$.

Thus U open in $\mathcal{T}_E$ => U open in $\mathcal{T}_B$ =>U open in $\mathcal{T}_c$ => U open in $\mathcal{T}_E$.
Consequently all three topologies are identical in $\mathbb{R}^2$.

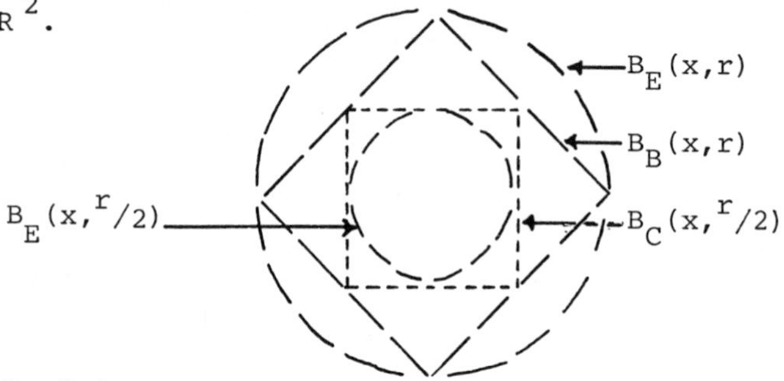

Fig.3.9

Suppose that $\mathcal{T}_1$ and $\mathcal{T}_2$ are two topologies on a space X. If any open set U in $\mathcal{T}_1$ is also an open set in $\mathcal{T}_2$ then say that $\mathcal{T}_2$ is <u>finer</u> than $\mathcal{T}_1$ and write $\mathcal{T}_1 \subset \mathcal{T}_2$. If $\mathcal{T}_1 \subset \mathcal{T}_2$ and $\mathcal{T}_2 \subset \mathcal{T}_1$ then $\mathcal{T}_1$ and $\mathcal{T}_2$ are identical, and we now write $\mathcal{T}_1 = \mathcal{T}_2$.

If d_1 and d_2 are two metrics on a space X, then under some conditions the topologies $\mathcal{T}_1$ and $\mathcal{T}_2$ induced by d_1 and d_2 are identical. Say the metrics d_1 and d_2 are <u>equivalent</u> iff for each $\varepsilon > 0$ there exist $\eta_1 > 0$ and $\eta_2 > 0$ such that

$$d_1(x,y) < \eta_1 \Rightarrow d_2(x,y) < \varepsilon$$
and
$$d_2(x,y) < \eta_2 \Rightarrow d_1(x,y) < \varepsilon .$$

Another way of expressing this is that

$$B_1(x,\eta_1) \subset B_2(x,\varepsilon)$$
and
$$B_2(x,\eta_2) \subset B_1(x,\varepsilon)$$

where $B_i(x,r) = \{y:d_i(x,y) < r\}$ for i=1 or 2.

Just as in lemma 3.3, the cartesian, Euclidean and city block metrics on $\mathbb{R}^n$ are equivalent. We can use this to show that the induced topologies are identical.

We now show that equivalent metrics induce identical topologies.

If $f:X \to \mathbb{R}$ is a function, and V is a set in X, define $\sup(f,V)$, the supremum of f on V to be the smallest number $M \in \mathbb{R}$ such that $f(x) \leq M$ for all $x \in V$.

Similarly define $\inf(f,V)$, the infimum of f on V to be the largest number $m \in \mathbb{R}$ such that $f(x) \geq m$ for all $x \in V$.

If $d: X \times X \to \mathbb{R}$ is a metric on X, and x a point in X, V a subset of X, define the distance from x to V to be $d(x,V) = \inf(d(x,-),V)$ where $d(x,-): V \to \mathbb{R}$ is the function $d(x,-)(y) = d(x,y)$.

Suppose now that U is an open set in the topology $\mathcal{J}_1$ induced by the metric d_1. For any point $x \in U$ there exists $r > 0$ such that $B_1(x,r) \subset U$, where $B_1(x,r) = \{y \in X: d_1(x,y) < r\}$. Since we assume the metrics d_1 and d_2 are equivalent, there must exist $s > 0$, say, such that

$$B_2(x,s) \subset B_1(x,r)$$

where $B_2(x,s) = \{y \in X: d_2(x,y) < s\}$. Indeed one may choose $s = d_2(x, \overline{B_1(x,r)})$ where $\overline{B_1(x,r)}$ is the complement of $B_1(x,r)$ in X (see Fig.3.10). Clearly the set U must be open in $\mathcal{J}_2$ and so $\mathcal{J}_2$ is finer than $\mathcal{J}_1$. In the same way, however, there exists $t > 0$ such that $B_1(x,t) \subset B_2(x,s)$, where again one may choose $t = d_1(x, \overline{B_2(x,s)})$. Hence if U is open in $\mathcal{J}_2$ it is open in $\mathcal{J}_1$; and so $\mathcal{J}_1$ is finer than $\mathcal{J}_2$. As a consequence $\mathcal{J}_1$ and $\mathcal{J}_2$ are identical.

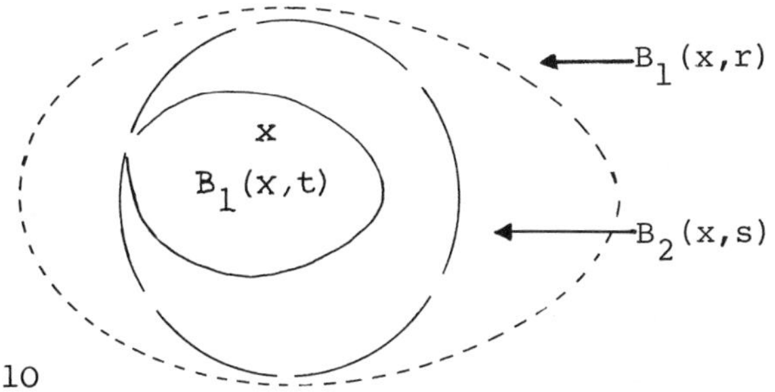

Fig.3.10

Thus we obtain the following lemma.

<u>Lemma 3.4</u>

The product topology $\mathcal{T}^n$, Euclidean topology $\mathcal{T}_E$, cartesian topology $\mathcal{T}_c$ and city block topology $\mathcal{T}_B$ are all identical on $\mathbb{R}^n$.

As a consequence we may use, as convenient, any one of these three metrics, or any other equivalent metric, on $\mathbb{R}^n$ knowing that topological results are unchanged.

3.2. CONTINUITY

Suppose that $(X,\mathcal{T})$ and $(Y,\mathcal{S})$ are two topological spaces, and $f:X \to Y$ is a function between X and Y. Say that f is <u>continuous</u> (with respect to the topologies $\mathcal{T}$ and $\mathcal{S}$) iff for any set U in $\mathcal{S}$ (ie U is $\mathcal{S}$-open) then the set $f^{-1}(U) = \{x \in X: f(x) \in U\}$ is $\mathcal{T}$-open.

This definition can be given an alternative form in the case when X and Y are metric spaces, with metrics d_1, d_2 say.

Consider a point x_o in the domain of f. For any $\varepsilon > 0$ the ball $B_2(f(x_o),\varepsilon) = \{y \in Y: d_2(f(x_o),y) < \varepsilon\}$ is open. For continuity, we require that the inverse image of this ball be open. That is to say there exists some δ, such that the ball $B_1(x_o,\delta) = \{x \in X: d_1(x_o,x) < \delta\}$ belongs to $f^{-1}(B_2(f(x_o),\varepsilon))$.

Thus $x \in B_1(x_o,\delta) \Rightarrow f(x) \in B_2(f(x_o),\varepsilon)$.

Therefore say f is continuous at $x_o \in X$ iff for any $\varepsilon > 0, \exists\, \delta > 0$ such that

$f(B_1(x_o,\delta)) \subset B_2(f(x_o),\varepsilon)$.

In the case that X and Y have norms $\| \ \|_X$ and $\| \ \|_Y$, then we may say that f is continuous at x_o iff for any $\varepsilon > 0$, $\exists\ \delta > 0$ such that

$$\|x-x_o\|_X < \delta \Rightarrow \|f(x) - f(x_o)\|_Y < \varepsilon.$$

Then f is continuous on X iff f is continuous at all x in X.

If X,Y are vector spaces then we may check the continuity of a function $f:X \to Y$ by using the metric or norm form of the definition.

For example suppose $f:\mathbb{R} \to \mathbb{R}$ has the graph given in Fig. 3.11. Clearly f is not continuous. To see this formally let $f(x_o) = y_o$ and choose ε such that $|y_1-y_o| > \varepsilon$. Clearly if $x\in(x_o-\delta,x_o)$ then $f(x) \in (y_o-\varepsilon,y_o)$.

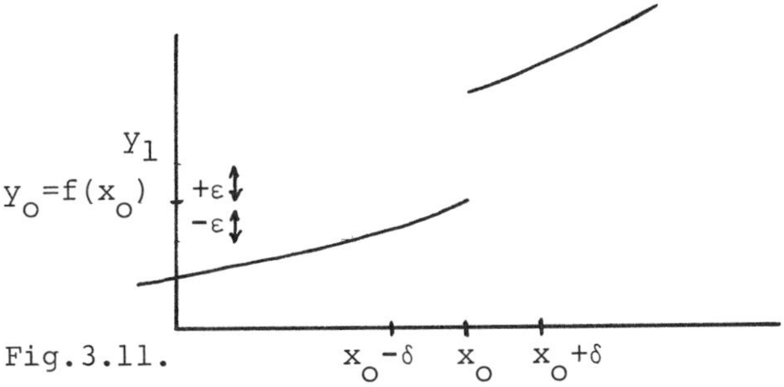

Fig.3.11.

However for any $\delta > 0$ it is the case that $x\in(x_o,x_o + \delta)$ implies $f(x) > y_o + \varepsilon$.

Thus there exists no $\delta > 0$ such that

$$x\in(x_o-\delta,x_o+ \delta) \Rightarrow f(x)\in (y_o-\varepsilon,y_o+ \varepsilon).$$

Hence f is not continuous at x_o.

We can give an alternative definition of continuity.

A sequence of points in a metric space X is a collection of points $\{x_n:n\in Z\}$, indexed by the positive integers Z. The sequence is written (x_n). The sequence (x_n) has a limit x iff

$\forall \varepsilon > 0 \ \exists n_o \in Z$ such that $n > n_o$ implies
$\|x_n - x\|_X < \varepsilon$.
In this case write $x_n \to x$ as $n \to \infty$, or $\underset{n\to\infty}{\text{Lim}}\, x_n = x$.
Note that x is then an accumulation point of the set $\{x_1, \ldots.\}$.
More generally $(x_n) \to x$ iff for any open set G containing x, all but a finite number of points in the sequence (x_n) belong to G.
Thus say f is continuous at x_o iff

$$x_n \to x_o \text{ implies } f(x_n) \to f(x_o).$$

Example 3.1 Consider the function $f : \mathbb{R} \to \mathbb{R}$ given by $f : x \to \begin{cases} x \sin \frac{1}{x} & \text{for } x \neq 0 \\ 0 & x = 0 \end{cases}$.
Now $x \sin \frac{1}{x} = \frac{\sin y}{y}$ where $y = \frac{1}{x}$.
Consider a sequence (x_n) where $\underset{n\to\infty}{\text{Lim}}\, x_n = 0$.
We shall write this $x \to 0$.
$\underset{x\to 0}{\text{Lim}}\, x \sin \frac{1}{x} = \underset{y\to\infty}{\text{Lim}} \frac{\sin y}{y} = 0$ since $|\sin y|$ is bounded above by 1, and $\underset{y\to\infty}{\text{Lim}} \frac{1}{y} = 0$.
Thus $\underset{x\to 0}{\text{Lim}}\, f(x) = 0$. But $f(0) = 0$, and so $x_n \to 0$ implies $f(x_n) \to 0$. Hence f is continuous at 0.
On the other hand suppose $g(x) = \sin \frac{1}{x}$. Clearly $g(x)$ has no limt as $x \to 0$. To see this observe that for any sequence $(x_n) \to 0$ it is impossible to find a nbd. G of some point $y \in [-1,1]$ such that $g(x_n) \in G$ whenver $n > n_o$.

Any linear function between finite-dimensional vector spaces is continuous, and thus the set of continuous functions contains the set of linear functions, when the domain is finite-dimensional. To see this suppose that $f : V \to W$ is a linear transformation between normed vector spaces. (Note that V and W may be infinite-dimensional.)

Let $\| \ \|_V$ and $\| \ \|_W$ be the norms on V,W respectively.

Say that f is <u>bounded</u> iff $\exists B > 0$ such that $\| f(x) \|_W \le B \| x \|_V$ for all $x \in V$.

Suppose now that $\| f(x) - f(x_0) \|_W < \varepsilon$.

Now $\| f(x) - f(x_0) \|_W = \| f(x - x_0) \|_W \le B \| x - x_0 \|_V$ since f is linear and bounded.

Choose $\delta = \frac{\varepsilon}{B}$.

Then $\| x - x_0 \|_V < \delta \Rightarrow \| f(x) - f(x_0) \|_W \le B \| x - x_0 \|_V$
$< \varepsilon.$

Thus if f is linear and bounded it is continuous.

Lemma 3.5

Any linear transformation $f : V \to W$ is bounded and thus continuous if V is finite-dimensional (of dimension n).

Proof

Use the cartesian norm $\| \ \|_C$ on V, and let $\| \ \|_W$ be the norm on W. Let $e_1, \ldots, e_n$ be a basis for V, $\| x \|_C = \sup\{ |x_i| : i = 1, \ldots, n\}$ and

$$e = \sup_n \{ \| f(e_i) \|_W : i = 1, \ldots, n\}.$$

Now $f(x) = \sum_{i=1} x_i f(e_i)$.

Thus $\| f(x) \|_W \le \sum_{i=1}^{n} \| f(x_i e_i) \|_W$ by the triangle inequality

$$\le \sum_{i=1}^{n} |x_i| \, \| f(e_i) \|_W \text{ since } \| ay \|_W = |a| \, \| y \|_W$$

$$\le n \, e \, \| x \|_C .$$

Thus f is bounded, and hence continuous with respect to the norms $\| \ \|_C$, $\| \ \|_W$. But for any other norm $\| \ \|_V$ it can be shown that there exists $B' > 0$ such that $\| x \|_C \le B' \| x \|_V$. Thus f is bounded, and hence continuous, with respect to the norms $\| \ \|_V$, $\| \ \|_W$.

Consider now the set $L(\mathbb{R}^n, \mathbb{R}^m)$ of linear functions from $\mathbb{R}^n$ to $\mathbb{R}^m$. Clearly if $f,g \in L(\mathbb{R}^n,\mathbb{R}^m)$ then the sum $f+g$ defined by $(f+g)(x) = f(x)+g(x)$ is also linear, and for any $\alpha \in \mathbb{R}$, αf, defined by $(\alpha f)(x) = \alpha(f(x))$ is linear. Hence $L(\mathbb{R}^n,\mathbb{R}^m)$ is a vector space over $\mathbb{R}$. Since $\mathbb{R}^n$ is finite dimensional, by lemma 3.5, any member of $L(\mathbb{R}^n,\mathbb{R}^m)$ is bounded. Therefore for any $f \in L(\mathbb{R}^n,\mathbb{R}^m)$ we may define

$$||f|| = \sup_{x \in \mathbb{R}^n} \left\{ \frac{||f(x)||}{||x||} : ||x|| \neq 0 \right\}.$$

Since f is bounded this is defined. Moreover $||f|| = 0$ only if f is the zero function.
By definition $||f||$ is the real number such that $||f|| \leq B$ for all B such that $||f(x)|| \leq B||x||$.
In particularly $||f(x)|| \leq ||f||\ ||x||$.
If $f,g \in L(\mathbb{R}^n,\mathbb{R}^m)$, then

$$\begin{aligned} ||(f+g)(x)|| &= ||f(x)+g(x)|| \leq ||f(x)|| + ||g(x)|| \\ &\leq ||f||\ ||x|| + ||g||\ ||x|| = (||f|| + ||g||)\,||x|| \end{aligned}$$

Thus $||f+g|| \leq ||f|| + ||g||$.
Hence $||\ ||$ on $L(\mathbb{R}^n,\mathbb{R}^m)$ satisfies the triangle inequality, and so $L(\mathbb{R}^n,\mathbb{R}^m)$ is a normed vector space. This in turn implies that $L(\mathbb{R}^n,\mathbb{R}^m)$ has a metric and thus a topology.
It is often useful to use the metrics
$d_1(f,g) = \sup\{||f(x) - g(x)|| : x \in \mathbb{R}^n\}$
or $d_2(f,g) = \sup\{|f_i(x) - g_i(x)| : i = 1,\ldots,m, x \in \mathbb{R}^n\}$
where $f = (f_1,\ldots,f_m)$, $g = (g_1,\ldots,g_m)$.
Alternatively, choose bases for $\mathbb{R}^n$ and $\mathbb{R}^m$ and consider the matrix representation function

$$M : (L(\mathbb{R}^n,\mathbb{R}^m), +) \to (M(n,m), +).$$

On the right hand side we add matrices element by element under the rule $(a_{ij}) + (b_{ij}) = (a_{ij} + b_{ij})$.
With this operation M(n,m) is also a vector space. Clearly we may choose a basis for M(n,m) to be

$\{E_{ij}: i=1,\ldots,n; j=1,\ldots,m\}$ where E_{ij} is the elementary matrix with 1 in the ith column and j^{th} row.

Thus $M(n,m)$ is a vector space of dimension nm.

Since M is a bijection, $L(\mathbb{R}^n,\mathbb{R}^m)$ is also of dimension nm.

A norm on $M(n,m)$ is given by

$$\|A\| = \sup \ \{|a_{ij}|: i=1,\ldots,n; j=1,\ldots,m\}$$

where $A = (a_{ij})$.

This in turn defines a metric and thus a topology on $M(n,m)$. Finally this defines a topology on $L(\mathbb{R}^n,\mathbb{R}^m)$ as follows. For any open set U in $M(n,m)$, let $V = M^{-1}(U)$ and call V open. The base for the topology on $L(\mathbb{R}^n,\mathbb{R}^m)$ then consists of all sets of this form. One can show that the topology induced on $L(\mathbb{R}^n,\mathbb{R}^m)$ in this way is independent of the choice of bases.

We have shown that the set $L(\mathbb{R}^n,\mathbb{R}^m)$ of linear maps from $\mathbb{R}^n$ to $\mathbb{R}^m$ is a normed vector space of dimension nm and thus has a topology.

When $L(\mathbb{R}^n,\mathbb{R}^m)$ is endowed with this topology we shall write it as $\mathcal{L}(\mathbb{R}^n,\mathbb{R}^m)$.

If V is an infinite dimensional vector space and $f \in L(V,W)$, then f need not be continuous or bounded. However the subset of $L(V,W)$ consisting of bounded, and thus continuous, maps in $L(V,W)$ admits a norm and thus a topology. So we may write this subset as $\mathcal{L}(V,W)$.

Now let $C_0(\mathbb{R}^n,\mathbb{R}^m)$ be the set of continuous functions from $\mathbb{R}^n$ to $\mathbb{R}^m$. We now show that $C_0(\mathbb{R}^n,\mathbb{R}^m)$ is a vector space.

Lemma 3.6

$C_0(\mathbb{R}^n,\mathbb{R}^m)$ is a vector space over $\mathbb{R}$.

Proof

Suppose that f,g are both continuous maps. At any $x_0 \in \mathbb{R}^n$, and any $\varepsilon > 0$, $\exists\, \delta_1, \delta_2 > 0$ such that

$$\| x-x_0 \| < \delta_1 \Rightarrow \| f(x)-f(x_0) \| < \tfrac{1}{2}\varepsilon$$
$$\| x-x_0 \| < \delta_2 \Rightarrow \| g(x)-g(x_0) \| < \tfrac{1}{2}\varepsilon .$$

Let $\delta = \min(\delta_1, \delta_2)$.

Then
$$\begin{aligned} \| x-x_0 \| < \delta \Rightarrow \| (f+g)(x)-(f+g)(x_0) \| &= \| f(x)-f(x_0)+g(x)-g(x_0) \| \\ &\leq \| f(x)-f(x_0) \| + \| g(x)-g(x_0) \| \\ &< \tfrac{1}{2}\varepsilon + \tfrac{1}{2}\varepsilon = \varepsilon. \end{aligned}$$

Thus $f+g \in C_0(\mathbb{R}^n, \mathbb{R}^m)$.

Also for any $\alpha \in \mathbb{R}$, any $\varepsilon > 0\ \exists\, \delta > 0$ st

$$\| x-x_0 \| < \delta \Rightarrow \| f(x)-f(x_0) \| < \frac{\varepsilon}{|\alpha|}.$$

Therefore $\| (\alpha f)(x)-(\alpha f)(x_0) \| = |\alpha|\, \| f(x)-f(x_0) \| < \varepsilon$.

Thus $\alpha f \in C_0(\mathbb{R}^n, \mathbb{R}^m)$. Hence $C_0(\mathbb{R}^n, \mathbb{R}^m)$ is a vector space.

Since $L(\mathbb{R}^n, \mathbb{R}^m)$ is closed under addition and scalar multiplication, it is a vector subspace of dimension nm of the vector space $C_0(\mathbb{R}^n, \mathbb{R}^m)$. Note however that $C_0(\mathbb{R}^n, \mathbb{R}^m)$ is an infinite-dimensional vector space.

Lemma 3.7

If $(X,\mathcal{T})$, $(Y,\mathcal{S})$ and $(Z,\mathcal{R})$ are topological spaces and $C_0((X,\mathcal{T}),(Y,\mathcal{S}))$, $C_0((Y,\mathcal{S}),(Z,\mathcal{R}))$ and $C_0((X,\mathcal{T}),(Z,\mathcal{R}))$ are the sets of functions which are continuous with respect to these topologies, then the composition operator, o, maps $C_0((X,\mathcal{T}),(Y,\mathcal{S})) \times C_0((Y,\mathcal{S}),(Z,\mathcal{R}))$ to $C_0((X,\mathcal{T}),(Z,\mathcal{R}))$

Proof

Suppose $f:(X,\mathcal{T}) \to (Y,\mathcal{S})$ and $g:(Y,\mathcal{S}) \to (Z,\mathcal{R})$ are continous.

We seek to show that $g \circ f : (X, \mathcal{T}) \to (Z, \mathcal{R})$ is continuous. Choose any open set U in Z. By continuity of g, $g^{-1}(U)$ is an $\mathcal{S}$-open set in Y. But by the continuity of f, $f^{-1}(g^{-1}(U))$ is a $\mathcal{T}$-open set in X. However $f^{-1}g^{-1}(U) = (g \circ f)^{-1}(U)$.
Thus gof is continuous.

Note therefore that if $f \in L(\mathbb{R}^n, \mathbb{R}^m)$ and $g \in L(\mathbb{R}^m, \mathbb{R}^k)$ then $g \circ f \in L(\mathbb{R}^n, \mathbb{R}^k)$ will also be continuous.

3.3. COMPACTNESS

Let $(X, \mathcal{T})$ be a topological space. An <u>open cover</u> for X is a family $\{U_j : j \in J\}$ of $\mathcal{T}$-open sets such that $X = \bigcup_{j \in J} U_j$.
If $U = \{U_j : j \in J\}$ is an open cover for X, a <u>subcover</u> of U is an open cover U' of X where $U' = \{U_j : j \in J'\}$ and the index set J' is a subset of J. The subcover is called <u>finite</u> if J' is a finite set (ie $|J'|$, the number of elements of J', is finite).

<u>Definition 3.5</u>

A topological space $(X, \mathcal{T})$ is called <u>compact</u> iff <u>any</u> open cover of X has a finite subcover. If Y is a subset of the topological space $(X, \mathcal{T})$ then Y is compact iff the topological space $(Y, \mathcal{T}_Y)$ is compact. Here $\mathcal{T}_Y$ is the topology induced on Y by $\mathcal{T}$. (see Def. 3.4).

Say that a family $C_J = \{C_j : j \in J\}$ of closed sets in a topological space $(X, \mathcal{T})$ has the <u>finite intersection property</u> (FIP) iff whenever J' is a finite subset of J then $\bigcap_{j \in J'} C_j$ is non-empty.

Lemma 3.8

A topological space $(X,\mathcal{J})$ is compact iff whenever C_J is a family of closed sets with the finite intersection property then $\bigcap_{j\in J} C_j$ is non-empty.

Proof

We establish first of all that $U_J = \{U_j : j\in J\}$ is an open cover of X iff the family $C_J = \{C_j = X\setminus U_j : j \in J\}$ of closed sets has empty intersection.

Now $\bigcup_J U_j = \bigcup_J (X\setminus C_j) = \bigcup_J (X\cap \overline{C_j})$

$$= X\cap(\bigcup_J \overline{C}_j) = X\cap(\overline{\bigcap_J C_j}).$$

Thus $\bigcup_J U_j = X$ iff $\bigcap_J C_j = \Phi$.

To establish necessity, suppose that X is compact and that the family C_J has FIP. If C_J in fact has empty intersection than $U_J = \{X\setminus C_j : j\in J\}$ must be an open cover. Since X is compact there exists a finite set $J'\subset J$ such that U_J' is a cover. But then C_J' has empty intersection contradicting FIP. Thus C_J has non-empty intersection.

To establish sufficiency, suppose that any family C_J, satisfying FIP, has non-empty intersection. Let $U_J = \{U_j : j\in J\}$ be an open cover for X. If U_J has no finite subcover, then for any finite J', the family $C_J' = \{X\setminus U_j : j\in J'\}$ must have non-empty intersection. By FIP, the family C_J must have non-empty intersection, contradicting the assumption that U_J was a cover. Thus $(X,\mathcal{J})$ is compact.

This lemma allows us to establish conditions under which a preference relation P on X has a non-empty choice $C_P(X)$, see page 25. Say the preference relation P on the topological space X is lower demi-continuous (ldc) iff the inverse correspondence $\phi_P^{-1} : X \to X : x \to \{y\in X : xPy\}$ is open for all x in X.

Lemma 3.9

If X is a compact topological space and P is an acyclic and lower demi-continuous preference on X, then there exists a choice $\bar{x}$ of P in X.

Proof

Suppose on the contrary that there is no choice. Thus for all $x \in X$ there exists some $y \in X$ such that yPx. Thus $x \in \phi_P^{-1}(y)$.
Hence $U = \{\phi_P^{-1}(y) : y \in X\}$ is a cover for X.
Moreover for each $y \in X$, $\phi_P^{-1}(y)$ is open.
Since X is compact, there exists a finite subcover of U. That is to say there exists a finite set A in X such that $U' = \{\phi_P^{-1}(y) : y \in A\}$ is a cover for X.
In particular this implies that for each $x \in A$, there is some $y \in A$ such that $x \in \phi_P^{-1}(y)$, or that yPx.
But then $C_P(A) = \{x \in A : \phi_P(x) = \Phi\} = \Phi$.
Now P is acyclic on X, and thus acyclic on A.
Hence, by the acyclicity of P and lemma 1.4, $C_P(A) \neq \Phi$. By the contradiction, $U = \{\phi_P^{-1}(y) : y \in X\}$ cannot be a cover. That is to say there is some $\bar{x} \in X$ such that $\bar{x} \in \phi_P^{-1}(y)$ for no $y \in X$. But then $yP\bar{x}$ for no $y \in X$, and so $\bar{x} \in C_P(X)$, or $\bar{x}$ is the choice on X.

This lemma can be used to show that a continuous function $f : X \to \mathbb{R}$ from a compact topological space X into the reals attains its bounds.
Remember that we defined the supremum and infimum of f on a set Y to be

i) $\sup(f,Y) = M$ such that $f(x) \leq M$ for all $x \in Y$ and if $f(x) \leq M'$ for all $x \in Y$ then $M' \geq M$

ii) $\inf(f,Y) = m$ such that $f(x) \geq m$ for all $x \in Y$ and if $f(x) \geq m'$ for all $x \in Y$ then $m \geq m'$.

Say f attains its upper bound on Y iff there

is some x_s in Y such that $f(x_s) = \sup(f,Y)$. Similarly say f attains its lower bound on Y iff there is some x_i in Y such that $f(x_i) = \inf(f,Y)$.

Given the function $f:X \to \mathbb{R}$ define a preference P on X x X by xPy iff $f(x) > f(y)$.

Clearly P is acyclic, since > on $\mathbb{R}$ is acyclic.

Moreover for any $x \in X$,

$$\phi_P^{-1}(x) = \{y:f(y) < f(x)\} \text{ is open, when f is continuous.}$$

To see this let $U = (-\infty, f(x))$.

Clearly U is an open set in $\mathbb{R}$. Moreover f(y) belongs to the open interval $(-\infty, f(x))$ iff $y \in \phi_P^{-1}(x)$. But f is continuous, and so $f^{-1}(U)$ is open in X. Since $y \in f^{-1}(U)$ iff $y \in \phi_P^{-1}(x)$, $\phi_P^{-1}(x)$ is open for any $x \in X$.

Weierstrass Theorem

Let $(X,\mathcal{T})$ be a topological space and $f:X \to \mathbb{R}$ a continuous real-valued function. If Y is a compact subset of X, then f attains its bounds on Y.

Proof

As above, for each $x \in Y$, define $U_x = (-\infty, f(x))$. Then

$$\phi_P^{-1}(x) = \{y \in Y: f(y) < f(x)\} = f^{-1}(U_x) \cap Y$$

is an open set in the induced topology on Y.

By lemma 3.9 there exists a choice $\bar{x}$ in Y such that $\phi_P^{-1}(\bar{x}) = \Phi$. But then $f(y) > f(\bar{x})$ for no $y \in Y$. Hence $f(y) \leq f(\bar{x})$ for all $y \in Y$. Thus $f(\bar{x}) = \sup(f,Y)$.

In the same way let Q be the relation on X given by xQy iff $f(x) < f(y)$. Then there is a choice $\bar{\bar{x}} \in Y$ such that $f(y) < f(\bar{\bar{x}})$ for no $y \in Y$. Hence $f(y) \geq f(\bar{\bar{x}})$ for all $y \in Y$, and so $f(\bar{\bar{x}}) = \inf(f,Y)$.

Thus f attains its bounds on Y.

We can develop this result further.

Lemma 3.10

If $f : (X,\mathcal{T}) \to (Z,\mathcal{S})$ is a continuous function between topological spaces, and Y is a compact subset of X, then

$$f(Y) = \{f(y) \in Z : Y \in Y\}$$

is compact.

Proof

Let $\{W_\alpha\}$ be an open cover for f(Y). Then each member W_α of this cover may be expressed in the form $W_\alpha = U_\alpha \cap f(Y)$ where U_α is an open set in Z. For each α, let $V_\alpha = f^{-1}(U_\alpha) \cap Y$. Now each V_α is open in the induced topology on Y. Moreover, for each $y \in Y$, there exists some W_α such that $f(y) \in W_\alpha$. Thus $\{V_\alpha\}$ is an open cover for Y. Since Y is compact, $\{V_\alpha\}$ has a finite subcover $\{V_\alpha : \alpha \in J\}$, and so $\{f(V_\alpha) : \alpha \in J\}$ is a finite subcover for $\{W_\alpha\}$. Thus f(Y) is compact.

Now a real-valued continuous function f is bounded on a compact set, Y (by the Weierstrass Theorem). So f(Y) will be contained in $[f(\bar{x}),f(\bar{\bar{x}})]$, say, for some $\bar{x},\bar{\bar{x}} \in Y$. Since f(Y) must also be compact, this suggests that a closed set of the form [a,b] must be compact.

For a set $Y \subset \mathbb{R}$ define sup(Y) = sup(id,Y), the <u>supremum</u> of Y, and inf(Y) = inf(id,Y), the <u>infimum</u> of Y. Here $id : \mathbb{R} \to \mathbb{R}$ is the identity on $\mathbb{R}$. The set $Y \subset \mathbb{R}$ is <u>bounded above</u> (or below) iff its supremum (or infimum) is finite. The set is <u>bounded</u> iff it is both bounded above and below. Thus a set of the form [a,b], say with $-\infty < a < b < +\infty$ is bounded.

Heine Borel Theorem

A closed bounded interval, [a,b], of the real line is compact.

Sketch of Proof

Consider a family $C = \{[a,c_i],[d_j,b]: i \in I, j \in J\}$ of subsets of $[a,b]$ with the finite intersection property. Suppose that neither I nor J is empty. Let $d = \sup(\{d_j : j \in J\})$ and suppose that for some $k \in I$, $c_k < d$. Then there exists $i \in I$ and $j \in J$ such that $[a,c_i] \cap [d_j,b] = \Phi$, contradicting the finite intersection property. Thus $c_i \geq d$, and so $[a,c_i] \cap [d,b] \neq \Phi$, for all $i \in I$. Hence the family C has non empty intersection. By lemma 3.8, $[a,b]$ is compact.

Definition 3.6

A topological space $(X,\mathcal{J})$ is called Hausdorff iff any two distinct points $x,y \in X$ have $\mathcal{J}$-open neighbourhoods U_x, U_y such that $U_x \cap U_y = \Phi$.

Lemma 3.11

If (X,d) is a metric space then $(X,\mathcal{J}_d)$ is Hausdorff, where $\mathcal{J}_d$ is the topology on X induced by the metric d.

Proof

For two points $x \neq y$, let $\varepsilon = d(x,y) \neq 0$. Define $U_x = B(x, \frac{\varepsilon}{3})$ and $U_y = B(y,\frac{\varepsilon}{3})$. Clearly, by the triangle inequality, $B(x,\frac{\varepsilon}{3}) \cap B(y,\frac{\varepsilon}{3}) = \Phi$. Otherwise there would exist a point z such that $d(x,z) < \varepsilon/3, d(z,y) < \varepsilon/3$, which would imply that

$$d(x,y) < d(x,z) + d(z,y) = \frac{2\varepsilon}{3}.$$

By contradiction the open balls of radius $\varepsilon/3$ do not intersect. Thus $(X,\mathcal{J}_d)$ is Hausdorff.

A Hausdorff topological space is therefore a natural generalisation of a metric space.

Lemma 3.12

If $(X,\mathcal{J})$ is a Hausdorff topological space any compact subset Y of X is closed.

Proof

We seek to show that $X\setminus Y$ is open, by showing that for any $x\in X\setminus Y$, there exists a neighbourhood G of x and an open set H containing Y such that $G\cap H = \Phi$. Let $x\in X\setminus Y$, and consider any $y\in Y$. Since X is Hausdorff. there exists a neighbourhood V(y) of y and a neighbourhood U(y), say, of x such that $V(y)\cap U(y) = \Phi$. Since the family $\{V(y):y\in Y\}$ is an open cover of Y, and Y is compact, there exists a finite subcover $\{V(y):y\in A\}$, where A is a finite subset of Y.

Let $H = \bigcup_{y\in A} V(y)$ and $G = \bigcap_{y\in A} U(y)$.

Suppose that $G\cap H \neq \Phi$. Then this implies there exists $y\in A$ such that $V(y)\cap U(y)$ is non-empty. Thus $G\cap H = \Phi$. Since A is finite, G is open. Moreover Y is contained in H. Thus $X\setminus Y$ is open and Y is closed.

Lemma 3.13

If $(X,\mathcal{J})$ is a compact topological space and Y is a closed subset of X, then Y is compact.

Proof

Let $\{U_\alpha\}$ be an open cover for Y, where each $U_\alpha \subset X$. Then $\{V_\alpha = U_\alpha \cap Y\}$ is also an open cover for Y.

Since $X\setminus Y$ is open, $\{X\setminus Y\}\cup\{V_\alpha\}$ is an open cover for X.

Since X is compact there is a finite subcover.

Since each $V_\alpha \subset Y$, $X\setminus Y$ must be a member of this subcover. Hence the subcover is of the form $\{X\setminus Y\}\cup\{V_j:j\in J\}$. But then $\{V_j:j\in J\}$ is a finite subcover of $\{V_\alpha\}$ for Y. Hence Y is compact.

Tychonoff's Theorem

If $(X,\mathcal{T})$ and $(Y,\mathcal{S})$ are two compact topological spaces then $(X \times Y, \mathcal{T} \times \mathcal{S})$, with the product topology, is compact.

Proof

To see this we need only consider a cover for $X \times Y$ of the form $\{U_\alpha \times V_\beta\}$ for $\{U_\alpha\}$ an open cover for X and $\{V_\beta\}$ an open cover for Y. Since both X and Y are compact, both $\{U_\alpha\}$ and $\{V_\alpha\}$ have finite subcovers $\{U_j\}_{j\in J}$ and $\{V_k\}_{k\in K}$, and so $\{U_j \times V_k : (j,k) \in J \times K\}$ is a finite subcover for $X \times Y$.

As a corollary of this theorem, let $I_k = [a_k, b_k]$ for $k=1,\ldots,n$ be a family of closed bounded intervals in $\mathbb{R}$. Each interval is compact by the Heine Borel Theorem.
Thus the closed <u>cube</u> $I^n = I_1 \times I_2 .. I_n$ in $\mathbb{R}^n$ is compact, by Tychonoff's Theorem.
Say that a set $Y \subset \mathbb{R}^n$ is bounded iff for each $y \in Y$ there exists some finite number $K(y)$ such that $\|x-y\| < K(y)$ for all $x \in Y$. Here $\| \ \|$ is any convenient norm on $\mathbb{R}^n$. If Y is bounded then clearly there exists some closed cube $I^n \subset \mathbb{R}^n$ such that $Y \subset I^n$. Thus we obtain:

Lemma 3.14

If Y is a closed bounded subset of $\mathbb{R}^n$ then Y is compact.

Proof

By the above, there is a closed cube I^n such that $Y \subset I^n$. But I^n is compact by Tychonoff's Theorem. Since Y is a closed subset of I^n, Y is compact, by lemma 3.13.

In $\mathbb{R}^n$ a compact set Y is one that is both closed and bounded. To see this note that $\mathbb{R}^n$ is certainly a metric space, and therefore Hausdorff. By lemma 3.12, if Y is compact then it must be closed. To see that it must be bounded, consider the unbounded closed interval $A = [0,\infty)$ in $\mathbb{R}$, and an open cover $\{U_n = (n-2,n);\ n = 1,\ldots,\infty\}$. Clearly $\{(-1,1),\ (0,2),\ (1,3)\ldots.\}$ cover $[0,\infty)$. A finite subcover must be bounded above by N, say, and so the point N does not belong to the subcover. Hence $[0,\infty)$ is non-compact.

Lemma 3.15

A compact subset Y of $\mathbb{R}$ contains its bounds.

Proof

Let $s = \sup(id,Y)$ and $i = \inf(id,Y)$ be the supremum and infimum of Y. Here $id:\mathbb{R} \to \mathbb{R}$ is the identity function. By the discussion above, Y must be bounded, and so i and s must be finite. We seek to show that Y contains these bounds, ie. that $i\in Y$ and $s\in Y$. Suppose for example that $s\notin Y$. By lemma 3.12, Y must be closed and hence $\mathbb{R}\setminus Y$ must be open. But then there exists a neighbourhood $(s-\varepsilon,s+\varepsilon)$ of s in $\mathbb{R}\setminus Y$, and so $s - \frac{\varepsilon}{2} \notin Y$. But this implies that $y \leq s - \frac{\varepsilon}{2}$ for all $y\in Y$, which contradicts the assumption that $s = \sup(id,Y)$. Hence $s\in Y$. A similar argument shows that $i\in Y$. Thus $Y = [i,y_1]\cup \ldots \cup[y_r,s]$ say, and so Y contains its bounds.

Lemma 3.16

Let $(X,\mathcal{T})$ be a topological space and $f:X \to \mathbb{R}$ a continuous real-valued function. If $Y\subset X$ is compact then there exist points x_o and x_1 in Y such that $f(x_o) \le f(y) \le f(x_1)$ for all $y \in Y$.

Proof

By lemma 3.10, $f(Y)$ is compact. By lemma 3.15, $f(Y)$ contains its infimum and supremum. Thus there exists $x_o, x_1 \in Y$ such that

$$f(x_o) \le f(y) \le f(x_1) \text{ for all } y \in Y.$$

Note that $f(Y)$ must be bounded, and so $f(x_o)$ and $f(x_1)$ must be finite.

We have here obtained a second proof of the Weierstrass Theorem that a continuous real-valued function on a compact set attains its bounds, and shown moreover that these bounds are finite. A useful application of this theorem is that if Y is a compact set in $\mathbb{R}^n$ and $x \notin Y$ then there is some point y in Y which is nearest to x. Remember that we defined the distance from a point x in a metric space (X,d) to a subset Y of X to be $d(x,Y) = \inf(f_x, Y)$ where $f_x : Y \to \mathbb{R}$ is defined by $f_x(y) = d(x,-)(y) = d(x,y)$. (See page 117).

Lemma 3.17

Suppose Y is a subset of a metric space (X,d) and $x \in X$. Then the function $f_x : Y \to \mathbb{R}$ given by $f_x(y) = d(x,y)$ is continuous.

Proof

Consider $y_1, y_2 \in Y$ and suppose that $d(x,y_1) \ge d(x,y_2)$. Then
$|d(x,y_1) - d(x,y_2)| = d(x,y_1) - d(x,y_2)$.
By the triangle inequality

$$d(x,y_1) \le d(x,y_2) + d(y_2,y_1).$$

Hence $|d(x,y_1) - d(x,y_2)| \le d(y_1,y_2)$

and so $d(y_1,y_2) < \varepsilon \Rightarrow |d(x,y_1) - d(x,y_2)| < \varepsilon$,

for any $\varepsilon > 0$.

Thus for any $\varepsilon > 0$,

$$d(y_1,y_2) < \varepsilon \Rightarrow |f_x(y_1) - f_x(y_2)| < \varepsilon,$$

and so f_x is continuous.

<u>Lemma 3.18</u>

If Y is a compact subset of a metric space X and $x \in X$, then there exists a point $y_0 \in Y$ such that $d(x,Y) = d(x,y_0)$, where $d(x,y_0) < \infty$.

<u>Proof</u>

By lemma 3.17, the function $d(x,-):Y \to \mathbb{R}$ is continuous. By lemma 3.16, this function attains its lower and upper bounds on Y.
Thus there exists $y_0 \in Y$ such that

$$d(x,y_0) = \inf(d(x,-),Y) = d(x,Y)$$

where $d(x,y_0)$ is finite.

The point y_0 in Y such that $d(x,y_0) = d(x,Y)$ is the nearest point in Y to x.
Note of course that if $x \in Y$ then $d(x,Y) = 0$.
More importantly, when Y is compact $d(x,Y) = 0$ <u>if and only if</u> $x \in Y$.
To see this necessity, suppose that $d(x,Y) = 0$.
Then by lemma 3.18, there exist $y_0 \in Y$ such that $d(x,y_0) = 0$. By the definition of a metric $d(x,y_0) = 0$ iff $x = y_0$ and so $x \in Y$.
The point $y \in Y$ that is nearest to x is dependent on the metric of course, and may also not be unique.

d_E: Euclidean distance

d_c: cartesian distance

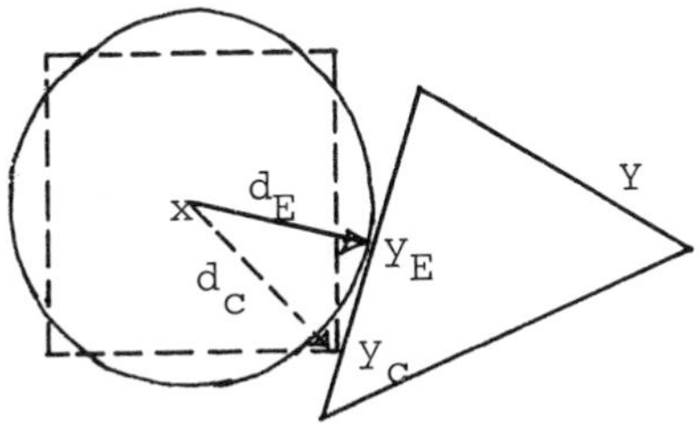

3.4 CONVEXITY

3.4.1 A convex set

If x,y are two points in a vector space, X, then the arc, [x,y], is the set $\{z \in X : \exists \lambda \in [0,1] \text{ s.t. } z = \lambda x + (1-\lambda)y\}$.
A point in the arc [x,y] is called a convex combination of x and y. If Y is a subset of X, then the convex hull, con(Y), of Y is the smallest set in X that contains, for every pair of points x,y in Y, the arc [x,y].
The set Y is called convex iff con(Y) = Y.
The set Y is strictly convex iff for any x,y the combination $\lambda x + (1-\lambda)y$, for $\lambda \in (0,1)$, belongs to the interior of Y.
Note that if Y is a vector subspace of the real vector space X then Y must be convex. For then if $x,y \in Y$ both $\lambda, (1-\lambda) \in \mathbb{R}$ and so $\lambda x + (1-\lambda)y \in Y$.

Definition 3.7

Let Y be a real vector space, or a convex subset of a real vector space, and let $f : Y \to \mathbb{R}$ be a function. Then f is said to be

i) convex iff $f(\lambda x + (1-\lambda)y) \leq \lambda f(x) + (1-\lambda)f(y)$
ii) concave iff $f(\lambda x + (1-\lambda)y) \geq \lambda f(x) + (1-\lambda)f(y)$
iii) quasi-concave iff $f(\lambda x + (1-\lambda)y) \geq \min[f(x),f(y)]$

for any $x,y \in Y$ and any $\lambda \in [0,1]$.

Suppose now that $f : Y \to \mathbb{R}$ and consider the preference correspondence $P : Y \to Y$ given by

$$P(x) = \{y \in Y : f(y) > f(x)\}.$$

If f is quasi-concave then when $y_1, y_2 \in P(x)$,

$$f(\lambda y_1 + (1-\lambda)y_2) \geq \min[f(y_1),f(y_2)] > f(x).$$

Hence $\lambda y_1 + (1-\lambda)y_2 \in P(x)$.
Thus for all $x \in Y$, $P(x)$ is convex.
We shall call a preference correspondence $P: Y \to Y$ <u>convex</u> when Y is convex and P is such that $P(x)$ is convex for all $x \in Y$. When a function $f: Y \to \mathbb{R}$ is quasi-concave then the strict preference relation P defined by f is convex. Note also that the weak preference $R: Y \to Y$ given by

$$R(x) = \{y \in Y: f(y) \geq f(x)\}$$

will also be convex.
Moreover if $f: Y \to \mathbb{R}$ is a concave function then it is quasi-concave. To see this consider $x, y \in Y$, and suppose that $f(x) \leq f(y)$.
By concavity,

$$\begin{aligned} f(\lambda x + (1-\lambda)y) &\geq \lambda f(x) + (1-\lambda)f(y) \\ &\geq \lambda f(x) + (1-\lambda)f(x) \\ &\geq \min[f(x), f(y)]. \end{aligned}$$

Thus f is quasi-concave.
Note however that a quasi-concave function need be neither convex nor concave.
Note that if f is a linear function then it is convex, concave and quasi-concave.
There is a partial order $>$ on $\mathbb{R}^n$ given by $x > y$ iff $x_i > y_i$ where $x = (x_1, \ldots, x_n), y = (y_1, \ldots, y_n)$. A function $f: \mathbb{R}^n \to \mathbb{R}$ is weakly monotonically increasing iff $f(x) \geq f(y)$ for any $x, y \in \mathbb{R}^n$ such that $x > y$. A function $f: \mathbb{R}^n \to \mathbb{R}$ has decreasing returns to scale iff f is weakly monotonically increasing and concave. A very standard assumption in economic theory is that feasible production of an output has decreasing returns to scale of inputs, and that consumers' utility or preference has decreasing returns to scale in consumption. We shall return to this point below.

3.4.2 Examples

Example 3.2

i) Consider the set $X_1 = \{(x_1,x_2)\in\mathbb{R}^2 : x_2 \geq x_1\}$.
Clearly if $x_2 \geq x_1$ and $x_2' \geq x_1'$ then
$\lambda x_2 + (1-\lambda)x_2' \geq \lambda x_1 + (1-\lambda)x_1'$ for $\lambda\in[0,1]$.
Thus $\lambda(x_1,x_2) + (1-\lambda)(x_1',x_2')$
$= (\lambda x_1 + (1-\lambda)x_1', \lambda x_2 + (1-\lambda)x_2') \in X_1$.
Hence X_1 is convex.
On the other hand consider the set
$X_2 = \{(x_1,x_2)\in\mathbb{R}^2 : x_2 \geq x_1^2\}$.
As Figure 3.12(i) indicates this is a strictly convex set.
However the set $X_3 = \{(x_1,x_2)\in\mathbb{R}^2 : |x_2| \geq x_1^2\}$ is not convex. To see this suppose $x_2 < 0$. Then $(x_1,x_2)\in X_3$ implies that $x_2 \leq -x_1^2$. But then $-x_2 \geq x_1^2$. Clearly $(x_1,0)$ belongs to the convex combination of (x_1,x_2) and $(x_1,-x_2)$ yet $(x_1,0) \notin X_3$.

ii) Consider now the set $X_4 = \{(x_1,x_2) : x_2 \geq x_1^3\}$.
As Figure 3.12(ii) shows it is possible to choose (x_1,x_2) and (x_1',x_2') with $x_1 < 0$, so that the convex combination of (x_1,x_2) and (x_1',x_2') does not belong to X_4.
However $X_5 = \{(x_1,x_2)\in\mathbb{R}^2 : x_2 \geq x_1^3 \text{ and } x_1 \geq 0\}$ and $X_6 = \{(x_1,x_2)\in\mathbb{R}^2 : x_2 \leq x_1^3 \text{ and } x_1 \leq 0\}$ are both convex sets.

iii) Now consider the set $X_7 = \{(x_1,x_2)\in\mathbb{R}^2 : x_1 x_2 \geq 1\}$.
From Figure 3.12(iii) it is clear that the restriction of the set X_7 to the positive quadrant $R_+^2 = \{(x_1,x_2)\in\mathbb{R}^2 : x_1 \geq 0 \text{ and } x_2 \geq 0\}$ is strictly convex, as is the restriction of

X_7 to the negative quadrant $\mathbb{R}^2_- = \{(x_1,x_2)\in\mathbb{R}^2:$
$x_1 \leq 0$ and $x_2 \leq 0\}$.
However if $(x_1,x_2)\in X_7 \cap \mathbb{R}^2_+$ then $(-x_1,-x_2)\in$
$X_7 \cap \mathbb{R}^2_-$.
Clearly the origin (0,0) belongs to the
convex hull of (x_1,x_2) and $(-x_1,-x_2)$, yet
does not belong to X_7.
Thus X_7 is not convex.
Finally a set of the form
$X_8 = \{(x_1,x_2)\in\mathbb{R}^2_+ : x_2 \leq x_1^{\alpha}$ for $\alpha\in(0,1)\}$
is also convex. See Figure 3.12(iv).

Example 3.3

i) Consider the set
$B = \{(x_1,x_2)\in\mathbb{R}^2: (x_1-a_1)^2 + (x_2-a_2)^2 \leq r^2\}$.
See Figure 3.12(v).
This is the closed ball centred on $(a_1,a_2)=a$,
of radius r.
Suppose that $x,y\in B$ and $z = \lambda x+(1-\lambda)y$ for
$\lambda\in[0,1]$.
Let $\|\ \|$ stand for the Euclidean norm.
Then x,y both satisfy $\|x-a\| \leq r$, $\|y-a\| \leq r$.
But $\|z-a\| \leq \lambda\|x-a\| + (1-\lambda)\|y-a\|$.
Thus $\|z-a\| \leq r$ and so $z\in B$.
Hence B is convex. Moreover B is a closed
and bounded subset of $\mathbb{R}^2$ and is thus compact.
For a general norm on $\mathbb{R}^n$, the closed ball
$B = \{x\in\mathbb{R}^n: \|x-a\| \leq r\}$ will be compact and
convex.

ii) In the next section we define the hyperplane
$H(\rho,\alpha)$ normal to a vector ρ in $\mathbb{R}^n$ to be
$\{x\in\mathbb{R}^n: (\rho,x) = \alpha\}$ where α is some real number.
Suppose that $x,y\in H(\rho,x)$.

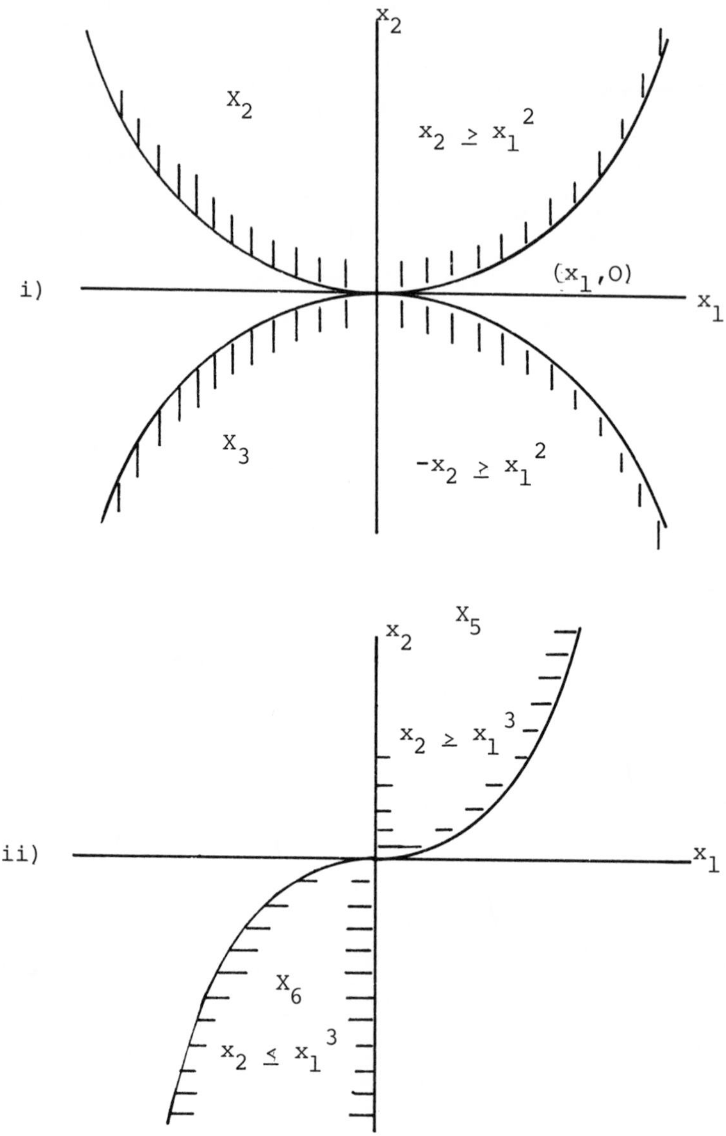

i)
x_2
X_2
$x_2 \geq x_1^2$
$(x_1, 0)$
x_1
X_3
$-x_2 \geq x_1^2$
ii)
x_2
X_5
$x_2 \geq x_1^3$
x_1
X_6
$x_2 \leq x_1^3$

Fig.3.12.

iii)

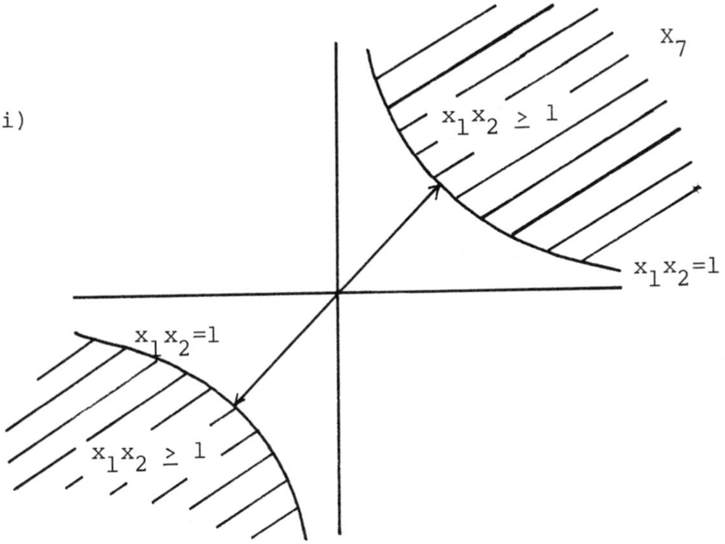

X_7
$x_1x_2 \geq 1$
$x_1x_2=1$
$x_1x_2=1$
$x_1x_2 \geq 1$

iv)

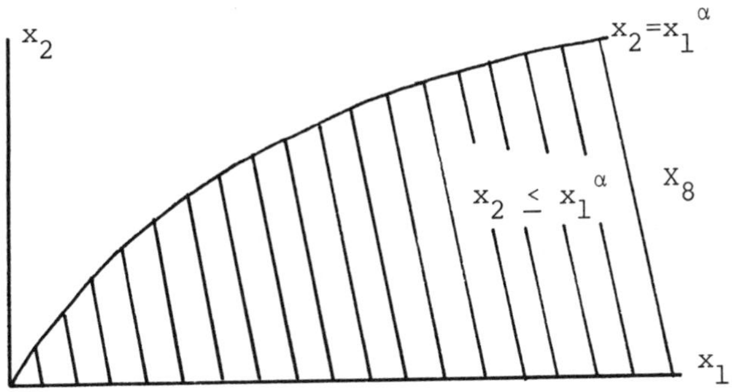

x_2
$x_2=x_1^\alpha$
$x_2 \leq x_1^\alpha$
X_8
x_1

v)

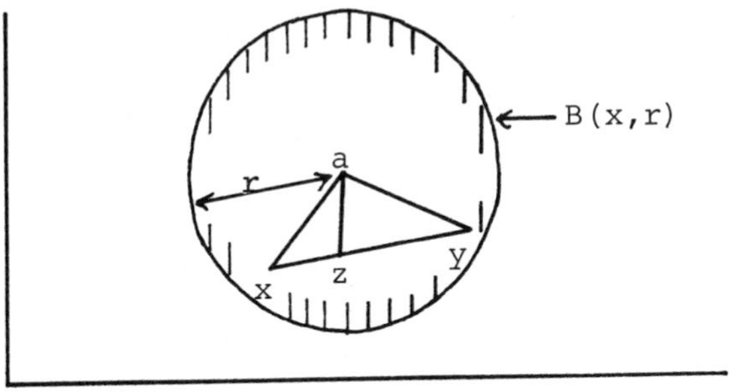

B(x,r)
a
r
x
z
y

Now $(\rho, \lambda x + (1-\lambda)y) = \lambda(\rho, x) + (1-\lambda)(\rho, y)$
$= \alpha \quad$, whenever $\lambda \in [0,1]$.

Thus $H(\rho, \alpha)$ is a convex set.

We also define the closed half-space $H_+(\rho, \alpha)$ by $H_+(\rho, \alpha) = \{x \in \mathbb{R}^n : (\rho, x) \geq \alpha\}$.

Clearly if $x, y \in H_+(\rho, \alpha)$ then

$(\rho, \lambda x + (1-\lambda)y) = \lambda(\rho, x) + (1-\lambda)(\rho, y) \geq \alpha$

and so $H_+(\rho, \alpha)$ is also convex.

Notice that if B is the compact convex ball in $\mathbb{R}^n$ then there exists some $\rho \in \mathbb{R}^n$ and some $\alpha \in \mathbb{R}$ such that $B \subset H_+(\rho, \alpha)$.

If A and B are two convex sets in $\mathbb{R}^n$ then $A \cap B$ must also be a convex set, while $A \cup B$ need not be. For example the union of two disjoint compact sets will not be convex.

We have called a function $f: Y \to \mathbb{R}$ convex on Y iff $f(\lambda x + (1-\lambda)y) \leq \lambda f(x) + (1-\lambda) f(y)$ for $x, y \in Y$. Clearly this is equivalent to the requirement that the set $F = \{(z, x) \in \mathbb{R} \times Y : z \geq f(x)\}$ is convex.

To see this suppose (z_1, x_1) and $(z_2, x_2) \in F$. Then

$\lambda(z_1, x_1) + (1-\lambda)(z_2, x_2) \in F$ iff

$\lambda z_1 + (1-\lambda) z_2 \geq f(\lambda x_1 + (1-\lambda) x_2))$.

But $(f(x_1), x_1)$ and $(f(x_2), x_2) \in F$ and so

$\lambda z_1 + (1-\lambda) z_2 \geq \lambda f(x_1) + (1-\lambda) f(x_2) \geq f(\lambda x_1 + (1-\lambda) x_2)$ for $\lambda \in [0,1]$.

In the same way f is concave on Y iff $G = \{(z, x) \in \mathbb{R} \times Y : z \leq f(x)\}$ is convex.

If $f: Y \to \mathbb{R}$ is concave then the function $(-f): Y \to \mathbb{R}$, given by $(-f)(x) = -f(x)$, is convex and vice versa.

To see this note that if $z \leq f(x)$ then

$-z \geq -f(x)$, and so

$G = \{(z,x) \in \mathbb{R} \times Y: z \leq f(x)\}$ is convex

implies that

$F = \{(z,x) \in \mathbb{R} \times Y: z \geq (-f)(x)\}$ is convex.

Finally f is quasi-concave on Y iff, for all $z \in \mathbb{R}$, the set $G(z) = \{x \in Y: z \leq f(x)\}$ is convex.

Notice that G(z) is the image of G under the projection mapping $p_z: \mathbb{R} \times Y \to Y: (z,x) \to x$. Since the image of a convex set under a projection is convex, clearly G(z) is convex for any z whenever G is convex. As we know already this means that a concave function is quasi-concave.

We now apply these observations.

<u>Example 3.4</u>

i) Let $f: \mathbb{R} \to \mathbb{R}$ by $x \to x^2$.
As example 3.4(i) showed, the set
$F = \{(x,z) \in \mathbb{R} \times \mathbb{R}: z \geq f(x) = x^2\}$ is convex.
Hence f is convex.

ii) Now let $f: \mathbb{R} \to \mathbb{R}$ by $x \to x^3$.
Example 3.4(ii) showed that the set
$F = \{(x,z) \in \mathbb{R}_+ \times \mathbb{R}: z \geq f(x) = x^3\}$ is convex
and so f is <u>convex</u> on the convex set
$\mathbb{R}_+ = \{x \in \mathbb{R}: x \geq 0\}$.
On the other hand
$F = \{(x,z) \in \mathbb{R}_- \times \mathbb{R}: z \leq f(x) = x^3\}$ is convex
and so f is <u>concave</u> on the convex set
$\mathbb{R}_- = \{x \in \mathbb{R}: x \leq 0\}$.

iii) Let $f: \mathbb{R} \to \mathbb{R}$ by $x \to \frac{1}{x}$.
By example 3.2(iii) the set
$F = \{(x,z) \in \mathbb{R}_+ \times \mathbb{R}: z \geq f(x) = \frac{1}{x}\}$ is convex

and so f is <u>convex</u> on $\mathbb{R}_+$ and <u>concave</u> on $\mathbb{R}_-$.

iv) Let $f(x) = x^\alpha$ where $0 < \alpha < 1$.
Then $F = \{(x,z) \in \mathbb{R}_+ \times \mathbb{R} : z \leq f(x) = x^\alpha\}$ is convex, and so f is concave.

v) Consider the exponential function $\exp: \mathbb{R} \to \mathbb{R} : x \to e^x$.
Figure 3.13(i) demonstrates that the exponential function is convex. Another way of showing this is to note that $e^x > f(x)$ for any geometric function $f: x \to x^r$ for $r > 1$, for any $x \in \mathbb{R}_+$.
Since the geometric functions are convex, so is e^x.
On the other hand as Figure 3.13(ii) shows the function $\log_e : \mathbb{R}_+ \to \mathbb{R}$, inverse to exp, is concave.

vi) Consider now $f: \mathbb{R}^2 \to \mathbb{R} : (x,y) \to xy$.
Just as in example 3.2(iii) the set $\{(x,y) \in \mathbb{R}^2_+ : xy \geq t\} = \mathbb{R}^2_+ \cap f^{-1}[t,\infty)\}$ is convex and so f is a quasi-concave function on $\mathbb{R}^2_+$. Similarly f is quasi-concave on $\mathbb{R}^2_-$.
However f is not quasi-concave on $\mathbb{R}^2$.

vii) Let $f: \mathbb{R}^2 \to \mathbb{R} : (x_1,x_2) \to r^2-(x_1-a_1)^2-(x_2-a_2)^2$.
Since the function $g(x)=x^2$ is convex, $(-g)(x) = -x^2$ is concave, and so clearly f is a concave function.
Moreover it is obvious that f has a supremum in $\mathbb{R}^2$ at the point $(x_1,x_2) = (a_1,a_2)$. On the other hand the functions in examples 3.4 (iv) to (vi) are monotonically increasing.

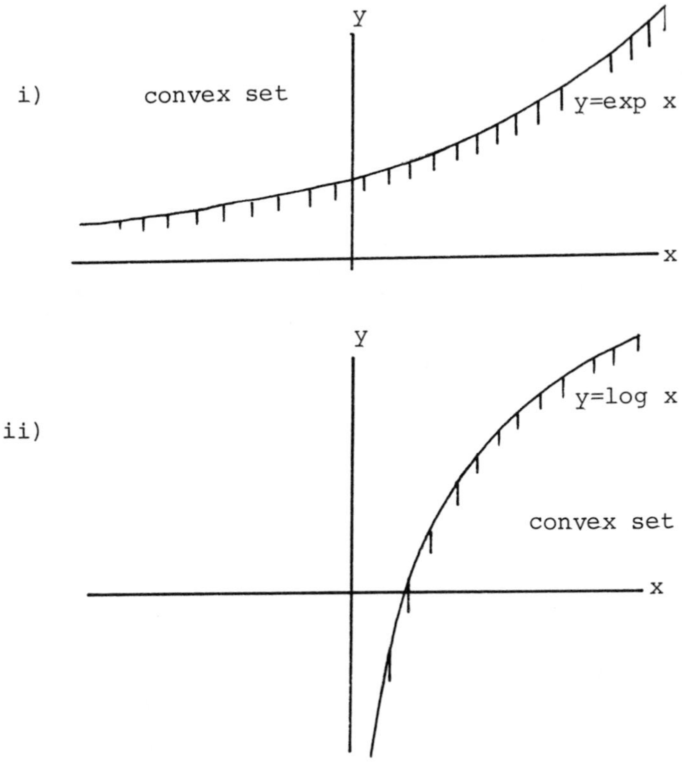

Fig.3.13.

3.4.3. Separation Properties of Convex Sets

Let X be a vector space of dimension n with a scalar product (,).

Define $H(\rho,\alpha) = \{x \in X: (\rho,x) = \alpha\}$ to be the hyperplane in X <u>normal</u> to the vector $\rho \in \mathbb{R}^n$.

It should be clear that $H(\rho,\alpha)$ is an (n-1) dimensional plane displaced some distance from the origin. To see this suppose that $x = \lambda\rho$ belongs to $H(\rho,\alpha)$. Then $(\rho,\lambda\rho) = \lambda\|\rho\|^2 = \alpha$.

Thus $\lambda = \frac{\alpha}{\|\rho\|^2}$. Hence the length of x is

$\| x \| = |\lambda| \; \|\rho\| = \frac{|\alpha|}{\|\rho\|}$ and so $x = \pm \frac{|\alpha|}{\|\rho\|^2} \rho$.

Clearly if $y = \lambda\rho + y_0$ belongs to $H(\rho,\alpha)$ then $(\rho,y) = (\rho,\lambda\rho+y_0) = \alpha+(\rho,y_0)$ and so $(\rho,y_0) = 0$.
Thus any vector y in $H(\rho,\alpha)$ can be written in the form $y = \lambda\rho+y_0$ where y_0 is orthogonal to ρ. Since there exists (n-1) linearly independent vectors $y_1,\ldots,y_{n-1}$, all orthogonal to ρ, any vector $y \in H(\rho,\alpha)$ can be written in the form

$$y = \lambda\rho + \sum_{i=1}^{n-1} a_i y_i,$$

where $\lambda\rho$ is a vector of length $\frac{|\alpha|}{\|\rho\|}$.

Now let $\{\rho^{\perp}\} = \{x \in \mathbb{R}^n : (\rho,x) = 0\}$.
Clearly $\{\rho^{\perp}\}$ is a vector subspace of $\mathbb{R}^n$, of dimension (n-1) through the origin.
Thus $H(\rho,\alpha) = \lambda\rho + \{\rho^{\perp}\}$
has the form of an (n-1)-dimensional vector subspace displaced a distance $\frac{|\alpha|}{\|\rho\|}$ along the vector ρ.

Clearly if ρ_1 and ρ_2 are colinear vectors (ie $\rho_2 = a\rho_1$ for some $a \in \mathbb{R}$) then $\{\rho^{\perp}\} = \{\rho_2^{\perp}\}$.
Suppose that $\frac{\alpha_1\rho_1}{\|\rho\|^2} = \frac{\alpha_2\rho_2}{\|\rho\|^2}$, then both $H(\rho_1,\alpha_1)$ and $H(\rho_2,\alpha_2)$ contain the same point and are thus identical.
Thus $H(\rho_1,\alpha_1) = H(a\rho_1,a\alpha_1) = H\left(\frac{\rho_1}{\|\rho_1\|}, \frac{\alpha_1}{\|\rho_1\|}\right)$.

The hyperplane $H(\rho,\alpha)$ separates X into two <u>closed</u> half-spaces :

$$H_+(\rho,\alpha) = \{x \in X: (\rho,x) \geq \alpha\}$$

and $H_-(\rho,\alpha) = \{x \in X: (\rho,x) \leq \alpha\}$.

we shall also write $\overset{o}{H}_+(\rho,\alpha) = \{x \in X: (\rho,x) > \alpha\}$

$$\overset{o}{H}_-(\rho,\alpha) = \{x \in X: (\rho,x) < \alpha\}$$

for the open half-spaces formed by taking the interiors of $H_+(\rho,\alpha)$ and $H_-(\rho,\alpha)$, in the case $\rho \neq 0$.

Lemma 3.19

Let Y be a non-empty compact convex subset of a finite dimensional real vector space X, and let x be a point in $X \setminus Y$.

Then there is a hyperplane $H(\rho,\alpha)$ through a point $y_0 \in Y$ such that

$$(\rho,x) < \alpha = (\rho,y_0) \leq (\rho,y) \text{ for all } y \in Y.$$

Proof

As in lemma 3.17 let $f_x : Y \to \mathbb{R}$ be the function $f_x(y) = \|x-y\|$, where $\| \ \|$ is the norm induced from the scalar product $(\ , \ )$ in X.

By lemma 3.18 there exists a point $y_0 \in Y$ such that $\|x-y_0\| = \inf(f_x,Y) = d(x,Y)$.

Thus $\|x-y_0\| \leq \|x-y\|$ for all $y \in Y$.

Now define $\rho = y_0 - x$ and $\alpha = (\rho,y_0)$.

Then

$$(\rho,x) = (\rho,y_0) - (\rho,(y_0-x))$$
$$= (\rho,y_0) - \|\rho\|^2 < (\rho,y_0).$$

Suppose now that there is a point $y \in Y$ such that $(\rho,y_0) > (\rho,y)$.

By convexity, $w = \lambda y + (1-\lambda)y_0 \in Y$, where λ belongs to the interval $(0,1)$.

But $\|x-y_0\|^2 - \|x-w\|^2 = \|x-y_0\|^2 - \|x-\lambda y - y_0 + \lambda y_0\|^2$

$$= 2\lambda(\rho,(y_0-y)) - \lambda^2\|y-y_0\|^2.$$

Now $(\rho,y_0) > (\rho,y)$ and so, for sufficiently small λ, the right hand side is positive.

Thus there exists a point w in Y, close to y_0, such that $\|x-y_0\| > \|x-w\|$.

But this contradicts the assumption that y_0 is the nearest point in Y to x.

Thus $(\rho,y) \geq (\rho,y_0)$ for all $y \in Y$.

Hence $(\rho,x) < \alpha = (\rho,y_0) \leq (\rho,y)$ for all $y \in Y$.

Note that the point y_0 belongs to the hyperplane $H(\rho,\alpha)$, the set Y belongs to the closed half-space $H_+(\rho,\alpha)$, while the point x belongs to the open half-space

$$\overset{o}{H}_-(\rho,\alpha) = \{z \in X: (\rho,z) < \alpha\}.$$

Thus the hyperplane separates the point x from the compact convex set Y (see Figure 3.14).

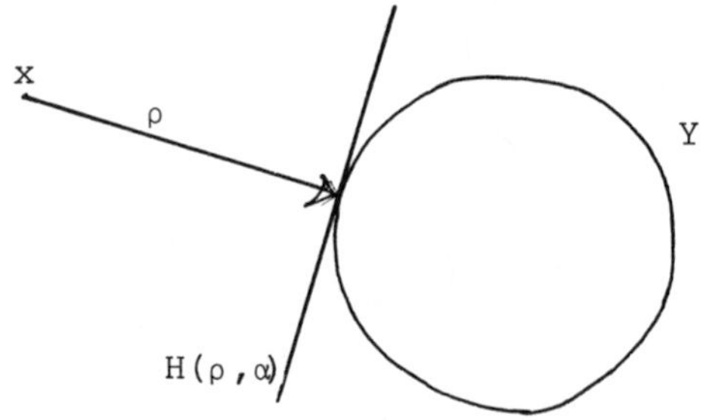

Fig.3.14.

While convexity is necessary for the proof of this theorem, the compactness requirement may be weakened to Y being closed. Suppose however that Y is an open set. Then it is possible to choose a point x outside Y, which is, none the less, an accumulation point of Y such that $d(x,y) = 0$.

On the other hand if Y is compact but not convex, then a situation such as Figure 3.15 is possible. Clearly no hyperplane separates x from Y.

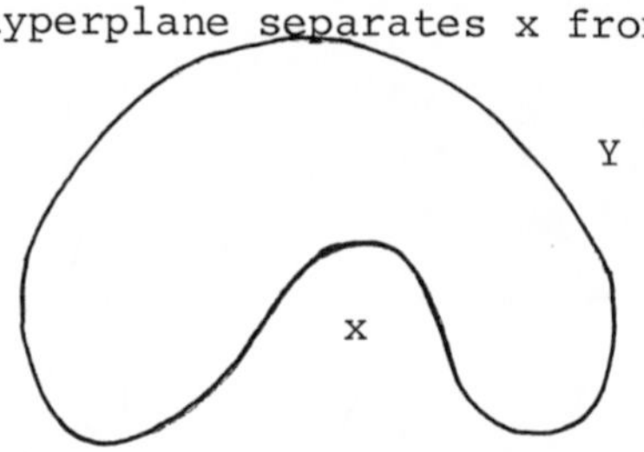

Fig.3.15.

If A and B are two sets, and $H(\rho,\alpha) = H$ is a hyperplane such that $A \subset H_-(\rho,\alpha)$ and $B \subset H_+(\rho,\alpha)$ then say that H weakly separates A and B. If H is such that $A \subset \overset{o}{H}_-(\rho,\alpha)$ and $B \subset \overset{o}{H}_+(\rho,\alpha)$ then say H strongly separates A and B. Note in the latter case that it is necessary that $A \cap B = \Phi$.

In lemma 3.19 we found a hyperplane $H(\rho,\alpha)$ such that $(\rho,x) < \alpha$. Clearly it is possible to find $\alpha_- < \alpha$ such that $(\rho,x) < \alpha_-$.

Thus the hyperplane $H(\rho,\alpha_-)$ strongly separates x from the compact convex set Y.

If Y is convex but not compact, then it is possible to find a hyperplane H that weakly separates x from Y.

We now extend this result to the separation of convex sets.

Separating Hyperplane Theorem

Suppose that A and B are two disjoint non-empty convex sets of a finite dimensional vector space X. Then there exists a hyperplane H that weakly separates A from B. If both A and B are compact then H strongly separates A from B.

Proof

Since A and B are convex the set

$A-B = \{w \in X: w=a-b \text{ where } a \in A, b \in B\}$

is also convex.

To see this suppose a_1-b_1 and $a_2-b_2 \in A-B$.

Then $\lambda(a_1-b_1)+(1-\lambda)(a_2-b_2) = [\lambda a_1+(1-\lambda)a_2]$
$+[\lambda b_1+(1-\lambda)b_2] \in A-B$.

Now $A \cap B = \Phi$. Thus there exists no point in both A and B, and so $\underline{0} \notin A-B$. By lemma 3.19, there exists a hyperplane $H(-\rho,\underline{0})$ weakly separating $\underline{0}$ from A-B.

ie. $(\rho,\underline{0}) = 0 \leq (\rho,w)$ for all $w \in B-A$.

But then $(\rho,a) \leq (\rho,b)$ for all $a\in A, b\in B$.

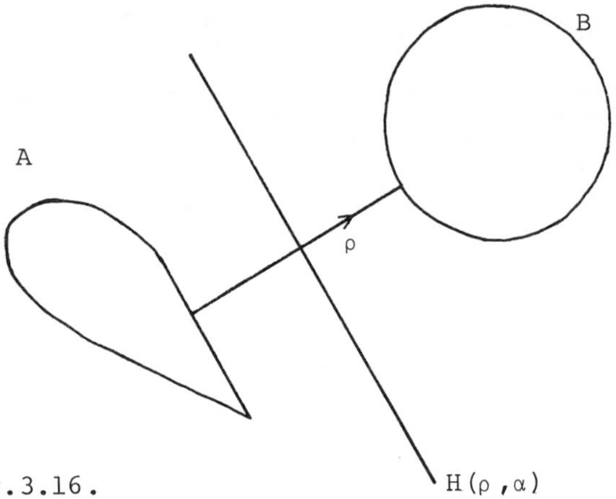

Fig.3.16.

Choose $\alpha\in[\sup_{a\in A}(\rho,a), \inf_{b\in B}(\rho,b)]$.

In the case that A,B are non-compact, it is possible that $\sup_{a\in A}(\rho,a) = \inf_{b\in B}(\rho,b)$

Thus $(\rho,a) \leq \alpha \leq (\rho,b)$ and so $H(\rho,\alpha)$ weakly separates A and B.

Consider now the case when A and B are compact. The function $\rho^*:X \to \mathbb{R}$ given by $\rho^*(x) = (\rho,x)$ is clearly continuous. By lemma 3.16, since both A and B are compact, there exists points $\bar{a}\in A$ and $\bar{b}\in B$ such that $(\rho,\bar{a}) = \sup_{a\in A}(\rho,a)$

$$(\rho,\bar{b}) = \inf_{b\in B.}(\rho,b) .$$

If $\sup_{a\in A}(\rho,a) = \inf_{b\in B}(\rho,b)$ then $(\rho,\bar{a}) = (\rho,\bar{b})$, and so $\bar{a} = \bar{b}$ contradicting $A\cap B = \Phi$.

Thus $(\rho,\bar{a}) < (\rho,\bar{b})$ and we can choose α such that

$$(\rho,a) \leq (\rho,\bar{a}) < \alpha < (\rho,\bar{b}) \leq (\rho,b)$$

for all a,b in A,B. Thus $H(\rho,\alpha)$ strongly separates A and B.

Example 3.5

Hildenbrand and Kirman (1976) have applied this theorem to find a price vector which supports a final allocation of economic resources. Consider a society $N = \{1,\dots,n\}$ in which each individual i has an initial endowment $e_i = (e_{i1},\dots,e_{im}) \in \mathbb{R}^m$ of m commodities. At price vector $p = (p_1,\dots,p_m)$, the budget set of individual i is $B_i(p) = \{x \in \mathbb{R}^m : (p,x) \leq (p,e_i)\}$. Each individual has a preference relation P_i on $\mathbb{R}^m \times \mathbb{R}^m$, and at the price vector p the demand $D_i(p)$ is the set

$$\{x \in B_i(p) : y \; P_i \; x \text{ for no } y \in B_i(p)\}.$$

Let $f_i = (f_{i1},\dots,f_{im}) \in \mathbb{R}^m$ be the final allocation to individual i, for $i=1,\dots,m$. Suppose there exists a price vector $p = (p_1,\dots,p_m)$ with the property (*) $x \; P_i \; f_i \Rightarrow (p,x) > (p,e_i)$. Then this would imply that $f_i \in B_i(p) \Rightarrow f_i \in D_i(p)$. If property (*) holds at some price vector p, for each i, then $f_i \in D_i(p)$ for each i. To show existence of such a price vector, let

$$\pi_i = P_i(f_i) - e_i \in \mathbb{R}^m.$$

Here as before $P_i(f_i) = \{x \in \mathbb{R}^m : x \; P_i \; f_i\}$. Suppose that there exists a hyperplane $H(p,0)$ strongly separating 0 from π_i. In this case $0 < (p, x - e_i)$ for all $x \in P_i(f_i)$. But this is equivalent to $(p,x) > (p,e_i)$ for all $x \in P_i(f_i)$

Hence let $\pi = \text{con}\left[\bigcup_{i \in N} \pi_i\right]$ be the convex hull of the sets $\pi_i, i \in N$. Clearly if $\underline{0} \notin \pi$ and there is a hyperplane $H(p,0)$ strongly separating $\underline{0}$ from π, then p is a price vector which supports the final allocation $f_1,\dots,f_m$.

3.5. OPTIMISATION ON CONVEX SETS

A key notion underlying economic theory is that of the maximisation of an objective function subject to one or a number of constraints. The most elementary case of such a problem is the one addressed by the Weierstrass Theorem: if $f:X \to \mathbb{R}$ is a continuous function, and Y is a compact constraint set then there exists some point $\bar{y}$ such that $f(\bar{y}) = \sup(f,Y)$. Here $\bar{y}$ is a maximum point of f on Y.

Using the Separating Hyperplane theorem we can extend this analysis to the optimisation of a convex preference correspondence on a compact convex constraint set.

3.5.1 Optimisation of a convex preference correspondence

Suppose that Y is a compact, convex constraint set in $\mathbb{R}^m$ and $P:\mathbb{R}^m \to \mathbb{R}^m$ is a preference correspondence which is convex (ie P(x) is convex for all $x \in \mathbb{R}^m$). A choice for P on Y is a point $\bar{y} \in Y$ such that $P(\bar{y}) \cap Y = \Phi$.

We shall say that P is non-satiated in $\mathbb{R}^m$ iff for no $y \in \mathbb{R}^m$ is it the case that $P(y) = \Phi$. A sufficient condition to ensure non-satiation for example is the assumption of monotonicity ie. $x > y$ (where as before this means $x_i > y_i$, for each of the coordinates $x_i, y_i, i=1,\ldots,m$) implies that $x \in P(y)$.

Say that P is locally non-satiated in $\mathbb{R}^m$ iff for each $y \in \mathbb{R}^m$ and any neighbourhood U_y of y in $\mathbb{R}^m$, then $P(y) \cap U_y \neq \Phi$.

Clearly monotonicity implies local non-satiation implies non-satiation.

Suppose that y belongs to the interior of the compact constraint set Y. Then there is a neighbourhood U_y of y within Y. Consequently $P(y) \cap U_y \neq \Phi$ and so y cannot be a choice from Y. On the other hand, since Y is compact it is closed, and so if y belongs to the boundary δY of Y, it belongs to Y itself. By definition if $y \in \delta Y$ then any neighbourhood U_y of y intersects $\mathbb{R}^m \setminus Y$. Thus when $P(y) \subset \mathbb{R}^m \setminus Y$, y will be a choice from Y. Alternatively if y is a choice of P from Y, then y must belong to the boundary of P.

<u>Lemma 3.20</u>

Let Y be compact, convex constraint set in $\mathbb{R}^m$ and let $P:\mathbb{R}^m \to \mathbb{R}^m$ be a preference correspondence which is locally non-satiated, and is such that, for all $x \in \mathbb{R}^m$, P(x) is open and convex. Then $\bar{y}$ is a choice of P from Y iff there is a hyperplane $H(p,\alpha)$ through $\bar{y}$ in Y which separates Y from $P(\bar{y})$ in the sense that

$$(p,y) \leq \alpha = (p,\bar{y}) < (p,x) \quad \text{for all } y \in Y \text{ and all } x \in P(\bar{y}).$$

<u>Proof</u>

Suppose that the hyperplane $H(p,\alpha)$ contains $\bar{y}$ and separates Y from $P(\bar{y})$ in the above sense. Clearly $\bar{y}$ must belong to the boundary of Y. Moreover $(p,y) < (p,x)$ for all $y \in Y, x \in P(\bar{y})$. Thus $Y \cap P(\bar{y}) = \Phi$ and so $\bar{y}$ is the choice of P from Y.

On the other hand suppose that $\bar{y}$ is a choice. Then $P(\bar{y}) \cap Y = \Phi$.

Moreover the local non-satiation property,

$P(\bar{y}) \cap U_{\bar{y}} \neq \Phi$ for $U_{\bar{y}}$ a nbd. of $\bar{y}$ in $\mathbb{R}^m$, guarantees that $\bar{y}$ must belong to the boundary of Y. Since Y and $P(\bar{y})$ are both convex, there exists a hyperplane $H(p,\alpha)$ through $\bar{y}$ such that

$$(p,y) \leq \alpha = (p,\bar{y}) \leq (p,x)$$

for all $y \in Y$, all $x \in P(\bar{y})$.
But $P(\bar{y})$ is open, and so the last inequality can be written $(p,\bar{y}) < (p,x)$.

Note that if either the constraint set, Y, or the correspondence P is such that P(y) is strictly convex, for all $y \in \mathbb{R}^m$, then the choice $\bar{y}$ is unique.

If $f:\mathbb{R}^m \to \mathbb{R}$ is a concave or quasi-concave function then application of this lemma to the preference correspondence $P:\mathbb{R}^m \to \mathbb{R}$, where $P(x) = \{y \in \mathbb{R}^m : f(y) > f(x)\}$, characterises the maximum point $\bar{y}$ of f on Y. Here $\bar{y}$ is a maximum point of f on Y if $f(\bar{y}) = \sup(f,Y)$. Note that local non-satiation of P requires that for any point x in $\mathbb{R}^m$, and any neighbourhood U_x of x in $\mathbb{R}^m$, there exists $y \in U_x$ such that $f(y) > f(x)$.

The vector $p = (p_1,\ldots,p_m)$ which characterises the hyperplane $H(p,\alpha)$ is called in economic applications the vector of <u>shadow prices</u>. The reason for this will become clear in the following example.

<u>Example 3.6</u>

As an example suppose that optimal use of (m-1) different inputs $(x_1,\ldots,x_{m-1})$ gives rise to an output y, say, where $y = y(x_1,\ldots,x_{m-1})$. Any m vector $(x_1,\ldots,x_{m-1},x_m)$ is <u>feasible</u> as long as $x_m \leq y(x_1,\ldots,x_{m-1})$. Here x_m is the output. Write $g(x_1,\ldots,x_{m-1},x_m) = y(x_1,\ldots,x_{m-1}) - x_m$.

Then a vector $x = (x_1,\ldots,x_{m-1},x_m)$ is feasible iff $g(x) \geq 0$.

Suppose now that $y = y(x_1,\ldots,x_{m-1})$ is a concave function in $x_1,\ldots,x_{m-1}$. Then clearly the set $G = \{x \in \mathbb{R}^m : g(x) \geq 0\}$ is a convex set.

Now let $\pi(x_1,\ldots,x_{m-1},x_m) = -\sum p_i x_i + p_m x_m$ be the profit function of the producer, when prices for inputs and outputs are given exogenously by $(-p_1,\ldots,-p_{m-1},p_m)$.

Again let $P: \mathbb{R}^m \to \mathbb{R}^m$ be the preference correspondence $P(x) = \{z \in \mathbb{R}^m : \pi(z) > \pi(x)\}$.

Since for each x, $P(x)$ is convex, and locally non-satiated, there is a choice $\bar{x}$ and a hyperplane $H(\rho,\alpha)$ separating $P(\bar{x})$ from G.

Indeed it is clear from the construction that

$$P(\bar{x}) \subset \overset{\circ}{H}_+(\rho,\alpha) \text{ and } G \subset H_-(\rho,\alpha).$$

Moreover the hyperplane $H(\rho,\alpha)$ must coincide with the set of points $\{x \in \mathbb{R}^m : \pi(x) = \pi(\bar{x})\}$.

Thus the hyperplane $H(\rho,\alpha)$ has the form

$$\{x \in \mathbb{R}^m : (p,x) = \pi(\bar{x})\}$$

and so may be written $H(p,\pi(\bar{x}))$.

Note that the intercept on the x_m axis is $\frac{\pi(\bar{x})}{p_m}$ while the distance of the hyperplane from the origin is $\frac{\pi(\bar{x})}{\|p\|} = \frac{\pi(\bar{x})}{\sqrt{\sum p_i^2}}$. Thus the intercept gives the profit measured in units of output, while the distance from the origin of the profit hyperplane gives the profit in terms of a normalized price vector $(\|p\|)$.

Figure 3.17 illustrates the situation with one input (x_1) and one output (x_2).

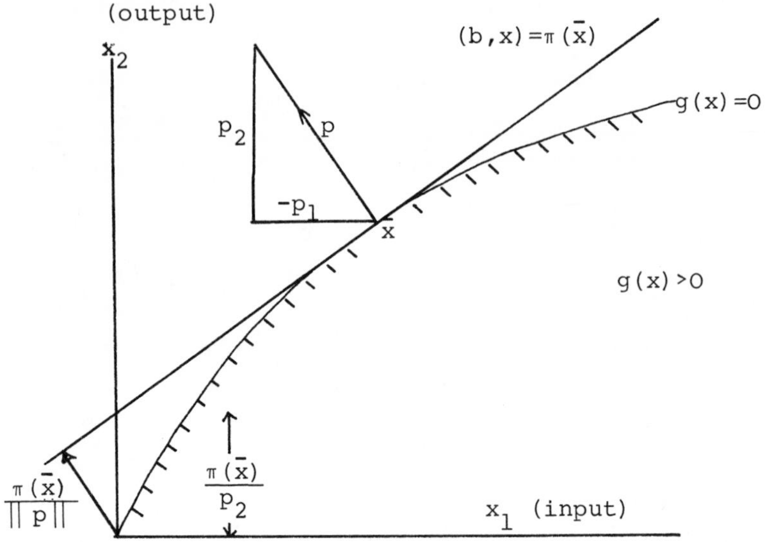

Fig.3.17.

Precisely the same analysis can be performed when optimal production is characterised by a general production function $F:\mathbb{R}^n \to \mathbb{R}$.

Here $x_1,\ldots,x_m$ are inputs, with prices $-p_1,\ldots,-p_m$ and $x_{m+1},\ldots,x_n$ are outputs with prices $p_{m+1},\ldots,p_n$.

Let $p = (-p_1,\ldots,-p_m,p_{m+1},\ldots,p_n)\in\mathbb{R}^n$.

Define F so that a vector $x\in\mathbb{R}^n$ is <u>feasible</u> iff $F(x) \geq 0$. Note that we also need to restrict all inputs and outputs to be non-negative.

Therefore define $\mathbb{R}^n_+ = \{x:x_i \geq 0 \text{ for } i=1,\ldots,n\}$.

Assume that the feasible set

$$G = \{x\in\mathbb{R}^n_+:F(x) \geq 0\} \text{ is convex.}$$

As before let $P:\mathbb{R}^n \to \mathbb{R}^n$ where

$P(x) = \{z\in\mathbb{R}^n:\pi(z) > \pi(x)\}$.

Then the point $\bar{x}$ is a choice of P from G iff $\bar{x}$ maximises the profit function

$$\pi(x) = \sum_{j=1}^{n-m} p_{m+j}\, x_{m+j} - \sum_{j=1}^{m} p_j x_j .$$

By the previous example $\bar{x}$ is a choice iff the hyperplane $H(p, \pi(\bar{x}))$ separates $P(\bar{x})$ and G: i.e. $P(\bar{x}) \subset \overset{o}{H}_+(p, \pi(\bar{x}))$ and $G \subset H_-(p, \pi(\bar{x}))$.

In the next chapter we shall use this optimality condition to characterise the choice $\bar{x}$ more fully in the case when F is "smooth".

<u>Example 3.7</u>

Consider now the case of a <u>consumer</u> maximising a preference correspondence $P: \mathbb{R}^n \to \mathbb{R}^n$ subject to a budget constraint B(p) which is dependent on a set of exogeneous prices $p_1, \ldots, p_n$.

For example the consumer may hold an initial set of endowments $(e_1, \ldots, e_n)$, so let

$I = \sum_{i=1}^{n} p_i e_i = (p,e)$.

The budget set is then

$$B(p) = \{x \in \mathbb{R}^n_+ : (p,x) \leq I\},$$

where for convenience we assume the consumer only buys a non-negative amount of each commodity. Suppose that P is monotonic, and P(x) is open, convex for all $x \in \mathbb{R}^n$. As before $\bar{x}$ is a choice from B(p) iff there is a hyperplane $H(\rho, \alpha)$ separating $P(\bar{x})$ from B(p).

Under these conditions the choice must belong to the upper boundary of B(p) and so satisfy $(p,\bar{x}) = (p,e) = I$. Thus the hyperplane has the form H(p, I), and so the optimality condition is

$P(\bar{x}) \subset \overset{o}{H}_+(p, I)$ and

$B(p) \subset H_-(p, I)$;

ie $(p,x) \leq I = (p,\bar{x}) < (p,y)$

for all $x \in B(p)$ and all $y \in P(\bar{x})$.

Figure 3.18 illustrates the situation with two commodities x_1 and x_2.

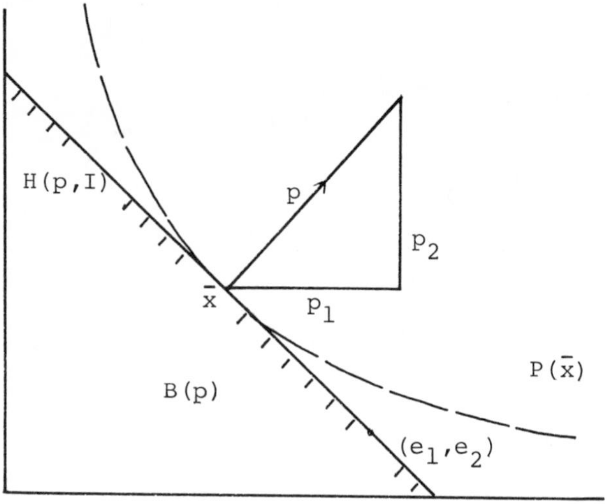

Fig.3.18.

In the next chapter we use this optimality condition to characterise a choice when preference is given by a smooth utility function $f: \mathbb{R}^n \to \mathbb{R}$.

In the previous two examples we considered
i) optimisation of a profit function, which is determined by exogenously given prices, subject to a fixed production constraint, and
ii) optimisation of a fixed preference correspondence, subject to a budget constraint, which is again determined by exogenous prices. Clearly at a given price vector each producer will "demand" a certain input vector and supply a particular output vector, so that the combination is his choice in the environment determined by p. In the same way a consumer will respond to a price

vector p by demanding optimal amounts of each commodity, and possibly supplying other commodities such as labour, or various endowments. In contrast to example 3.7, regard all prices as positive, and consider a commodity x_j demanded by an agent i as an input to be negative, and positive when supplied as an output. Let $\bar{x}_{ij}(p)$ be the optimal demand or supply of commodity j by agent i at the price vector p.

Then market equilibrium of supply and demand in a society {1,...,i,...N} occurs when

$\sum_{i=1}^{N} \sum_{j=1}^{n} \bar{x}_{ij}(p) = 0$. A price vector which leads to market equilibrium in demand and supply is called an <u>equilibrium price vector</u>.

<u>Example 3.8</u>

To give a simple example, consider two agents. The first agent controls a machine which makes use of labour, x, to produce a single output y. Regard $x \in (-\infty, 0]$ and consider price vectors $p \in \mathbb{R}^2_+$, where p = (w,r) and w is the price of labour, and r the price of the output. An output is feasible for Agent One iff $F(x,y) \geq 0$.

Agent Two is the only supplier of labour, but is adverse to working. His preference is described by a quasi-concave utility function $f: \mathbb{R}^2 \to \mathbb{R}$ and we restrict attention to a domain $D = \{(x,y) \in \mathbb{R}^2 : x \leq 0, y \geq 0\}$.

Assume that f is monotonic:

ie. if $x_1 < x_2$ and $y_1 < y_2$ then $f(x_1,y_1) < f(y_2,y_2)$. The budget constraint of Agent Two at (w,r) is therefore

$$B(w,r) = \{(x_1,y_2) \in D: ry_2 \leq w|x|\},$$

where $|x|$ is the quantity of labour supplied, and y_2 is the amount of commodity y consumed.

Profit for Agent One is $\pi(x,y) = ry - wx$, and we shall assume that this agent then consumes an amount $y_1 = \frac{\pi(x,y)}{r}$ of commodity y.

For equilibrium of supply and demand at prices $(\bar{w},\bar{r})$

i) $\bar{y} = \bar{y}_1 + \bar{y}_2$

ii) $(\bar{x},\bar{y})$ maximises $\pi(x,y) = \bar{r}y - \bar{w}x$ subject to $F(x,y) \geq 0$

iii) $(\bar{x},\bar{y}_2)$ maximises $f(x,y_2)$ subject to $\bar{r}y_2 = \bar{w}x$.

At any point $(x,y) \in D$, and vector (w,r) define

$P(x,y) = \{(x',y') \in D : f(x',y' - y_1) > f(x,y - y_1)\}$

where as above $y_1 = \frac{ry-wx}{r}$ is the amount of commodity y consumed by the producer.

Thus $P(x,y)$ is the preference correspondence of Agent One displaced by the distance y_1 up the y-axis.

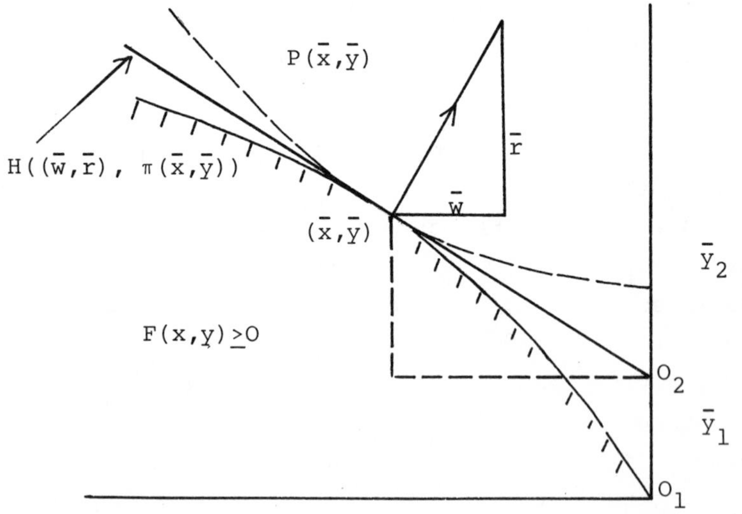

Fig.3.19.

Figure 3.19 illustrates that it is possible to find a vector (w,r) such that $H = H((w,r),\pi(\bar{x},\bar{y}))$ separates $P(\bar{x},\bar{y})$ and the production set

$$G = \{(x,y)\in D: F(x,y) \geq 0\}.$$

As in example 3.6, the intersect of H with the y-axis is $\bar{y}_1 = \frac{\pi(\bar{x},\bar{y})}{r}$, the consumption of y by Agent One.

The hyperplane H is the set

$$\{(x,y): ry + wx = r\bar{y}_1\}.$$

Hence for all $(x,y)\in H$, $(x,y-\bar{y}_1)$ satisfies $r(y-\bar{y}_1) + wx = 0$. Thus H is the boundary of the second Agent's budget set

$\{(x,y_2): ry_2+wx = 0\}$ displaced up the y-axis by $\bar{y}_1$.

Consequently $\bar{y} = \bar{y}_1 + \bar{y}_2$ and so $(\bar{x},\bar{y})$ is a market equilibrium.

Note that the hyperplane separation satisfies:

$$py - rx \leq \pi(\bar{x},\bar{y}) < ry' - wx'$$

for all $(x,y)\in G$, and all $(x',y')\in P(\bar{x},\bar{y})$.

As above $(x',y')\in P(\bar{x},\bar{y})$ iff $f(x',y'-\bar{y}_1) > f(\bar{x},\bar{y}_2)$.

So the right hand side implies that if $(x',y')\in P(\bar{x},\bar{y})$ then

$$ry' - wx' > \pi(\bar{x},\bar{y}).$$

Since $y_2' = y' - \bar{y}_1, ry_2' - wx' > 0$ or $(x',y' - \bar{y}_1)\in \overset{o}{H}_+((\bar{w},\bar{r}),0)$ and so $(x',y'-\bar{y}_1)$ is infeasible for Agent Two.

Finally $(\bar{x},\bar{y})$ maximises $\pi(x,y)$ subject to $(x,y)\in G$, and so $(\bar{x},\bar{y})$ results from optimising behaviour by both agents at the price vector (w,r).

As this example illustrates it is possible to show existence of a market equilibrium in economies characterised by compact convex constraint sets, and convex preference correspondences. To do this in a general context however requires more powerful mathematical tools, which we shall introduce in the next chapter. Before this however we consider one further application of the hyperplane separation theorem to a situation where we wish to optimise a concave objective function subject to a number of concave constraints.

3.5.2. Kuhn Tucker Theorem

Here we consider a family of contraints in $\mathbb{R}^n$.
Let $g = (g_1,\ldots,g_m): \mathbb{R}^n \to \mathbb{R}^m$. As before let $\mathbb{R}^m_+ = \{(y_1,\ldots,y_m): y_i \geq 0 \text{ for } i=1,\ldots,n\}$.
A point x is feasible iff $x \in \mathbb{R}^n_+$ and $g(x) \in \mathbb{R}^m_+$ (ie $g_i(x) \geq 0$ for $i=1,\ldots,m$).
Let $f: \mathbb{R}^n \to \mathbb{R}$ be the objective function.
Say that $x^* \in \mathbb{R}^n$ is an optimum of the constrained optimisation problem (f,g) iff x^* solves the problem:
Maximise $f(x)$ subject to the feasibility constraint $g(x) \in \mathbb{R}^m_+$, $x \in \mathbb{R}^n_+$.
Call the problem (f,g) solvable iff there is some $x \in \mathbb{R}^n_+$ such that $g_i(x) > 0$ for $i=1,\ldots,m$.
The Lagrangian to the problem (f,g) is:

$$L(x,\lambda) = f(x) + \sum_{i=1}^{m} \lambda_i g_i(x) = f(x) + (\lambda, g(x))$$

where $x \in \mathbb{R}^n_+$ and $\lambda = (\lambda_1,\ldots,\lambda_m) \in \mathbb{R}^m_+$.
The pair $(x^*,\lambda^*) \in \mathbb{R}^{n+m}_+$ is called a global saddle point for the problem (f,g) iff

$$L(x,\lambda^*) \leq L(x^*,\lambda^*) \leq L(x^*,\lambda)$$

for all $x \in \mathbb{R}^n_+, \lambda \in \mathbb{R}^m_+$.

Kuhn Tucker Theorem 1

Suppose $f, g_1,\ldots,g_m: \mathbb{R}^n \to \mathbb{R}$ are concave functions for all $x \in \mathbb{R}^n_+$.
Then if x^* is an optimum to the solvable problem $(f,g): \mathbb{R}^n \to \mathbb{R}^{m+1}$ there exists a $\lambda^* \in \mathbb{R}^m_+$ such that

(x^*,λ^*) is a saddle point for (f,g).

Proof

Let $A = \{y \in \mathbb{R}^{m+1} : \exists x \in \mathbb{R}^n_+ \text{ s.t. } y \leq (f,g)(x)\}$.

Here $(f,g)(x) = (f(x), g,(x), \ldots g_m(x))$.

Thus $y = (y_1,\ldots,y_{m+1}) \in A$ iff $\exists x \in \mathbb{R}^n_+$ such that

$$y_1 \leq f(x)$$
$$y_{j+1} \leq g_j(x) \text{ for } j=1,\ldots,m.$$

Let x^* be an optimum and

$$B = \{z = (z_1,\ldots,z_{m+1}) \in \mathbb{R}^m : z_1 > f(x^*) \text{ and } (z_2,\ldots,z_{m+1}) > 0\}.$$

Since f,g are concave, A is convex.

To see this suppose $y_1, y_2 \in A$.

But since both f and g are concave $af(x_1)+(1-a)f(x_2) \leq f(ax_1+(1-a)x_2)$

and similarly for g, for any $a \in [0,1]$.

Thus
$$ay_1+(1-a)y_2 \leq a(f,g)(x_1)+(1-a)(f,g)(x_2) \leq (f,g)(ax_1+(1-a)x_2).$$

Since $x_1,x_2 \in \mathbb{R}^n_+$, $ax_1+(1-a)x_2 \in \mathbb{R}^n_+$ and so $ay_1+(1-a)y_2 \in \mathbb{R}^n_+$.

Clearly B is convex, since $az_{11}+(1-a)z_{12} > f(x^*)$ if $a \in [0,1]$ and $z_{11}, z_{12} > f(x^*)$.

To see $A \cap B = \Phi$, consider $x \in \mathbb{R}^n$ such that $g(x) < 0$.

Then $(y_2,\ldots,y_{m+1}) \leq g(x) < \underline{0} \leq (z_2,\ldots,z_{m+1})$.

If $g(x) \in \mathbb{R}^m_+$ then x is feasible.

In this case $y_1 \leq f(x) \leq f(x^*) < z_1$.

By the separating hyperplane theorem, there exists $(p_1,\ldots,p_{m+1}) \in \mathbb{R}^{m+1}$ and $\alpha \in \mathbb{R}$ such that $H(p,\alpha) = \{w \in \mathbb{R}^{m+1} : \sum_{j=1}^{m+1} w_j p_j = \alpha\}$ separates A and B

ie. $\sum_{j=1}^{m+1} p_j y_j \leq \alpha \leq \sum_{j=1}^{m+1} p_j z_j$

for any $y \in A$ and $z \in B$. Moreover $p \in \mathbb{R}^{m+1}_+$.

By the definition of A, for any $y \in A$, $\exists x \in \mathbb{R}^n_+$ such that $y \leq (f,g)(x)$. Thus for any $x \in \mathbb{R}^n_+$,

$$p_1 f(x) + \sum_{j=2}^{m} p_j g_j(x) \leq \sum_{j=1}^{m+1} p_j z_j .$$

Since $(f(x^*),0,\ldots,0)$ belongs to the boundary of B,

$$p_1 f(x) + \sum_{j=2}^{m} p_j g_j(x) \leq p_1 f(x^*).$$

Suppose $p_1 = 0$. Since $p \in \mathbb{R}^{m+1}_+$, there exists $p_j > 0$. Since the problem is solvable, $\exists\, x \in \mathbb{R}^n_+$ such that $g_j(x) > 0$. But this gives $\sum_{j=2}^{m} p_j g_j(x) > 0$, contradicting $p_1 = 0$.

Hence $p_1 > 0$. Let $\lambda^*_j = \dfrac{p_{j+1}}{p_1}$ for $j=1,\ldots,m$.

Then $L(x,\lambda^*) = f(x) + \sum_{j=1}^{m} \lambda^*_j g_j(x) \leq f(x^*)$ for all $x \in \mathbb{R}^n_+$, where $\lambda^* = (\lambda^*_1,\ldots,\lambda^*_m) \in \mathbb{R}^m_+$.

Since x^* is feasible, $g(x^*) \in \mathbb{R}^m_+$, and $(\lambda^*,g(x^*)) \geq 0$.
But $f(x^*) + (\lambda^*,g(x^*)) \leq f(x^*)$ implying $(\lambda^*,g(x^*)) \leq 0$. Thus $(\lambda^*,g(x^*)) = 0$.
Clearly $(\lambda,g(x^*)) \geq 0$ if $\lambda \in \mathbb{R}^m_+$.
Thus $L(x,\lambda^*) \leq L(x^*,\lambda^*) \leq L(x^*,\lambda)$ for any $x \in \mathbb{R}^n_+$, $\lambda \in \mathbb{R}^m_+$.

Kuhn Tucker Theorem 2

If the pair (x^*,λ^*) is a global saddle point for the problem (f,g), then x^* is an optimum.

Proof

By the assumption

$$L(x,\lambda^*) \leq L(x^*,\lambda^*) \leq L(x^*,\lambda)$$

for all $x \in \mathbb{R}^n_+$, $\lambda \in \mathbb{R}^m_+$.
Choose $\lambda = (\lambda^*_1,\ldots 2\lambda^*_i,\ldots,\lambda^*_m)$.
Then $L(x^*,\lambda) \geq L(x^*,\lambda^*)$ implies $g_i(x^*)\lambda^*_i \geq 0$.
If $\lambda^*_i \neq 0$ then $g_i(x^*) \geq 0$, and so $(\lambda^*,g(x^*)) \geq 0$.
On the other hand $L(x^*,\lambda^*) \leq L(x^*,0)$ implies

$$(\lambda^*,g(x^*)) \leq 0.$$

Thus $(\lambda^*,g(x^*)) = 0$.
Hence $f(x) + (\lambda^*,g(x)) \leq f(x^*) \leq f(x^*) + (\lambda,g(x^*))$.

If x is feasible, $g(x) \geq 0$ and so $(\lambda^*, g(x)) \geq 0$.
Thus $f(x) \leq f(x) + (\lambda^*, g(x)) \leq f(x^*)$
for all $x \in \mathbb{R}^n_+$, whenever $g(x) \in \mathbb{R}^m_+$.
Hence x^* is an optimum for the problem (f,g).
Note that for a concave optimisation problem (f,g), x^* is an optimum for (f,g) iff (x^*, λ^*) is a global saddle point for the Lagrangian $L(x, \lambda), \lambda \in \mathbb{R}^m_+$.
Moreover (x^*, λ^*) are such that $(\lambda^*, g(x^*))$ <u>minimises</u> $(\lambda, g(x))$ for all $\lambda \in \mathbb{R}^m_+$, $x \in \mathbb{R}^n_+$, $g(x) \in \mathbb{R}^m_+$.
Since $(\lambda^*, g(x^*)) = 0$ this implies that if $g_i(x^*) > 0$ then $\lambda_i^* = 0$ and if $\lambda_i^* > 0$ then $g_i(x^*) = 0$.

The coefficients $(\lambda_1^*, \ldots, \lambda_n^*)$ are called <u>shadow prices</u>. If the optimum is such that $g_i(x^*) > 0$ then the shadow price $\lambda_i^* = 0$. In other words if the optimum does not lie in the boundary of the ith constraint set $\partial B_i = \{x : g_i(x) = 0\}$, then this constraint is <u>slack</u>, with zero shadow price. If the shadow price is non zero then the constraint cannot be slack, and the optimum lies on the boundary of the constraint set. See Heal (1973) for further discussion of the uses of the Kuhn Tucker Theorem.

In the case of a single constraint, the assumption of non-satiation was sufficient to guarantee that the constraint was not slack.
In this case

$$f(x) + \frac{p_2}{p_1} g(x) \leq f(x^*) \leq f(x^*) + \lambda g(x^*)$$

for any $x \in \mathbb{R}^n_+$, and $\lambda \in \mathbb{R}^n_+$, where $\frac{p_2}{p_1} > 0$.

The Kuhn Tucker theorem is of particular use when objective and constraint functions are smooth. In this case the Lagrangean permits computation of the optimal points of the problem. We deal with these procedures in the next chapter.

Chapter 4

DIFFERENTIAL CALCULUS AND SMOOTH OPTIMISATION

Under certain conditions a continuous function $f:\mathbb{R}^n \to \mathbb{R}^m$ can be approximated at each point x in $\mathbb{R}^n$ by a linear function $df(x):\mathbb{R}^n \to \mathbb{R}^m$, known as the differential of f at x. In the same way the differential df may be approximated by a bilinear map $d^2f(x)$. When all differentials are continuous then f is called smooth. For a smooth function f, Taylor's Theorem gives a relationship between the differentials at a point x and the value of f in a neighbourhood of a point. This in turn allows us to characterise maximum points of the function by features of the first and second differential. For a real-valued function whose preference correspondence is convex we can virtually identify critical points (where $df(x) = 0$) with maxima.

In the maximisation problem for a smooth function on a "smooth" constraint set, we seek critical points of the Lagrangian, introduced in the previous chapter. In particular in economic situations with exogenous prices we may characterise optimum points for consumers and producers to be points where the differential of the utility or production function is given by the price vector. Finally we use these results to show that for a society the set of pareto optimal points belongs to a set of generalised critical points of a function which describes the preferences of the society.

4.1 DIFFERENTIAL OF A FUNCTION

A function $f:\mathbb{R} \to \mathbb{R}$ is <u>differentiable</u> at $x \in \mathbb{R}$ if $\underset{h \to 0}{\text{Limit}} \dfrac{f(x+h) - f(x)}{h}$ exists (and is neither $+\infty$ nor $-\infty$).

When this limit exists we shall write it as $\left.\dfrac{df}{dx}\right|_x$.

Another way of writing this is that as $(x_n) \to x$ then $\dfrac{f(x_n) - f(x)}{x_n - x} \to \left.\dfrac{df}{dx}\right|_x$, the <u>derivative</u> of f at x.

Again this means that there is a real number $\lambda(x) = \left.\dfrac{df}{dx}\right|_x \in \mathbb{R}$ such that $f(x+h) - f(x) = \lambda(x)h + \varepsilon|h|$ where $\varepsilon \to 0$ as $h \to 0$.

Let $df(x)$ be the linear function $\mathbb{R} \to \mathbb{R}$ given by $df(x)(h) = \lambda(x)h$.

Then the map $\mathbb{R} \to \mathbb{R}$ given by

$$h \to f(x) + df(x)(h) = g(x+h)$$

is a "first order approximation" to the map

$$h \to f(x+h).$$

In other words the maps $h \to g(x+h)$ and $h \to f(x+h)$ are "tangent" to one another where "tangent" means that

$$\frac{|f(x+h) - g(x+h)|}{|h|}$$

approaches zero as $h \to 0$.

Note that the map $h \to f(x) + df(x)(h) = g(x+h)$ has a straight line graph, and so $df(x)$ is a "linear approximation" to the function f at x.

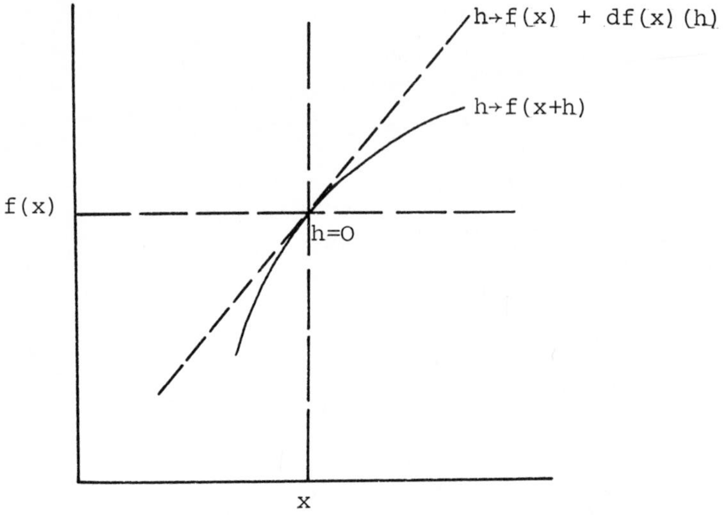

Fig.4.1.

<u>Example 4.1</u>

i) Suppose $f:\mathbb{R} \to \mathbb{R} : x \to x^2$.

Then $\lim_{h\to 0}\frac{f(x+h)-f(x)}{h} = \lim_{h\to 0}\frac{(x+h)^2-x^2}{h} = \lim_{h\to 0}\frac{2hx+h^2}{h}$

$= 2x + \lim_{h\to 0} h = 2x.$

Similarly if $f:\mathbb{R} \to \mathbb{R} : x \to x^r$ then $df(x) = rx^{r-1}$.

ii) Suppose $f:\mathbb{R} \to \mathbb{R} : x \to \sin x$.

Then $\lim_{h\to 0}\left(\frac{\sin(x+h)-\sin x}{h}\right) = \lim_{h\to 0}\left(\frac{\sin x(\cos h - 1) + \cos x \sin h}{h}\right)$

$= \lim_{h\to 0}\frac{\sin x}{h}\left(\frac{-h^2}{2}\right) + \lim_{h\to 0}\frac{\cos x}{h}\left(h\right)$

$= \cos x.$

iii) $f:\mathbb{R} \to \mathbb{R} : x \to e^x$.

$\lim_{h\to 0}\frac{e^{x+h}-e^x}{h} = \lim_{h\to 0}\frac{e^x}{h}\left[1+h+\frac{h^2}{2} \ \ldots \ -1\right] = e^x.$

iv) $f:\mathbb{R}\to\mathbb{R}:x \to x^4$ if $x \geq 0$

x^2 if $x < 0$.

Consider the limit as h approaches 0 from above (ie $h \to 0_+$). Then

$$\lim_{h\to 0_+} \frac{f(0+h)-f(0)}{h} = \frac{h^4-0}{h} = h^3 = 0.$$

The limit as h approaches 0 from below is

$$\lim_{h\to 0_-} \frac{f(0+h)-f(0)}{h} = \frac{h^3-0}{h} = h^2 = 0.$$

Thus df(0) is defined and equal to 0.

v) $f: \mathbb{R} \to \mathbb{R}$, by $x \to -x^2$ $\quad x \leq 0$

$x \to (x-1)^2-1$ $\quad 0 < x \leq 1$

$x \to -x$ $\quad x > 1$.

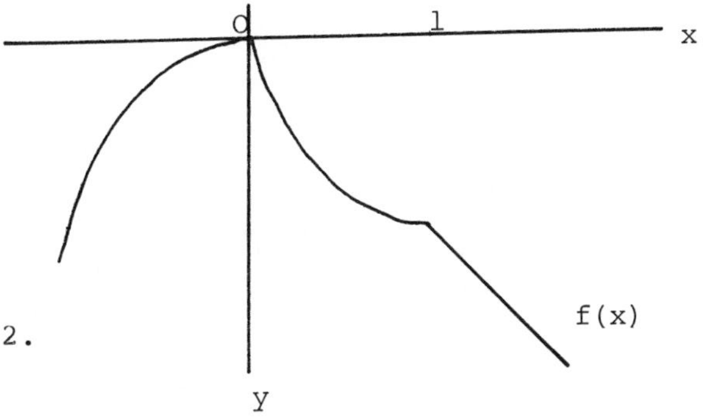

Fig.4.2.

$$\lim_{x\to 0_-} f(x) = 0$$

$\lim_{x\to 0_+} f(x) = 0.$ Thus f is continuous at x = 0.

$$\lim_{x\to 1_-} f(x) = -1$$

$\lim_{x\to 1_+} f(x) = -1.$ Thus f is continuous at x = 1.

$$\lim_{x\to 0_-} df(x) = \lim_{x\to 0_-} (-2x) = 0.$$

$$\lim_{x \to 0_+} df(x) = \lim_{x \to 0_+} 2(x-1) = -2.$$

$$\lim_{x \to 1_-} df(x) = \lim_{x \to 1_-} 2(x-1) = 0.$$

$$\lim_{x \to 1_+} df(x) = \lim_{1_+} (-1) = -1.$$

Hence $df(x)$ is not continuous at $x = 0$ and $x = 1$.
To extend the definition to the higher dimension case, we proceed as follows:

<u>Definition 4.1</u> Let X,Y be two normed vector spaces, with norms $\| \ \|_X$, $\| \ \|_Y$, and suppose $f,g:X \to Y$. Then say f and g are <u>tangent</u> at $x \in X$ iff

$$\lim_{\|h\|_X \to 0} \frac{\|f(x+h)-g(x+h)\|_Y}{\|h\|_X} = 0$$

If there exists a linear map $df(x): X \to Y$ such that the function $g:X \to Y$ given by

$$g(x+h) = f(x) + df(x)(h)$$

is tangent to f at x, then f is said to be differentiable at x, and $df(x)$ is called the <u>differential</u> of f at x.

In other words $df(x)$ is the differential of f at x iff there is a linear approximation $df(x)$ to f at x, in the sense that

$$f(x+h) - f(x) = df(x)(h) + \|h\|_X \, \mu(h)$$

where $\mu:X \to Y$ and $\|\mu(h)\|_Y \to 0$ as $\|h\|_X \to 0$.

Note that since $df(x)$ is a linear map from X to Y, then its image is a vector subspace of Y, and $df(x)(\underline{0})$ is the origin, $\underline{0}$, in Y.
Suppose now that f is defined on an open ball U in X.
For some $x \in U$, consider an open neighbourhood V of x in U. The image of the map

$h \to g(x+h)$ for each $h \in U$

will be of the form $f(x) + df(x)(h)$, which is to say a linear subspace of Y, but translated by the vector f(x) from the origin.

If f is differentiable at x, then we can regard df(x) as a linear map from X to Y, so $df(x) \in L(X,Y)$, the set of linear maps from X to Y. As we showed in §3.2 of the previous chapter, L(X,Y) is a normed vector space, when X is finite dimensional. For example, for $k \in L(X,Y)$ we can define $\|k\|$ by

$\|k\| = \sup \{ \|k(x)\|_Y : x \in X \text{ st } \|x\|_X = 1 \}$.

Let $\mathcal{L}(X,Y)$ be L(X,Y) with the topology induced from this norm.

When $f: U \subset X \to Y$ is continuous we shall call f a C^0-map. If f is C^0, and df(x) is defined at x, then df(x) will be linear and thus continuous, in the sense that $df(x) \in \mathcal{L}(X,Y)$.

Hence we can regard df as a map

$$df: U \to \mathcal{L}(X,Y).$$

It is important to note here that though the map df(x) may be continuous, the map $df: U \to \mathcal{L}(X,Y)$ need not be continuous at x. However when f is C^0, and the map

$$df: U \to \mathcal{L}(X,Y)$$

is continuous for all $x \in U$, then we shall say that f is a C^1-differentiable map on U. Let $C_0(U,Y)$ be the set of maps from U to Y which are continuous on U, and let $C_1(U,Y)$ be the set of maps which are C^1-differentiable on U. Clearly $C_1(U,Y) \subset C_0(U,Y)$. If f is a differentiable map, then df(x), since it is linear, can be represented by a matrix. Suppose therefore that $f: \mathbb{R}^n \to \mathbb{R}$, and let $\{e_1,\dots,e_n\}$ be the standard basis for $\mathbb{R}^n$.

Then for any $h \in \mathbb{R}^n$, $h = \sum_{i=1}^{n} h_i e_i$ and so

$$df(x)(h) = \sum_{i=1}^{n} h_i \, df(x)(e_i) = \sum_{i=1}^{n} h_i \alpha_i \text{ say.}$$

Consider the vector $(0,\ldots,h_i,\ldots,0) \in \mathbb{R}^n$.

Then by the definitions

$$\alpha_i = df(x)(0,\ldots,h_i,\ldots,0) =$$

$$= \lim_{h_i \to 0} \left\{ \frac{f(x_1,\ldots,x_i+h_i,\ldots) - f(x_1,\ldots x_i,\ldots x_n)}{h_i} \right\}$$

$$= \left.\frac{\partial f}{\partial x_i}\right|_x ,$$

where $\left.\frac{\partial f}{\partial x_i}\right|_x$ is called the partial derivative of f at x with respect to the ith coordinate, x_i.

Thus the linear function $df(x): \mathbb{R}^n \to \mathbb{R}$ can be represented by a "row vector" or matrix

$$Df(x) = \left(\left.\frac{\partial f}{\partial x_1}\right|_x , \ldots\ldots, \left.\frac{\partial f}{\partial x_n}\right|_x \right).$$

Note that this representation is dependent on the particular choice of the basis for $\mathbb{R}^n$. This matrix Df(x) can also be regarded as a vector in $\mathbb{R}^n$, and is then called the direction gradient of f at x. The ith coordinate of Df(x) is the partial derivative of f with respect to x_i at x.

If h is a vector in $\mathbb{R}^n$ with coordinates $(h_1,\ldots h_n)$ with respect to the standard basis, then

$$df(x)(h) = \sum_{i=1}^{n} h_i \left.\frac{\partial f}{\partial x_i}\right|_x = (Df(x),h)$$

where (Df(x),h) is the scalar product of h and the direction gradient Df(x).

In the same way if $f: \mathbb{R}^n \to \mathbb{R}^m$ and f is differentiable at x, then df(x) can be represented by the nxm matrix

$$Df(x) = \left(\frac{\partial f_j}{\partial x_i} \right)_x \qquad \begin{array}{l} i = 1,\ldots,n \\ j = 1,\ldots,m \end{array}$$

where $f(x) = f(x_1,\ldots,x_n) = (f_1(x),\ldots f_j(x),\ldots f_m(x))$.

This matrix is called the Jacobian of f at x.

We may define the norm of Df(x) to be

$$\| Df(x) \| = \sup \left\{ \left| \frac{\partial f_j}{\partial x_i} \Big|_x \right| : i=1,\ldots,n;\ j=1,\ldots,m \right\}.$$

When f has domain $U \subset \mathbb{R}^n$, then continuity of $Df: U \to M(n,m)$, where $M(n,m)$ is the set of $n \times m$ matrices, implies the continuity of each partial derivative

$$U \to \mathbb{R}: \quad x \to \frac{\partial f_j}{\partial x_i}\Big|_x .$$

Note that when $f: \mathbb{R} \to \mathbb{R}$ then $\frac{\partial f}{\partial x}\Big|_x$ is written simply as $\frac{df}{dx}\Big|_x$ and is a real number.

Then the linear function $df(x): \mathbb{R} \to \mathbb{R}$ is given by

$$df(x)(h) = \left(\frac{df}{dx}\Big|_x \right) h.$$

To simplify notation we shall not distinguish between the linear function df(x) and the real number $\frac{df}{dx}\Big|_x$ when $f: \mathbb{R} \to \mathbb{R}$.

Suppose now that $f: U \subset X \to Y$ and $g: V \subset Y \to Z$ such that $g \circ f: U \subset X \to Z$ exists. If f is differentiable at x, and g is differentiable at f(x) then $g \circ f$ is differentiable at x and is given by

$$d(g \circ f)(x) = dg(f(x)) \circ df(x).$$

In terms of Jacobian matrices this is

$$D(g \circ f)(x) = Dg(f(x)) \circ Df(x) \text{ or}$$

$$\frac{\partial g_k}{\partial x_i} = \sum_{j=1}^{m} \frac{\partial g_k}{\partial f_j} \frac{\partial f_j}{\partial x_i}$$

i.e.

$$\text{kth row}\begin{pmatrix} \frac{\partial g_k}{\partial f_1} & \cdots & \frac{\partial g_k}{\partial f_m} \end{pmatrix} \begin{pmatrix} \frac{\partial f_1}{\partial x_i} \\ \cdot \\ \cdot \\ \cdot \\ \frac{\partial f_m}{\partial x_i} \end{pmatrix}$$

ith column

This is also known as the chain-rule.

If Id: $\mathbb{R}^n \to \mathbb{R}^n$ is the identity map then clearly the Jacobian matrix of Id must be the identity matrix.

Suppose now that f: $U \subset \mathbb{R}^n \to V \subset \mathbb{R}^n$ is differentiable at x, and has an inverse $g = f^{-1}$ which is differentiable. Then g o f = Id and so

$\text{Id} = D(g \circ f)(x) = Dg(f(x)) \circ Df(x)$.

Thus $D(f^{-1})(f(x)) = [Df(x)]^{-1}$.

In particular, for this to be the case Df(x) must be a nxn matrix of rank n. When this is so, f is called a diffeomorphism.

On the other hand suppose $f: X \to \mathbb{R}$ and $g: Y \to \mathbb{R}$, where f is differentiable at $x \in X$ and g is differentiable at $y \in Y$.

Let $fg: X \times Y \to \mathbb{R} : (x,y) \to f(x)\, g(y)$.

From the chain rule, $d(f\,g)(x,y)(h,k)$

$$= f(x)\, dg(y)(k) + g(y)\, df(x)(h)$$

and so $d(fg)(x,y) = f(x)\, dg(y) + g(y)\, df(x)$

Hence fg is differentiable at the point $(x,y) \in X \times Y$.

When $X = Y = \mathbb{R}$, and $(fg)(x) = f(x)\, g(x)$ then $d(fg)(x) = f\, dg(x) + g\, df(x)$, where this is called the product rule.

Example 4.2

i) Consider the function $f: \mathbb{R} \to \mathbb{R}$ given by

$$x \to x^2 \sin \frac{1}{x} \quad \text{if } x \neq 0$$
$$0 \qquad\qquad x = 0.$$

We first of all verify that f is continuous.

Let $g(x) = x^2$, $h(x) = \sin \frac{1}{x} = \rho[m(x)]$

where $m(x) = \frac{1}{x}$ and $\rho(y) = \sin(y)$.

Since m is continuous at any non zero point, both h and g are continuous. Thus f is continuous at $x \neq 0$. (Compare with Example 3.1, page 120).

Now $\lim_{x \to 0_+} x^2 \sin \frac{1}{x} = \lim_{y \to +\infty} \frac{\sin y}{y^2}$.

But $-1 \leq \sin y \leq 1$, and so $\lim_{y \to +\infty} \frac{\sin y}{y^2} = 0$.

Hence $(x_n) \to 0$ implies $f(x_n) \to 0 = f(0)$.

Thus f is also continuous at $x = 0$.

Consider now the differential of f.

By the product rule, since $f = gh$

$$d(gh)(x) = x^2\, dh(x) + \left(\sin \frac{1}{x}\right) dg(x).$$

Since $h(x) = \rho[m(x)]$, by the chain rule,

$$\begin{aligned} dh(x) &= d\rho(m(x)).\ dm(x) \\ &= \cos(m(x)) \left(\frac{-1}{x^2}\right) \\ &= -\frac{1}{x^2} \cos\left(\frac{1}{x}\right). \end{aligned}$$

Thus $df(x) = d(gh)(x) = x^2\left[-\frac{1}{x^2}\cos\left(\frac{1}{x}\right)\right] + 2x \sin \frac{1}{x}$

$= -\cos\left(\frac{1}{x}\right) + 2x \sin \frac{1}{x}$, for any $x \neq 0$.

Clearly $df(x)$ is defined and continuous at any $x \neq 0$.

To determine if $df(0)$ is defined, let $k = \frac{1}{h}$.

Then $\lim_{h \to 0_+} \frac{f(0+h) - f(0)}{h} = \lim_{h \to 0_+} \frac{h^2 \sin \frac{1}{h}}{h}$

$= \lim_{h \to 0_+} h \sin \frac{1}{h} = \lim_{k \to +\infty} \frac{\sin k}{k}$.

But again $-1 \leq \sin k \leq 1$ for all k, and so

$$\lim_{k \to +\infty} \frac{\sin k}{k} = 0.$$

In the same way $\lim_{h \to 0_-} \frac{h^2 \sin \frac{1}{h}}{h} = 0.$

Thus $\lim_{h \to 0} \frac{f(0+h)-f(0)}{h} = 0$ and so $df(0) = 0$.

Hence $df(0)$ is defined and equal to zero.

On the other hand consider $(x_n) \to 0_+$.

We show that $\lim_{x_n \to 0_+} df(x_n)$ does not exist.

By the above $\lim_{x \to 0_+} df(x) = \lim_{x \to 0_+} \left[2\, x \sin \frac{1}{x} - \cos \frac{1}{x}\right]$.

While $\lim_{x \to 0_+} 2\, x \sin \frac{1}{x} = 0$, there is no limit for $\cos \frac{1}{x}$ as $x \to 0_+$ (see example 3.1). Thus the function $df: \mathbb{R} \to \mathcal{L}(\mathbb{R}, \mathbb{R})$ is not continuous at the point $x = 0$.

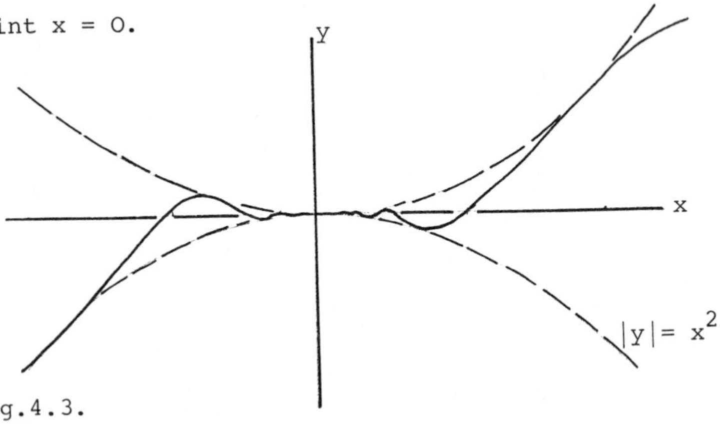

Fig.4.3.

The reason for the discontinuity of the function df at $x = 0$, is that in any neighbourhood U of the origin, there exist an "infinite" number of non-zero points, x', such that $df(x') = 0$. We return to this below.

4.2 C^r - DIFFERENTIABLE FUNCTIONS

4.2.1. The Hessian

Suppose that $f:X \to Y$ is a C^1 - differentiable map, with domain $U \subset X$.

Then as we have seen $df:U \to \mathcal{L}(X,Y)$ where $\mathcal{L}(X,Y)$ is the vector space of linear maps from X to Y with the norm

$$\|k\| = \sup\{\|k(x)\|_Y : x \in X \text{ s.t. } \|x\|_X = 1\}.$$

Since both U and $\mathcal{L}(X,Y)$ are normed vector spaces, and df is continuous, df may itself be differentiable at a point $x \in U$. If df is differentiable, then its derivative at x is written $d^2f(x)$, and will itself be a linear approximation of df from X to $\mathcal{L}(X,Y)$. Since df is C^1, df must be continuous, and so $d^2f(x)$ must be a continuous map.

Thus $d^2f(x) \in \mathcal{L}(X,\mathcal{L}(X,Y))$.

When

$$d^2f: U \to \mathcal{L}(X,\mathcal{L}(X,Y))$$

is itself continuous, and f is C^1 - differentiable, then say f is C^2 - differentiable. Let $C_2(U,Y)$ be the set of C^2 - differentiable maps on U. In precisely the same way say that f is C^r - differentiable iff f is C^{r-1}-differentiable, and the rth derivative $df:U \to \mathcal{L}(X,\mathcal{L}(X,\mathcal{L}(X,\mathcal{L}(X....)$ is continuous.

The map is called <u>smooth</u> or C^∞ if d^rf is continuous for all r.

Now the second derivative $d^2f(x)$ satisfies

$d^2f(x)(h)(k) \in Y$ for vectors $h,k \in X$.

Moreover $d^2f(x)(h)$ is a linear map from X to Y and $d^2f(x)$ is a linear map from X to $\mathcal{L}(X,Y)$.

Thus $d^2f(x)$ is linear in both factors h and k.

Hence $d^2f(x)$ may be regarded as a map

$H(x): X \times X \to Y$

where $H(x)(h,k) = d^2f(x)(h)(k) \in Y$.

Moreover $d^2f(x)$ is linear in both h and k, and so $H(x)$ is linear in both h and k.

Let $L^2(X;Y)$ be the set of <u>bilinear maps</u> $X \times X \to Y$. Thus $M \in L^2(X;Y)$ iff

$$M(\alpha_1h_1+\alpha_2h_2,k) = \alpha_1M(h_1,k) + \alpha_2M(h_2,k)$$
$$M(h,\beta_1k_1+\beta_2k_2) = \beta_1M(h,k_1) + \beta_2M(h,k_2)$$

for any $\alpha_1,\alpha_2,\beta_1,\beta_2 \in \mathbb{R}, h,h_1,h_2,k,k_1,k_2 \in X$.

Since X is a finite-dimensional normed vector space, so is X x X, and thus the set of bilinear maps $L^2(X;Y)$ has a norm topology. Write $\mathcal{L}^2(X;Y)$ when the set of bilinear maps has this topology.

The continuity of the second differential $d^2f: U \to \mathcal{L}(X,\mathcal{L}(X,Y))$ is equivalent to the continuity of the map $H:U \to \mathcal{L}^2(X;Y)$, and we may therefore regard d^2f as a map $d^2f:U \to \mathcal{L}^2(X;Y)$.

In the same way we may regard d^rf as a map $d^rf:U \to \mathcal{L}^r(X;Y)$ where $\mathcal{L}^r(X;Y)$ is the set of maps $X^r \to Y$ which are linear in each component, and is endowed with the norm topology.

Suppose now that $f:\mathbb{R}^n \to \mathbb{R}$ is a C^2 - map, and consider a point $x = (x_1,\ldots,x_n)$ where the co-ordinates are chosen with respect to the standard basis.

As we have seen the differential

$$df:U \to \mathcal{L}(\mathbb{R}^n,\mathbb{R})$$

can be represented by a continuous function

$$Df: x \to \left(\frac{\partial f}{\partial x_1}\bigg|_x, \ldots\ldots\ldots, \frac{\partial f}{\partial x_n}\bigg|_x\right).$$

Now let $\partial f_j:U \to \mathbb{R}$ be the continuous function

$$x \to \frac{\partial f}{\partial x_j}\bigg|_x .$$

Clearly the differential of ∂f_j will be

$$x \to \left(\frac{\partial}{\partial x_1} (\partial f_j)\Big|_x , \ldots\ldots, \frac{\partial}{\partial x_n} (\partial f_j)\Big|_x\right);$$

write $\frac{\partial}{\partial x_i} \left(\partial f_j\right)\Big|_x = \partial f_{ji} = \frac{\partial}{\partial x_i}\left(\frac{\partial f}{\partial x_j}\right)\Big|_x$.

Then the differential $d^2 f(x)$ can be represented by the matrix array

$$\left(\partial f_{ji}\right) = \begin{pmatrix} \frac{\partial}{\partial x_1}\left(\frac{\partial f}{\partial x_1}\right) & \cdot\ \cdot & \frac{\partial}{\partial x_1}\left(\frac{\partial f}{\partial x_n}\right) \\ \vdots & & \vdots \\ \frac{\partial}{\partial x_n}\left(\frac{\partial f}{\partial x_1}\right) & \cdot\ \cdot & \frac{\partial}{\partial x_n}\left(\frac{\partial f}{\partial x_n}\right) \end{pmatrix}_x .$$

This n x n matrix we shall also write as Hf(x) and call the Hessian matrix of f at x. Note that Hf(x) is dependent on the particular basis, or coordinate system for X.

From elementary calculus it is known that

$$\frac{\partial}{\partial x_i}\left(\frac{\partial f}{\partial x_j}\right)\Big|_x = \frac{\partial}{\partial x_j}\left(\frac{\partial f}{\partial x_i}\right)\Big|_x$$

and so the matrix Hf(x) is symmetric.

Consequently, as in §2.3.3, Hf(x) may be regarded as a quadratic form given by

$$D^2 f(x)(h,k) = (h, Hf(x)(k))$$

$$= (h_1,\ldots,h_n)\left(\frac{\partial}{\partial x_i}\left(\frac{\partial f}{\partial x_j}\right)\right)\begin{pmatrix} k_1 \\ \\ k_n \end{pmatrix}$$

$$= \sum_{i=1}^{n}\sum_{j=1}^{n} h_i \frac{\partial}{\partial x_i}\left(\frac{\partial f}{\partial x_j}\right) k_j .$$

As an illustration if $f:\mathbb{R}^2 \to \mathbb{R}$ is C^2 then $D^2 f(x):\mathbb{R}^2 \times \mathbb{R}^2 \to \mathbb{R}$ is given by

$$D^2 f(x)(h,h) =$$

$$(h_1 \quad h_2)\begin{pmatrix} \dfrac{\partial^2 f}{\partial x_1^2} & \dfrac{\partial^2 f}{\partial x_1 \partial x_2} \\ \dfrac{\partial^2 f}{\partial x_2 \partial x_1} & \dfrac{\partial^2 f}{\partial x_2^2} \end{pmatrix} \begin{pmatrix} h_1 \\ h_2 \end{pmatrix}$$

$$= \left(h_1^2 \quad \frac{\partial^2 f}{\partial x_1^2} + 2\, h_1 h_2 \, \frac{\partial^2 f}{\partial x_1 \partial x_2} \quad + \quad h_2^2 \quad \frac{\partial^2 f}{\partial x_2^2} \right)\bigg|_x .$$

In the case that $f: \mathbb{R} \to \mathbb{R}$ is C^2, then $\dfrac{\partial^2 f}{\partial x^2}\bigg|_x$ is simply written as $\dfrac{d^2 f}{dx^2}\bigg|_x$, a real number.

Consequently the second differential $D^2 f(x)$ is given by

$$D^2 f(x)(h,h) \quad = \quad h \left(\frac{d^2 f}{dx^2}\bigg|_x \right) h$$

$$= \quad h^2 \quad \frac{d^2 f}{dx^2}\bigg|_x .$$

We shall not distinguish in this case between the linear map $D^2 f(x): \mathbb{R}^2 \to \mathbb{R}$ and the real number $\dfrac{d^2 f}{dx^2}\bigg|_x$.

4.2.2. Taylor's Theorem

From the definition of derivative of a function $f: X \to Y, df(x)$ is the linear approximation to f in the sense that $f(x+h)-f(x) = df(x)(h) + \|h\|_X \mu(h)$ where the "error" $\|h\|_X \mu(h)$ approaches zero as h approaches zero. Taylor's Theorem is concerned with the "accuracy" of this approximation for a small vector h, by using the higher order derivatives

Our principal tool in this is the following. If $f: U \subset X \to \mathbb{R}$ and the convex hull $[x, x+h]$ of the points x and $x+h$ belongs to U, then there is some point $z \in [x, x+h]$ such that

$$f(x+h) = f(x) + df(z)(h).$$

To prove this result we proceed as follows.

<u>Lemma 4.1</u> (Rolle's Theorem)

Let $f: U \to \mathbb{R}$ where U is an open set in $\mathbb{R}$ containing the compact interval $I = [a,b]$, and $a < b$. Suppose that f is continuous and differentiable on U, and that $f(a) = f(b)$. Then there exists a point $c \in (a,b)$ such that $df(c) = 0$.

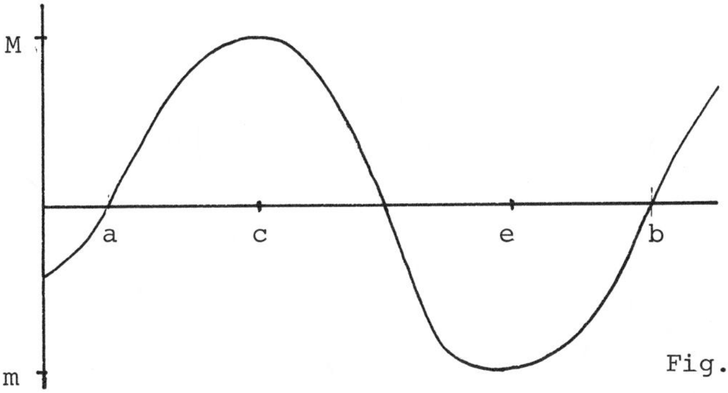

Fig.4.4.

<u>Proof</u>

From the Weierstrass Theorem (and lemma 3.16) f attains its upper and lower bounds on the compact interval, I.

Thus there exists finite $m, M \in \mathbb{R}$ such that

$$m \leq f(x) \leq M \quad \text{for all } x \in I.$$

If f is constant on I, so $m=f(x)=M$, $\forall x \in I$, then clearly $df(x) = 0$ for all $x \in I$.

Then there exists a point c in the interior (a,b) of I such that $df(c) = 0$. Suppose that f is not constant. Since f is continuous and I is compact, there exist points $c, e \in I$ such that $f(c) = M$ and $f(e) = m$.

Suppose that neither c nor e belong to (a,b). In this case we obtain a = e and b = c, say. But then M = m and so f is the constant function. When f is not the constant function either c or e belongs to the interior (a,b) of I.

i) suppose $c \in (a,b)$. Clearly $f(c)-f(x) \geq 0$ for all $x \in I$.

Since $c \in (a,b)$ there exists $x \in I$ s.t. $x > c$, in which case $\frac{f(x)-f(c)}{x-c} \leq 0$.

On the other hand there exists $x \in I$ s.t. $x < c$ and $\frac{f(x)-f(c)}{x-c} \geq 0$

By the continuity of df at x,

$$df(c) = \lim_{x \to c_+} \frac{f(x)-f(c)}{x-c} = \lim_{x \to c_-} \frac{f(x)-f(c)}{x-c} = 0$$

Since $c \in (a,b)$ and $df(c) = 0$ we obtain the result.

ii) if $e \in (a,b)$ then we proceed in precisely the same way to show $df(e) = 0$.

Thus there exists some point $c \in (a,b)$, say, such that $df(c) = 0$.

Note that when both c and e belong to the interior of I, then these maximum and minimum points for the function f are critical points in the sense that the derivative is zero.

Lemma 4.2

Let $f: \mathbb{R} \to \mathbb{R}$ where f is continuous on the interval $I = [a,b]$ and df is continuous on (a,b). Then there exists a point $c \in (a,b)$ such that $df(c) = \frac{f(b)-f(a)}{b-a}$.

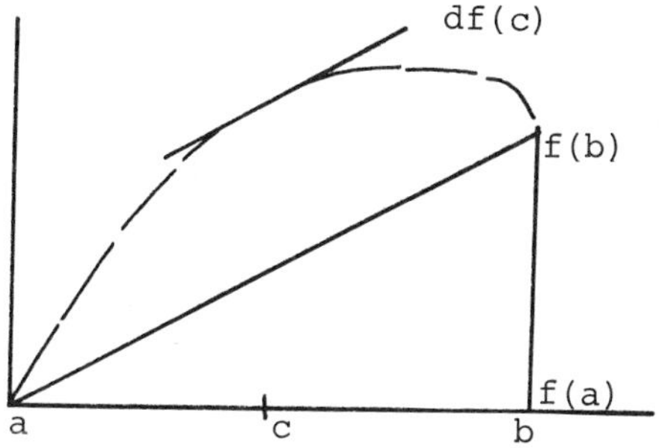

Fig.4.5.

Proof

Let $g(x) = f(b)-f(x)-k(b-x)$

and $k = \dfrac{f(b)-f(a)}{b-a}$.

Clearly $g(a) = g(b) = 0$.

By Rolle's Theorem, there exists some point $c \in (a,b)$ such that $dg(c) = 0$. But

$dg(c) = k-df(c)$.

Thus $df(c) = \dfrac{f(b)-f(a)}{b-a}$.

Lemma 4.3

Let $f:\mathbb{R} \to \mathbb{R}$ be continuous and differentiable on an open set containing the interval $[a,a+h]$. Then there exists a number $t \in (0,1)$ such that

$f(a+h) = f(a) + df(a+th)(h)$.

Proof

Put $b = a+h$. By the previous lemma there exists $c \in (a,a+h)$ such that

$df(c) = \dfrac{f(b)-f(a)}{b-a}$.

Let $t = \dfrac{c-a}{b-a}$. Clearly $t \in (0,1)$ and $c = a+th$.

But then $df(a+th):\mathbb{R} \to \mathbb{R}$ is the linear map given by $df(a+th)(h) = f(b)-f(a)$

and so $f(a+h) = f(a) + df(a+th)(h)$.

Mean Value Theorem

Let $f:U \subset X \to \mathbb{R}$ be a differentiable function

on U, where U is an open set in the normed vector space X.
Suppose that the line segment
$[x,x+h] = \{z:z = x+th \text{ where } t\in [0,1]\}$
belongs to U. Then there is some number $t \in (0,1)$ such that

$$f(x+h) = f(x) + df(x+th)(h) .$$

Proof

Define $g:[0,1] \to \mathbb{R}$ by

$$g(t) = f(x+th).$$

Now g is the composition of the function

$$\rho: [0,1] \to U: t \to x+th$$

with $f: [x,x+h] \to \mathbb{R}$.
Since both ρ and f are differentiable, so is g.
By the chain rule $dg(t) = df(\rho(t))\circ d\rho(t)$
$= df(x+th)(h)$.

By lemma 4.3, there exists $t \in (0,1)$ such that $dg(t) = \dfrac{g(1)-g(0)}{1-0}$.

But $g(1) = f(x+h)$ and $g(0) = f(x)$.
Hence $df(x+th)(h) = f(x+h)-f(x)$.

Lemma 4.4

Suppose $g:U \to \mathbb{R}$ is a C^2 - map on an open set U in $\mathbb{R}$ containing the interval $[0,1]$. Then there exists $\theta\in(0,1)$ such that $g(1) = g(0) + dg(0) + \tfrac{1}{2}d^2g(\theta)$.

Proof

(Note here that we regard $dg(t)$ and $d^2g(t)$ as real numbers).
Now define
$k(t) = g(t) - g(0) -tdg(0) -t^2[g(1) -g(0) -dg(0)]$.
Clearly $k(0) = k(1) = 0$, and so by Rolle's Theorem, there exists $\theta\in(0,1)$ such that $dk(\theta) = 0$.
But $dk(t) = dg(t) - dg(0) - 2t[g(1) - g(0) -dg(0)]$.

Hence $dk(0) = 0$.
Again by Rolle's Theorem, there exists $\theta' \in (0,\theta)$ such that $d^2k(\theta') = 0$.
But $d^2k(\theta') = d^2g(\theta') - 2[g(1)-g(0)-dg(0)]$.
Hence $g(1)-g(0)-dg(0) = \frac{1}{2}d^2g(\theta')$ for some $\theta' \in (0,1)$.

<u>Lemma 4.5</u>

Let $f: U \subset X \to \mathbb{R}$ be a C^2 - function on an open set U in the normed vector space X.
If the line segment $[x,x+h]$ belongs to U, then there exists $z \in (x,x+h)$ such that

$$f(x+h) = f(x) + df(x)(h) + \tfrac{1}{2}d^2f(z)(h,h).$$

<u>Proof</u>

Let $g: [0,1] \to \mathbb{R}$ by $g(t) = f(x+th)$.
As in the mean value theorem, $dg(t) = df(x+th)(h)$.
Moreover $d^2g(t) = d^2f(x+th)(h,h)$.
By lemma 4.4, $g(1) = g(0) + dg(0) + \frac{1}{2}d^2g(\theta')$ for some $\theta' \in (0,1)$. Let $z = x+\theta'h$.
Then $f(x+h) = f(x) + df(x)(h) + \frac{1}{2}d^2f(z)(h,h)$.

<u>Taylor's Theorem</u>

Let $f:U \subset X \to \mathbb{R}$ be a smooth (or C^∞-) function on an open set U in the normed vector space X. If the line segment $[x,x+h]$ belongs to U, then

$$f(x+h) = f(x) + \sum_{r=1}^{n} \frac{1}{r!} d^rf(x)(h,\dots,h) + R_n(h)$$

where the error term $R_n(h) = \frac{1}{(n+1)!} d^{n+1}f(z)(h,\dots,h)$ and $z \in (x,x+h)$.

<u>Proof</u>

By induction on lemma 4.5, using the mean value theorem.

The <u>Taylor series of f at x to order k</u> is

$$[f(x)]_k = f(x) + \sum_{r=1}^{k} \frac{1}{r!} d^r f(x)(h,\ldots,h).$$

When f is C^∞, then $[f(x)]_k$ exists for all k.
In the case when $X = \mathbb{R}^n$ and the error term $R_k(h)$ approaches zero as $k \to \infty$, then the Taylor series $[f(x)]_k$ will converge to f(x+h).

In general however $[f(x)]_k$ need not converge, or if it does converge then it need not converge to f(x+h).

Example 4.3

To illustrate this, consider the _flat_ function $f: \mathbb{R} \to \mathbb{R}$ given by

$$f(x) = \exp\left(-\frac{1}{x^2}\right) \qquad x \neq 0$$

$$= 0 \qquad x = 0.$$

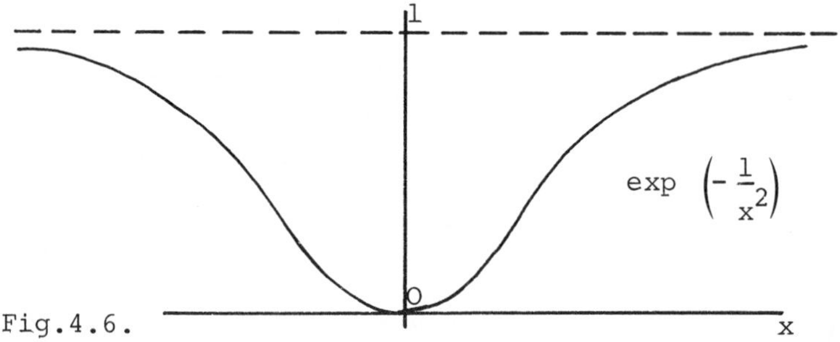

Fig.4.6.

Now $Df(x) = -\frac{2}{x^3} \exp\left(-\frac{1}{x^2}\right)$ for $x \neq 0$. Since $y^{3/2}e^{-y} \to 0$ as $y \to \infty$, we obtain $Df(x) \to 0$ as $x \to 0$.

However $Df(0) = \lim_{h \to 0} \frac{f(0+h)-f(0)}{h} = \lim_{H \to 0} \frac{1}{h} \exp\left(-\frac{1}{h^2}\right) = 0.$

Thus f is both continuous and C^1 at x = 0.
In the same way f is C^r and $D^r f(0) = 0$ for all $r > 1$.
Thus the Taylor series is $[f(0)]_k = 0$.
However for small $h > 0$ it is evident that $f(0+h) \neq 0$. Hence the Taylor series cannot converge to f.

These remarks lead directly to classification theory in differential topology, and are beyond the scope of this work. The interested reader may refer to Chillingsworth (1976) for further discussion.

4.2.3 Critical Points of a Function

Suppose now that $f: U \subset \mathbb{R}^n \to \mathbb{R}$ is a C^2 - map. Once a coordinate basis is chosen for $\mathbb{R}^n$, then $D^2f(x)$ may be regarded as a quadratic form. In matrix notation this means that

$$D^2f(x)(h,h) = h^t\, Hf(x)h\,.$$

As we have seen in Chapter 2 if the Hessian matrix $Hf(x) = (\partial f_{ji})_x$ has all its eigenvalues positive, then $D^2f(x)(h,h) > 0$ for all $h \in \mathbb{R}^n$, and so $Hf(x)$ will be positive definite.

Conversely $Hf(x)$ is negative definite iff all its eigenvalues are strictly negative.

Lemma 4.6

If $f: U \subset \mathbb{R}^n \to \mathbb{R}$ is a C^2 map on U, and the Hessian matrix $Hf(x)$ is positive (negative) definite at x, then there is a neighbourhood V of x in U s.t. $Hf(y)$ is positive (negative) definite for all $y \in V$.

Proof

If $Hf(x)$ is positive definite, then as we have seen there are n different algebraic relationships between the partial derivatives $\partial f_{ji}(x)$ for $j=1,\ldots,n$ and $i=1,\ldots,n$, which characterise the roots $\lambda_1(x),\ldots,\lambda_n(x)$ of the characteristic equation

$$|Hf(x) - \lambda(x)I| = 0.$$

But since f is C^2, the map $D^2f : U \to L^2(\mathbb{R}^n;\mathbb{R})$

is continuous. In particular this implies that for each i j the map $x \to \frac{\partial}{\partial x_i}\left(\frac{\partial f}{\partial x_j}\right)\Big|_x = \partial f_{ji}(x)$

is continuous. Thus if $\partial f_{ji}(x) > 0$ then there is a neighbourhood V of x in U such that $\partial f_{ji}(y) > 0$ for all $y \in V$. Moreover if

$$C(x) = C(\partial f_{ji}(x): i=1,\ldots,n; j=1,\ldots n)$$

is an algebraic sentence in $\partial f_{ji}(x)$ such that $C(x) > 0$ then again there is a neighbourhood V of x in U such that $C(y) > 0$ for all $y \in V$.

Thus there is a neighbourhood V of x in U such that $\lambda_i(x) > 0$ for $i=1,\ldots,n$ implies $\lambda_i(y) > 0$ for $i=1,\ldots,n$, and all $y \in V$. Hence $Hf(x)$ is positive definite at $x \in U$ implies that $Hf(y)$ is positive definite for all y in some neighbourhood of x in U. The same argument holds if $Hf(x)$ is negative definite at x.

<u>Definition 4.2</u>

Let $f: U \subset \mathbb{R}^n \to \mathbb{R}$ where U is an open set in $\mathbb{R}^n$.

A point x in U is called

i) a <u>local strict maximum</u> of f in U iff there exists a neighbourhood V of x in U such that $f(y) < f(x)$ for all $y \in V$ with $y \neq x$.

ii) a <u>local strict minimum</u> of f in U iff there exists a neighbourhood V of x in U such that $f(y) > f(x)$ for all $y \in V$ with $y \neq x$

iii) a <u>local maximum</u> of f in U iff there exists a neighbourhood V of x in U such that $f(y) \leq f(x)$ for $y \in V$.

iv) a <u>local minimum</u> of f in U iff there exists a neighbourhood V of x in U such that $f(y) \geq f(x)$ for all $y \in V$.

v) Similarly a global (strict) maximum (or minimum) on U is defined by requiring $f(y) < (\leq, >, \geq) f(x)$ respectively on U.

vi) If f is C^1 - differentiable then x is called a critical point iff $df(x) = 0$, the zero map from $\mathbb{R}^n$ to $\mathbb{R}$.

Lemma 4.7

Suppose that $f: U \subset \mathbb{R}^n \to \mathbb{R}$ is a C^2-function on an open set U in $\mathbb{R}^n$.
Then f has a local strict maximum (minimum) at x if i) x is a critical point of f and
ii) the Hessian $Hf(x)$ is negative (positive) definite.

Proof

Suppose that x is a critical point and $Hf(x)$ is negative definite.
By lemma 4.5

$$f(y) = f(x) + df(x)(h) + \tfrac{1}{2} d^2 f(z)(h,h)$$

whenever the line segment $[x,y] \in U$, $h = y-x$ and $z = x + \theta h$ for some $\theta \in (0,1)$.
Now by the assumption there is a coordinate base for $\mathbb{R}^n$ such that $Hf(x)$ is negative definite.
Let V be the neighbourhood of x in U such that $Hf(x)$ is negative definite for all y in V, and let $N_\varepsilon(x) = \{x+h: \|h\| < \varepsilon\}$ be an ε-nbd in V of x.
Let $S_{\varepsilon/2}(\underline{O}) = \{h \in \mathbb{R}^n: \|h\| = \tfrac{1}{2}\varepsilon\}$.

Clearly any vector $x+h$, where $h \in S_{\varepsilon/2}(\underline{O})$, belongs to $N_\varepsilon(x)$, and thus V. Hence $Hf(z)$ is negative definite for any $z = x + \theta h$, where $h \in S_{\varepsilon/2}(\underline{O})$ and $\theta \in (0,1)$.
Thus $Hf(z)(h,h) < 0$, and so $d^2(z)(h,h) < 0$ for all $h \in S_{\varepsilon/2}(\underline{O})$, and any $z \in [x, x+h]$.
But also by assumption $df(x) = 0$ and so $df(x)(h) = 0$

for all $h \in \mathbb{R}^n$.

Hence $f(x+h) = f(x) + \frac{1}{2} d^2f(z)(h,h)$

and so $f(x+h) < f(x)$ for $h \in S_{\varepsilon/2}(\underline{0})$.

But the same argument is true for any h satisfying $\|h\| < \varepsilon/_2$. Thus

$$f(y) < f(x)$$

for all y in the open ball of radius $\varepsilon/_2$ about x.

Hence x is a local strict maximum.

The same argument when Hf(x) is positive definite shows that x must be a local strict minimum.

In section 2.3 we defined a quadratic form $A^*: \mathbb{R}^n \times \mathbb{R}^n \to \mathbb{R}$ to be non-degenerate iff the <u>nullity</u> of A^*, namely $\{x: A^*(x,x) = 0\}$, is $\{\underline{0}\}$.

If x is a critical point of a C^2-function $f: U \subset \mathbb{R}^n \to \mathbb{R}$ such that $d^2f(x)$ is non-degenerate (when regarded as a quadratic form), then call x a non-degenerate critical point.

The dimension (s) of the subspace of $\mathbb{R}^n$ on which $d^2f(x)$ is negative definite is called the <u>index</u> of f at x, and x is called a critical point of index s.

If x is a non-degenerate critical point, then when any coordinate system for $\mathbb{R}^n$ is chosen, the Hessian Hf(x) will have s eigenvalues which are negative, and n-s which are positive.

For example if $f: \mathbb{R} \to \mathbb{R}$ then only three cases can occur at a critical point

i) $d^2f(x) > 0$: x is a local minimum

ii) $d^2f(x) < 0$: x is a local maximum

iii) $d^2f(x) = 0$: x is a degenerate critical point or point of inflection.

If $f: \mathbb{R}^2 \to \mathbb{R}$ then a number of different cases can occur. There are three non-degenerate cases :

i) $Hf(x) = \begin{bmatrix} 1 & 0 \\ 0 & 1 \end{bmatrix}$, say, with respect to a suitable basis; x is a local minimum since both eigenvalues are positive. Index = 0.

ii) $Hf(x) = \begin{bmatrix} -1 & 0 \\ 0 & -1 \end{bmatrix}$; x is a local maximum, both eigenvalues are negative. Index = 2.

iii) $Hf(x) = \begin{bmatrix} 1 & 0 \\ 0 & -1 \end{bmatrix}$; x is a <u>saddle point</u> or index 1 non-degenerate critical point.

In the degenerate cases one eigenvalue is zero and so $\det(Hf(x)) = 0$.

Example 4.4

Let $f:\mathbb{R}^2 \to \mathbb{R}:(x,y) \to xy$.

The differential at (x,y) is $Df(x,y) = (y,x)$.

Thus $H = Hf(x,y) = \begin{pmatrix} 0 & 1 \\ 1 & 0 \end{pmatrix}$.

Clearly $(0,0)$ is the critical point. Moreover $|H| = -1$ and so $(0,0)$ is non-degenerate. The eigenvalues λ_1, λ_2 of the Hessian satisfy $\lambda_1+\lambda_2 = 0, \lambda_1\lambda_2 = -1$. Thus $\lambda_1 = 1, \lambda_2 = -1$.

Eigenvectors of $Hf(x,y)$ are $v_1 = (1,1)$ and $v_2 = (1,-1)$ respectively.

Let $P = \frac{1}{\sqrt{2}}\begin{pmatrix} 1 & 1 \\ 1 & -1 \end{pmatrix}$ be the normalized eigenvector (basis change) matrix, so $P^{-1} = P$.

Then $\Lambda = \frac{1}{2}\begin{pmatrix} 1 & 1 \\ -1 & 1 \end{pmatrix}\begin{pmatrix} 0 & 1 \\ 1 & 0 \end{pmatrix}\begin{pmatrix} 1 & 1 \\ -1 & 0 \end{pmatrix} = \begin{pmatrix} 1 & 0 \\ 0 & -1 \end{pmatrix}$.

Consider a vector $h = (h_1,h_2) \in \mathbb{R}^2$.

In matrix notation, $h^t H h = h^t P \Lambda P^{-1} h$.

Now $P(h) = \frac{1}{\sqrt{2}}\begin{pmatrix} 1 & 1 \\ 1 & -1 \end{pmatrix}\begin{pmatrix} h_1 \\ h_2 \end{pmatrix} = \frac{1}{\sqrt{2}}\begin{pmatrix} h_1 + h_2 \\ h_1 - h_2 \end{pmatrix}$.

Thus $h^t H h = \frac{1}{2}[(h_1+h_2)^2 - (h_1-h_2)^2] = 2h_1h_2$.

It is clear that $D^3f(0,0) = 0$. Hence from Taylor's Theorem,

$f(0+h_1,0+h_2) = f(0) + Df(0)(h) + \frac{1}{2} D^2f(0)(h,h)$

and so $f(h_1,h_2) = \frac{1}{2}h^t H h = h_1h_2$.

Suppose we make the basis change represented by P.

Then with respect to the new basis $\{v_1,v_2\}$ the point (x,y) has coordinates $\left(\frac{1}{\sqrt{2}}(h_1+h_2), \frac{1}{\sqrt{2}}(h_1-h_2)\right)$

Thus f can be represented in a neighbourhood of the origin as

$$(h_1,h_2) \to \frac{1}{\sqrt{2}}(h_1+h_2)\frac{1}{\sqrt{2}}(h_1-h_2) = \frac{1}{2}(h_1^2 - h_2^2).$$

Notice that with respect to this new coordinate system $Df(h_1,h_2) = (h_1,-h_2)$

and $Hf(h_1,h_2) = \begin{pmatrix} 1 & 0 \\ 0 & -1 \end{pmatrix}$.

In the eigenspace $E_1 = \{(x,y) \in \mathbb{R}^2 : x = y\}$ the Hessian has eigenvalue 1 and so f has a local minimum at 0, when restricted to E_1.

Conversely in the eigenspace $E_{-1} = \{(x,y) \in \mathbb{R}^2 : x+y=0\}$ f has a local maximum at 0.

More generally when $f:\mathbb{R}^2 \to \mathbb{R}$ is a quadratic function in x,y, then at a critical point f can be represented either as

i) $(x,y) \to x^2+y^2$ an index 0, minimum.

ii) $(x,y) \to -x^2-y^2$ an index 2, maximum

iii) $(x,y) \to x^2-y^2$ an index 1 saddle

after a suitable linear transformation of coordinates.

Example 4.5

Let $f:\mathbb{R}^3 \to \mathbb{R} : (x,y,z) \to x^2+2y^2+3z^2+xy+xz$.

$\therefore Df(x,y,z) = (2x+y+z, 4y+x, 6z+x)$.

Clearly (0,0,0) is the only critical point.

$$H = Hf(x,y,z) = \begin{pmatrix} 2 & 1 & 1 \\ 1 & 4 & 0 \\ 1 & 0 & 6 \end{pmatrix}$$

$|H| = 38$ and so $(0,0,0)$ is non-degenerate.
It can be shown that the eigenvalues of the matrix are strictly positive, and so H is positive definite and $(0,0,0)$ is a minimum of the function. Thus f can be written in the form

$$(u,v,w) \to au^2+bv^2+cw^2, \text{ where } a,b,c > 0$$

and (u,v,w) are the new coordinates after a (linear) basis change.

Notice that lemma 4.7 does not assert that a local strict maximum (or minimum) of a C^1-function must be a critical point where the Hessian is negative (respectively positive) definite.

For example consider the "flat" function $f:\mathbb{R} \to \mathbb{R}$ given by $f(x) = -\exp(-\frac{1}{x^2})$, and $f(0) = 0$. As we showed in Example 4.3, $df(0) = d^2f(0) = 0$. Yet clearly $0 > -\exp(-\frac{1}{a^2})$ for any $a \neq 0$. Thus 0 is a global strict maximum of f on $\mathbb{R}$, although d^2f is not negative definite.

Fig.4.7.

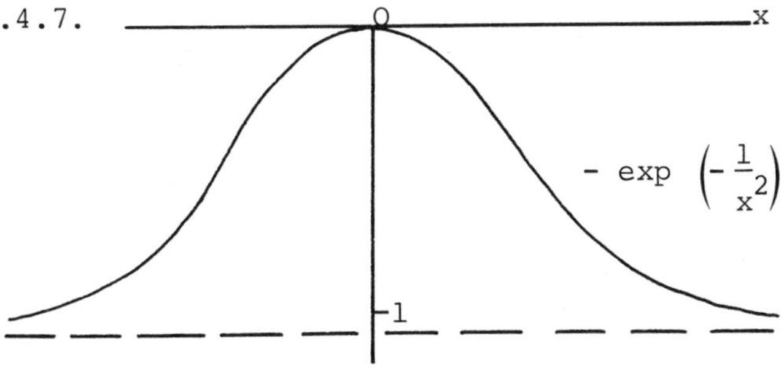

A local maximum or minimum must however be a critical point. If the point is a local maximum for example then the Hessian can have no positive eigenvalues. Consequently $D^2f(x)(h,h) \leq 0$ for all h, and so the Hessian must be negative semi-definite. As the flat function indicates, the Hessian may be identically zero at the local maximum.

Lemma 4.8

Suppose that $f: U \subset \mathbb{R}^n \to \mathbb{R}$ is a C^1 - function on an open set U in $\mathbb{R}^n$. Then f has a local maximum or minimum at x only if x is a critical point of f.

Proof

Suppose that $df(x) \neq 0$. Then we seek to show that x can be neither a local maximum nor minimum at x.

Since df(x) is a linear map from $\mathbb{R}^n$ to $\mathbb{R}$ it is possible to find some vector $h \in \mathbb{R}^n$ such that $df(x)(h) > 0$.

Choose h sufficiently small so that the line segment [x,x+h] belongs to U.

Now f is C^1, and so $df: U \to \mathcal{L}(\mathbb{R}^n, \mathbb{R})$ is continuous.

In particular since $df(x) \neq 0$ then for some neighbourhood V of x in U, $df(y) \neq 0$ for all $y \in V$.

Thus for all $y \in V$, $df(y)(h) > 0$ (See lemma 4.18 for more discussion of this phenomenon).

By the mean value theorem there exists $t \in (0,1)$ such that $f(x+h) = f(x) + df(x+th)(h)$.

By choosing h sufficiently small, the vector $x+th \in V$. Hence $f(x+h) > f(x)$.

Consequently x cannot be a local maximum.

But in precisely the same way if $df(x) \neq 0$ then it is possible to find h such that $df(x)(h) < 0$.

A similar argument can then be used to show that $f(x+h) < f(x)$ and so x cannot be a local minimum.

Hence if x is either a local maximum or minimum of f then it must be a critical point of f.

Lemma 4.9

Suppose that $f:U\subset\mathbb{R}^n \to \mathbb{R}$ is a C^2-function on an open set U in $\mathbb{R}^n$. If f has a local maximum at x then the Hessian d^2f at the critical point must be negative semi-definite (ie. $d^2f(x)(h,h) \leq 0$ for all $h\in\mathbb{R}^n$).

Proof

We may suppose that x is a critical point. Suppose further that for some coordinate basis at x, and vector $h\in\mathbb{R}^n$, $d^2f(x)(h,h) > 0$. As in lemma 4.7, by the continuity of d^2f there is a neighbourhood V of x in U such $d^2f(x')(h,h) > 0$ for all $x'\in V$.

Choose a ε-neighbourhood of x in V, and choose $\alpha > 0$ such that $\|\alpha h\| = \frac{1}{2}\varepsilon$. Clearly $x+\alpha h\in V$. By Taylor's Theorem, there exists $z = x+\theta\alpha h, \theta\in(0,1)$, such that $f(x+\alpha h) = f(x) + df(x)(h) + \frac{1}{2}\, d^2f(z)(\alpha h,\alpha h)$. But $d^2f(z)$ is bilinear, so $d^2f(z)(\alpha h,\alpha h) = \alpha^2 d^2f(z)(h,h) > 0$ since $z\in V$.

Moreover $df(x)(h) = 0$.

Thus $f(x+\alpha h) > f(x)$.

Moreover for any neighbourhood U of x it is possible to choose ε sufficiently small so that $x + \alpha h$ belongs to U. Thus x cannot be a local maximum.

Similarly if f has a local minimum at x then x must be a critical point with positive semi-definite Hessian.

Example 4.6

Let $f: \mathbb{R}^2 \to \mathbb{R} : (x,y) \to x^2y^2 - 4yx^2 + 4x^2$;
$Df(x,y) = (+2xy^2 - 8xy + 8x, 2x^2y - 4x^2)$.
Thus (x,y) is a critical point when

i) $x(2y^2-8y+8) = 0$ and

ii) $2x^2(y-2) = 0$.

Now $2y^2-8y+8 = 2(y-2)^2$.
Thus (x,y) is a critical point <u>either</u> when $y = 2$ or $x = 0$.
Let $S(f)$ be the set of critical points. Then
$S(f) = V_1 \cup V_2$ where $V_1 = \{(x,y) \in \mathbb{R}^2 : x = 0\}$

$V_2 = \{(x,y) \in \mathbb{R}^2 : y = 2\}$.

Now $Hf(x,y) = \begin{pmatrix} +2(y-2)^2 & -4x(2-y) \\ -4x(2-y) & +2x^2 \end{pmatrix}$

and so when $(x,y) \in V_1$ then $Hf(x,y) = \begin{pmatrix} \mu^2 & 0 \\ 0 & 0 \end{pmatrix}$

and when $(x,y) \in V_2$ then $Hf(x,y) = \begin{pmatrix} 0 & 0 \\ 0 & \tau^2 \end{pmatrix}$.

For suitable μ and τ, any point in $S(f)$ is degenerate.
On $V_1 \setminus \{(0,0)\}$ clearly a critical point is not negative semi-definite, and so such a point cannot be a local maximum. The same is true for a point on $V_2 \setminus \{(0,0)\}$.
Now $(0,0) \in V_1 \cap V_2$, and $Hf(0,0) = (0)$.
Lemma 4.9 does not rule out $(0,0)$ as a local maximum. However it should be obvious that the origin is a local minimum.

Unlike examples 4.4 and 4.5 no linear change of coordinate bases transforms the function into a quadratic canonical form.

To find a local maximum point we therefore seek all critical points. Those which have negative definite Hessian must be local maxima. Those points remaining which do not have a negative semi-definite Hessian cannot be local maxima, and may be rejected. The remaining critical points must then be examined.

A C^2-function $f: \mathbb{R}^n \to \mathbb{R}$ with a non-degenerate Hessian at every critical point is called a Morse function. Below we shall show that any Morse function can be represented in a canonical form such as we found in example 4.4. For such a function, local maxima are precisely those critical points of index n. Moreover, any smooth function with a degenerate critical point can be "approximated" by a morse function.

Suppose now that we wish to maximise a C^2-function on a compact set K. As we know from the Weierstrass theorem, there does exist a maximum. However, lemmas 4.8 and 4.9 are now no longer valid and it is possible that a point on the boundary of K will be a local or global maximum but not a critical point. However, lemma 4.7 will still be valid, and a negative definite critical point will certainly be a local maximum.

A further difficulty arises since a local maximum need not be a global maximum. However, for concave functions, local and global maxima coincide. We discuss maximisation by smooth optimisation on compact convex sets in the next section.

4.3. CONSTRAINED OPTIMISATION

4.3.1. Concave and Quasi-concave Functions

In the previous section we obtained necessary and sufficient conditions for a critical point to be a local maximum on an open set U. When the set is not open then a local maximum need not be a critical point. Previously we have defined the differential of a function only on an open set. Suppose now that $Y \subset \mathbb{R}^n$ is compact and therefore closed with a boundary ∂Y. If df is continuous at each point in the interior, Int(Y), of Y, then we may extend df over Y by defining df(x), at each point x in the boundary, ∂Y, of Y to be limit $df(x_n)$ for any sequence, (x_n), of points in Int(Y), which converge to x. More generally we shall say a function $f: Y \subset \mathbb{R}^n \to \mathbb{R}$ is C^1 on the <u>admissible</u> set Y if $df: Y \to \mathcal{L}(\mathbb{R}^n, \mathbb{R})$ is defined and continuous in the above sense at each $x \in Y$. We now give an alternative definition of the differential of a C^1-function $f: Y \to \mathbb{R}$. Suppose that Y is convex and both x and x+h belong to Y. Then the arc $[x, x+h] = \{z \in \mathbb{R}^n: z = x + \lambda h, \lambda \in [0,1]\}$ belongs to Y.

$$\text{Now } df(x)(h) = \lim_{\lambda \to 0_+} \frac{f(x + \lambda h) - f(x)}{\lambda}$$

and thus df(x)(h) is often called the <u>directional derivative</u> of f at x in the direction h.

If f is a concave function then we may relate df(x)(y-x) to f(y) and f(x).

<u>Lemma 4.10</u> If $f: Y \subset \mathbb{R}^n \to \mathbb{R}$ is a concave C^1-function on a convex admissible set Y then

$$df(x)(y-x) \geq f(y) - f(x).$$

<u>Proof</u> Since f is concave

$$f(\lambda y + (1-\lambda) x) \geq \lambda f(y) + (1-\lambda) f(x)$$

for any $\lambda \in [0,1]$ whenever $x, y \in Y$.

But then $f(x + \lambda (y-x)) - f(x) \geq \lambda [f(y) - f(x)]$.

$$\text{and so } df(x)(y-x) = \lim_{\lambda \to 0_+} \frac{f(x + \lambda (y-x)) - f(x)}{\lambda}$$

$$\geq f(y) - f(x).$$

This enables us to show that for a concave function, f, a critical point of f must be a global maximum when Y is open.

First of all call a function $f:Y \subset \mathbb{R}^n \to \mathbb{R}$ <u>strictly quasi-concave</u> iff Y is convex and for all $x,y \in Y$

$$f(\lambda y+(1-\lambda)x) > \min (f(x),f(y)) \text{ for all } \lambda \in (0,1).$$

Remember that f is quasi concave if

$$f(\lambda y+(1-\lambda)x) \geq \min (f(x),f(y)) \text{ for all } \lambda \in [0,1].$$

As above let $P(x;Y) = \{y \in Y: f(y) > f(x)\}$ be the preferred set of a function f on the set Y. A point $x \in Y$ is a global maximum of f on Y iff $P(x;Y) = \Phi$. When there is no chance of misunderstanding we shall write P(x) for P(x;Y).

<u>Lemma 4.11</u>

i) If $f:Y \subset \mathbb{R}^n \to \mathbb{R}$ is a concave or strictly quasi-concave function on a convex admissible set, then any point which is a local maximum of f is also a global maximum.

ii) If $f:U \subset \mathbb{R}^n \to \mathbb{R}$ is a concave C^1 - function where U is <u>open</u> and <u>convex</u> then any critical point of f is a global maximum on U.

<u>Proof</u>

i) Suppose that f is concave or strictly quasi-concave, and that x is a local maximum but not a global maximum on Y. Then there exists $y \in Y$ such that $f(y) > f(x)$.

Since Y is convex, the line segment [x,y] belongs to Y. For any neighbourhood U of x in Y there exists some $\lambda^* \in (0,1)$ such that, for $\lambda \in (0,\lambda^*)$, $z = \lambda y+(1-\lambda)x \in U$. But by concavity

$$f(z) \geq \lambda f(y)+(1-\lambda)f(x) > f(x).$$

Hence in any neighbourhood U of x in Y there exists a point z such that $f(z) > f(x)$. Hence x cannot

be a local maximum.
Similarly by strict quasi-concavity

$f(z) > \min(f(x), f(y)) = f(x)$, and so, again, x cannot be a local maximum. By contradiction a local maximum must be a global maximum.

ii) If f is C^1 and U is open then by lemma 4.8, a local maximum must be a critical point. By lemma 4.10, $df(x)(y-x) \geq f(y)-f(x)$.
Thus $df(x) = 0$ implies that $f(y)-f(x) \leq 0$ for all $y \in Y$. Hence x is a global maximum of f on Y.

Clearly if x were a critical point of a concave function on an open set then the Hessian $d^2f(x)$ must be negative semi-definite. By the above lemma the critical point must be a global maximum, and thus a local maximum. By lemma 4.9, $d^2f(x)$ must be negative semi-definite.

<u>Lemma 4.12</u>

If $f: U \subset \mathbb{R}^n \to \mathbb{R}$ is a quasi-concave C^2-function on an open set, then at any critical point, x, $d^2f(x)$ is negative semi-definite.

<u>Proof</u>

Suppose on the contrary that $df(x) = 0$ and $d^2f(x)(h,h) > 0$ for some $h \in \mathbb{R}^n$. As in lemma 4.6, there is a neighbourhood V of x in U such that $d^2f(z)(h,h) > 0$ for all z in V.
Thus there is some $\lambda^* \in (0,1)$ such that, for all $\lambda \in (0,\lambda^*)$, there is some z in V such that

$f(x+\lambda h) = f(x)+df(x)(\lambda h)+ \lambda^2 \; d^2f(z)(h,h)$

and $f(x-\lambda h) = f(x)+df(x)(-\lambda h)+(-\lambda h)^2 d^2f(z)(h,h)$,
where $[x-\lambda h, x+\lambda h]$ belongs to U.
Then $f(x+\lambda h) > f(x)$ and $f(x-\lambda h) > f(x)$.
Now $x \in [x-\lambda h, x+\lambda h]$ and so by quasi-concavity,

$f(x) \geq \min\ (f(x+\lambda h), f(x-\lambda h))$.

By contradiction $d^2f(x)(h,h) \leq 0$ for all $h \in \mathbb{R}^n$.

For a concave function, f, on a convex set Y, $d^2f(x)$ is negative semi-definite not just at critical points, but at every point in the interior of Y.

<u>Lemma 4.13</u>

i) If $f: U \subset \mathbb{R}^n \to \mathbb{R}$ is a concave C^2-function on an open convex set U, then $d^2f(x)$ is negative semi-definite for all $x \in U$.

ii) If $f: Y \subset \mathbb{R}^n \to \mathbb{R}$ is a C^2-function on an admissible convex set Y and $d^2f(x)$ is negative semi-definite for all $x \in Y$ then f is concave.

<u>Proof</u>

i) Suppose there exists $x \in U$ and $h \in \mathbb{R}^n$ such that $d^2f(x)(h,h) > 0$.

By the continuity of d^2f, there is a neighbourhood V of x in U such that $d^2f(z)(h,h) > 0$, for $z \in V$.

Choose $\theta \in (0,1)$ such that $x+\theta h \in V$. Then by Taylor's theorem there exists $z \in (x, x+\theta h)$ such that

$$f(x+\theta h) = f(x) + df(x)(\theta h) + \tfrac{1}{2}d^2f(z)(\theta h, \theta h)$$
$$> f(x) + df(x)(\theta h).$$

But then $df(x)(\theta h) < f(x+\theta h) - f(x)$.

This contradicts $df(x)(y-x) \geq f(y)-f(x), \forall x, y$ in U.

Thus $d^2f(x)$ is negative semi-definite.

ii) If $x, y \in Y$ then the arc $[x,y] \subset Y$ (see p.136).

Hence for some $z = \lambda x + (1-\lambda)y$, where $\lambda \in (0,1)$,

$$f(y) = f(x) + df(x)(y-x) + d^2f(z)(y-x, y-x)$$
$$\leq f(x) + df(x)(y-x).$$

But in the same way

$f(x) - f(z) \leq df(z)(x-z)$ and $f(y) - f(z) \leq df(z)(y-z)$.

Hence $f(z) \geq \lambda[f(x)-df(z)(x-z)] + (1-\lambda)[f(y)-df(z)(y-z)]$

Now $\lambda df(z)(x-z) + (1-\lambda)\ df(z)(y-z)$

$= \quad df(z)[\lambda x + (1-\lambda)y-z]$, by the linearity of $df(z)$,

$= \quad df(z)(0) = 0.$

Hence $f(z) \geq \lambda f(x) + (1-\lambda)f(y)$ for any $\lambda \in [0,1]$ and so f is concave.

We now extend the analysis to a quasi-concave function and characterise the preferred set $P(x;Y)$.

Lemma 4.14

If $f: Y \subset \mathbb{R}^n \to \mathbb{R}$ is a quasi-concave C^1 - function on the convex admissible set Y, then for any $x,y \in Y$,

i) $f(y) \geq f(x) \Rightarrow df(x)(y-x) \geq 0$,

ii) if $df(x)(y-x) > 0$ then there exists some $\lambda^* \in (0,1)$ such that $f(z) > f(x)$ for any

$z = \lambda y + (1-\lambda)x$ where $\lambda \in (0,\lambda^*)$.

Proof

i) By the definition of quasi-concavity

$f(\lambda y+(1-\lambda)x) > f(x)$ for all $\lambda \in [0,1]$.

But then, as in the analysis of a concave function,

$f(x+\lambda(y-x)) - f(x) \geq 0$

and so $df(x)(y-x) = \lim_{\lambda \to 0_+} \dfrac{f(x+\lambda(y-x)) - f(x)}{\lambda} \geq 0.$

ii) Now suppose $f(x) \geq f(z)$ for all z in the line segment $[x,y]$.

Then $df(x)(y-x) = \lim_{\lambda \to 0_+} \dfrac{f(x+\lambda(y-x))-f(x)}{\lambda} \leq 0$

contradicting $df(x)(y-x) > 0$.

Thus there exists $z^* = \lambda^*y+(1-\lambda^*)x$ such that $f(z^*) > f(x)$. But then for all $z \in (x,\lambda^*y+(1-\lambda^*)x)$ $f(z) > f(x)$.

The property that $f(y) \geq f(x) \Rightarrow df(x)(y-x) \geq 0$ is often called pseudo-concavity.

We shall also say that $f:Y \subset \mathbb{R}^n \to \mathbb{R}$ is <u>strictly pseudo-concave</u> iff for any x,y in Y, with $y \neq x$ then $f(y) \geq f(x)$ implies that $df(x)(y-x) > 0$.
(Note we do not require Y to be convex, but we do require it to be admissible).

<u>Lemma 4.15</u>

If $f:Y \subset \mathbb{R}^n \to \mathbb{R}$ is a strictly pseudo-concave function on an admissible set Y then

i) f is strictly quasi-concave when Y is convex.

ii) when x is a critical point it is a global strict maximum.

<u>Proof</u>

i) Suppose that f is not strictly quasi-concave. Then for some $x,y \in Y$, $f(\lambda^* y+(1-\lambda^*)x) \leq \min(f(x),f(y))$ for some $\lambda^* \in (0,1)$.

Without loss of generality suppose $f(x) \leq f(y)$, and $f(\lambda y+(1-\lambda)x) \leq f(x)$ for all $\lambda \in (0,1)$.

Then $df(x)(y-x) = \lim_{\lambda \to 0_+} \frac{f(\lambda y+(1-\lambda x))-f(x)}{\lambda} \leq 0$.

But by strict pseudo-concavity, we require that $df(x)(y-x) > 0$.

Thus f must be strictly quasi-concave.

ii) If $df(x) = 0$ then $df(x)(y-x) = 0$ for all $y \in U$.

Hence $f(y) < f(x)$ for all $y \in U$, $y \neq x$. Thus x is a global strict maximum.

As we know from previous results, when f is a quasi-concave function on Y, the preferred set $P(x;Y)$ belongs to an open half-space in Y. Lemma 4.14 establishes that the weakly preferred set

$$R(x;Y) = \{y \in Y: f(y) \geq f(x)\}$$

belongs to the closed half-space

$$H(x;Y) = \{y \in Y: df(x)(y-x) \geq 0\}.$$

When Y is open and convex the boundary of $H(x;Y)$ is the hyperplane $\{y \in Y: df(x)(y-x) = 0\}$ and $H(x;Y)$ has relative interior $\overset{\circ}{H}(x;Y) = \{y \in Y: df(x)(y-x) > 0\}$. Write $H(x), R(x), P(x)$ for $H(x;Y), R(x;Y), P(x;Y)$ etc. when convenient.

Lemma 4.16

If $f: U \subset \mathbb{R}^n \to \mathbb{R}$ is C^1, U open and convex

i) and f is quasi-concave, with $df(x) \neq 0$ then $P(x) \subset \overset{\circ}{H}(x)$,

ii) and f is concave or strictly pseudo-concave then $P(x) \subset \overset{\circ}{H}(x)$ for all $x \in U$.

Proof

i) Suppose that $df(x) \neq 0$ but that $P(x) \not\subset \overset{\circ}{H}(x)$. However both $P(x)$ and $\overset{\circ}{H}(x)$ are open sets in U. By lemma 4.14, $R(x) \subset H(x)$, and thus the closure of $P(x)$ belongs to the closure of $\overset{\circ}{H}(x)$ in U. Consequently there must exist a point y which belongs to $P(x)$ yet $df(x)(y-x) = 0$, so y belongs to the boundary of $\overset{\circ}{H}(x)$. Since $P(x)$ is open there exists a neighbourhood V of y in $P(x)$, and thus in $R(x)$.

Since y is a boundary point of $\overset{\circ}{H}(x)$ in any neighbourhood V of y there exists z such that $z \notin H(x)$. But this contradicts $R(x) \subset H(x)$.

Hence $P(x) \subset \overset{\circ}{H}(x)$.

ii) Since a concave or strictly pseudo-concave function is a quasi-concave function, (i) establishes that $P(x) \subset \overset{\circ}{H}(x)$ for all $x \in U$ such that $df(x) \neq 0$. By lemma 4.11 if $df(x) = 0$ then x is a critical point and thus a global maximum. Hence $P(x) = \overset{\circ}{H}(x) = \Phi$.

Lemma 4.8 shows that if $\overset{\circ}{H}(x) \neq \Phi$ then x cannot be a global maximum on the open set U.

Moreover for a concave or strictly pseudo-concave function P(x) is empty if $\overset{o}{H}(x)$ is empty (ie. when df(x) = 0).

Figure 4.8 illustrates these observations.

Let P(x) be the preferred set of a quasi-concave function to a (non-critical) point x.

Point y_1 satisfies $f(y_1) = f(x)$ and thus belongs to $\overset{o}{R}(x)$ and hence H(x). Point $y_2 \in H(x)-P(x)$ but there exists an open interval (x,z) belonging to $[x,y_2]$ and to P(x).

We may identify the linear map $df(x): \mathbb{R}^n \to \mathbb{R}$ with a vector $Df(x) \in \mathbb{R}^n$ where $df(x)(h) = (Df(x),h)$ the scalar product of Df(x) with h. Df(x) is the <u>direction</u> <u>gradient</u>, or <u>normal</u> to the indifference surface at x, and therefore to the hyperplane $\partial H(x) = \{y \in Y: df(x)(y-x) = 0\}$.

Fig.4.8.

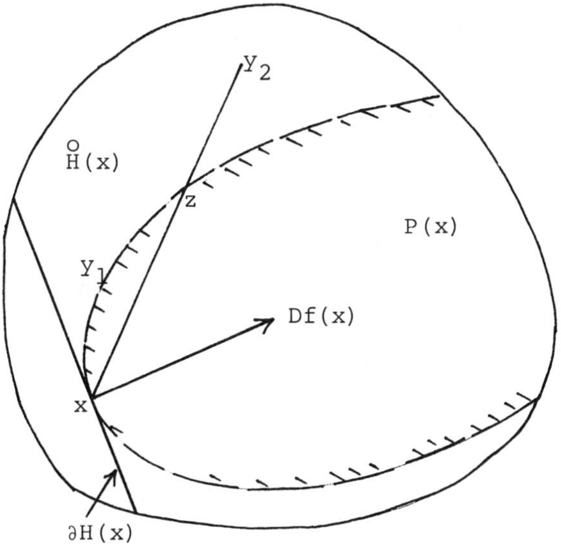

As we know, for a quasi-concave function it might be the case that $\overset{o}{H}(x) = \Phi$ (ie when $df(x) = \underline{0}$) yet $P(x) \neq \Phi$. Lemma 4.16 establishes that this cannot happen when f is concave, since on an open set a critical point for such a function must be a global maximum. The final lemma establishes similar results for a function on an admissible set.

Lemma 4.17

i) If f is a quasi-concave C^1-function on a convex admissible set Y, and x is a local maximum then $\overset{o}{H}(x;Y) = \Phi$. If $\overset{o}{H}(x;Y) \neq \Phi$ then $P(x) \neq \Phi$

ii) If f is a strictly pseudo-concave function on an admissible set Y, and x is a local maximum then it is a global strict maximum.

iii) If f is a concave C^1 - function or a strictly pseudo-concave function on an admissible convex set Y, then $P(x;Y) \subset \overset{o}{H}(x;Y)$. Hence $\overset{o}{H}(x;Y) = \Phi \Rightarrow P(x;Y) = \Phi$.

Proof

i) If $\overset{o}{H}(x;Y) \neq \Phi$ then $df(x)(y-x) > 0$ for some $y \in Y$. Then by lemma 4.14 (ii), in any neighbourhood U of x in Y there exists z such that $f(z) > f(x)$. Hence x cannot be a local maximum, and indeed $P(x) \neq \Phi$.

ii) Since f must be quasi-concave, when x is a local maximum then $df(x)(y-x) \leq 0$ for all $y \in Y$. By definition this implies that $f(y) < f(x)$ for all $y \in Y$ s.t. $y \neq x$. Thus x is a global strict maximum.

iii) If f is concave and $y \in P(x;Y)$ then $f(y) > f(x)$ and so $df(x)(y-x) \geq f(y)-f(x) > 0$. Thus $y \in \overset{o}{H}(x)$.

If f is strictly pseudo-concave then $f(y) > f(x)$ implies $df(x)(y-x) > 0$ and so $P(x;Y) \subset \overset{o}{H}(x;Y)$.

These observations are illustrated in Figure 4.9.

i) For the general function f_1, b is a critical point and local maximum, but not a global maximum(e). On the compact interval [a,d], d is a local maximum but not a global maximum.

ii) For the quasi-concave function f_2, a is a degenerate critical point but neither a local nor global maximum, while b is a degenerate critical point which is also a global maximum.

Point c is a critical point which is also a local maximum. However on [b,c], c is not a global maximum.

iii) For the concave function f_3, clearly b is a degenerate (but negative semi-definite) critical point, which is also a local and global maximum. Moreover on the interval [a,c], c is the local and global maximum, even though it is not a critical point. Note that $df_3(c)(a-c) < 0$.

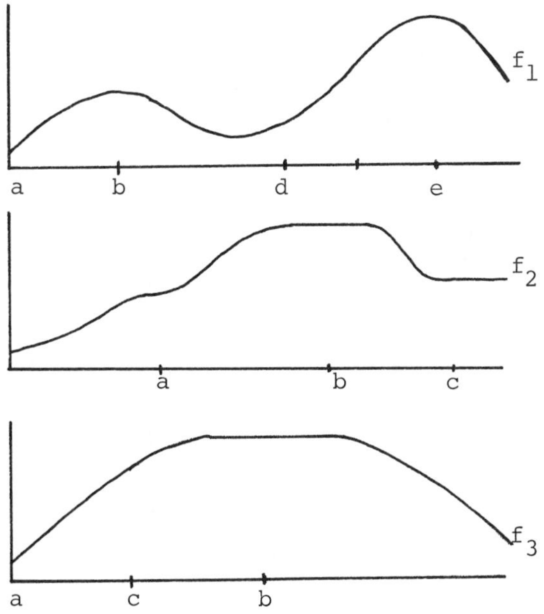

Fig.4.9.

This lemma suggests that we call any point x in an admissible set Y a <u>generalised critical point in Y</u> iff $\overset{o}{H}(x;Y) = \Phi$ (note of course that if $df(x) = 0$ then $\overset{o}{H}(x;Y) = \Phi$, but that the converse is not true when x is a boundary point).

Lemma 4.17 shows that (i) for a quasi-concave C^1-function, a global maximum is a local maximum is a generalised critical point (ii) for a concave C^1- or strictly pseudo-concave function a critical point is a generalised critical point is a local maximum is a global maximum.

4.3.2. Economic Optimisation with Exogenous Prices

Suppose now that we wish to find the maximum of a quasi-concave C^1-function $f:Y \to \mathbb{R}$ subject to a constraint $g(x) \geq 0$ where g is also a quasi-concave C^1-function $g:Y \to \mathbb{R}$.

As we know from the previous section, when $P_f(x) = \{y \in Y: f(y) > f(x)\}$ and $df(x) \neq 0$, then $P_f(x) \subset \overset{o}{H}_f(x) = \{y \in Y: df(x)(x-y) \geq 0\}$.

Suppose now that $H_g(x) = \{y \in Y: dg(x)(x-y) \geq 0\}$ has the property that $H_g(x) \cap \overset{o}{H}_f(x) = \Phi$, and x satisfies $g(x) = 0$.

In this case, there exists no point y such that

$g(y) \geq 0$ and $f(y) > f(x)$.

A condition that is sufficient for the disjointness of the two half-spaces $\overset{o}{H}_f(x)$ and $H_g(x)$ is clearly that $\lambda dg(x) + df(x) = 0$ for some $\lambda > 0$.

In this case if $df(x)(v) > 0$ then $dg(x)(v) < 0$, for any $v \in \mathbb{R}^n$.

Now let $L = L_\lambda(f,g)$ be the Lagrangian $f+\lambda g:Y \to \mathbb{R}$.

A <u>sufficient</u> condition for x to be a solution to the optimisation problem is that $dL(x) = 0$.

subject to the boundary problem).

e 4.8

aximise $f: \mathbb{R}^2 \to \mathbb{R} : (x,y) \to xy$

t to the constraint $g(x,y) = 1-x^2-y^2 \geq 0$.

k a solution to the first order condition:

$L(x,y) = Df(x,y) + \lambda\, Dg(x,y) = 0$.

$y,x) + \lambda(-2x,-2y) = 0$

$= y/_{2x} = x/_{2y}$ so $x^2 = y^2$.

$= -y$, $\lambda < 0$ and so $Df(x,y) = |\lambda| Dg(x,y)$,

sponding to a minimum of f on the feasible set

$) \geq 0)$.

we choose $x = y$ and $\lambda = \tfrac{1}{2}$.

$x,y)$ on the boundary of the constraint set we

re $1-x^2-y^2 = 0$. Hence $x=y= \pm \frac{1}{\sqrt{2}}$.

agrangian is therefore $L=xy+\tfrac{1}{2}(1-x^2-y^2)$ with

rential (with respect to x,y)

$DL(x,y) = (y-x,x-y)$ and Hessian

$$HL(x,y) = \begin{pmatrix} -1 & 1 \\ 1 & -1 \end{pmatrix}.$$

eigenvalues of HL are -2,0 corresponding to

nvectors (1,-1) and (1,1) respectively.

e HL is negative semi-definite, and so for

ple the point $\left(\frac{1}{\sqrt{2}}, \frac{1}{\sqrt{2}}\right)$ is a local maximum for

Lagrangian. As we have observed in Example

vi) the function $f(x,y) = xy$ is not quasi-

cave on $\mathbb{R}^2_o$, and hence it is not the case that

H_f. However on $\mathbb{R}^2_+ = \{(x,y) \in \mathbb{R}^2 : x \geq 0, y \geq 0\}$

s quasi-concave, and so the optimality condition

$,y) \cap H_f(x,y) = \Phi$ is sufficient for an optimum.

Note also that $Df(x,y) = (y,x)$ and so the

gin (0,0) is a critical point of f.

ever setting $DL(x,y) = 0$ at $(x,y) = (0,0)$

Note however that this is not a necessary condition. As we know from the previous section it might well be the case for some point x on the boundary of the admissible set Y that $dL(x) \neq 0$ yet there exists no $y \in Y$ such that

$$dg(x)(x-y) \geq 0 \text{ and } df(x)(x-y) > 0.$$

Figure 4.10 illustrates such a case when

$$Y = \{(x,y) \in \mathbb{R}^2 : x \geq 0,\ y \geq 0\}.$$

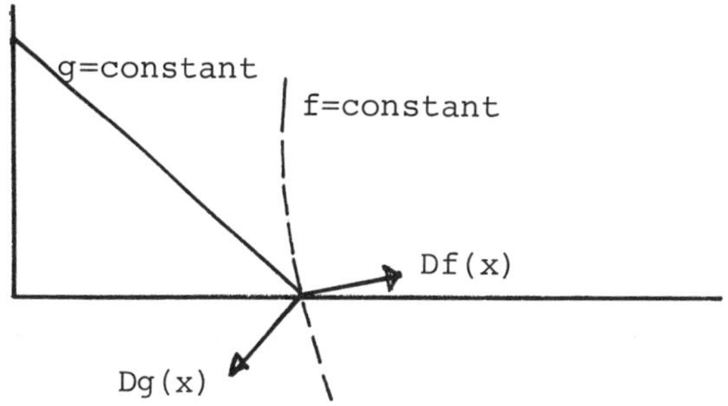

Fig.4.10.

We shall refer to this possibility as the boundary problem.

As we know we may represent the linear maps $df(x), dg(x)$ by the direction gradients, or vectors normal to the indifference surfaces, labelled $Df(x), Dg(x)$.

When $df(x), dg(x)$ satisfy $df(x)+\lambda dg(x) = 0$, $\lambda > 0$, then the direction gradients are positively dependent and satisfy $Df(x) + \lambda Dg(x) = 0$.

In the example $Df(x)$ and $Dg(x)$ are not positively dependent, yet x is a solution to the optimisation problem.

It is often common to make some boundary assumption so that the solution does not belong to the boundary of the feasible or admissible set Y.

In the more general optimisation problem $(f,g): Y \to \mathbb{R}^{m+1}$, the Kuhn Tucker theorem implies that a global saddle point (x^*, λ^*) to the

Lagrangian $L_\lambda(f,g) = f + \sum \lambda_i g_i$

gives a solution x^* to the optimisation problem. Aside from the boundary problem, we may find the global maxima of $L_\lambda(f,g)$ by finding the critical points of $L_\lambda(f,g)$.

Thus we must choose x^* such that

$$df(x^*) + \sum_{i=1}^{m} \lambda_i dg_i(x^*) = 0$$

Once a coordinate system is chosen this is equivalent to finding x^*, and coefficients $\lambda_1, \ldots, \lambda_m$ all non-negative such that

$$Df(x^*) + \sum_{i=1}^{m} \lambda_i Dg_i(x^*) = 0.$$

The Kuhn Tucker theorem also showed that if x^* is such that $g_i(x^*) > 0$ then $\lambda_i = 0$ and if $g_i(x^*) = 0$ then $\lambda_i > 0$.

Example 4.7

Maximise the function $f: \mathbb{R} \to \mathbb{R}: x \to x^2 : x \geq 0$
$x \to 0 : x < 0$

subject to $g_1(x) = x \geq 0$ and $g_2(x) = 1-x \geq 0$.

Now $L_\lambda(x) = x^2 + \lambda_1 x + \lambda_2(1-x)$;

$$\frac{\partial L}{\partial x} = 2x + \lambda_1 - \lambda_2 = 0, \quad \frac{\partial L}{\partial \lambda_1} = x = \frac{\partial L}{\partial \lambda_2} = 1-x=0.$$

Clearly these equations have no solution. By inspection the solution cannot satisfy $g_1(x) = 0$. Hence choose $\lambda_1 = 0$ and solve

$$L_\lambda(x) = x^2 + \lambda(1-x).$$

Then $\frac{\partial L}{\partial x} = 2x - \lambda$, $\frac{\partial L}{\partial \lambda} = 1-x = 0$.

Thus $x = 1$ and $\lambda = 2$ is a solution.

Suppose now that $f, g_1, \ldots, g_m$ are all concave functions on the convex admissible set $Y = \{x \in \mathbb{R}^n : x_i \geq 0, i=1,\ldots,n\}$.

Obviously if $z = \alpha y + (1-\alpha)x$

then $L_\lambda(f,g)(z) = f(z) + \sum_{i=1}^{m} \lambda_i g_i($

$\geq \alpha f(y) + (1-\alpha) f(x$

$+ \sum_{i=1}^{m} \lambda_i \, [\alpha g_i(y) + ($

$= \alpha L_\lambda(f,g)(y) + (1-$

Thus $L_\lambda(f,g)$ is a concave functio

By lemma 4.11, x^* is a global maxi

iff $dL(f,g)(x^*) = 0$ (aside from th

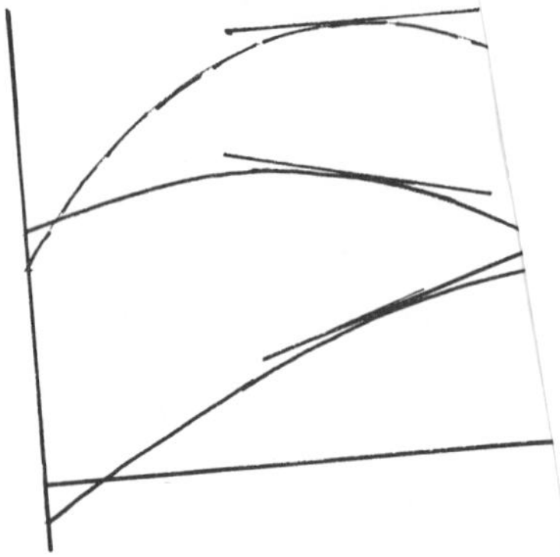

Fig.4.11.

For more general functions, to find
maximum of the Lagrangian $L_\lambda(f,g)$, a
optimum to the problem (f,g), we fin
points of $L_\lambda(f,g)$. Those critical p
negative definite Hessian will then b
maxima of $L_\lambda(f,g)$. However we still
critical points where the Hessian of
is negative semi-definite and then ex
maxima to find the global maxima. Ev
general case, any solution x^* to the
must be a global maximum for a suitabl
Lagrangian $L_\lambda(f,g)$, and thus must sati
order condition

$$Df(x^*) + \sum_{i=1}^{m} \lambda_i Dg_i(x^*) = 0$$

(again

Exampl

M
subje
We see
Thus
or λ
For x
(corr
g(x,y
Thus
For (
requi
The
diffe

The
eige
Henc
exam
the
3.4
cond
P_f
f i
H_g
ori
How

requires $\lambda = 0$. In this case however

$$HL(x,y) = \begin{pmatrix} 0 & 1 \\ 1 & 0 \end{pmatrix}$$

and as in Example 4.4, HL is non-degenerate with eigenvalies +1,-1. Hence HL is not negative semi-definite, and so (0,0) cannot be a local maximum for the Lagrangian.

However if we were to maximise $f(x,y) = -xy$ on the feasible set $\mathbb{R}^2_+$ subject to the same constraint then L would be maximised at (0,0) with $\lambda = 0$.

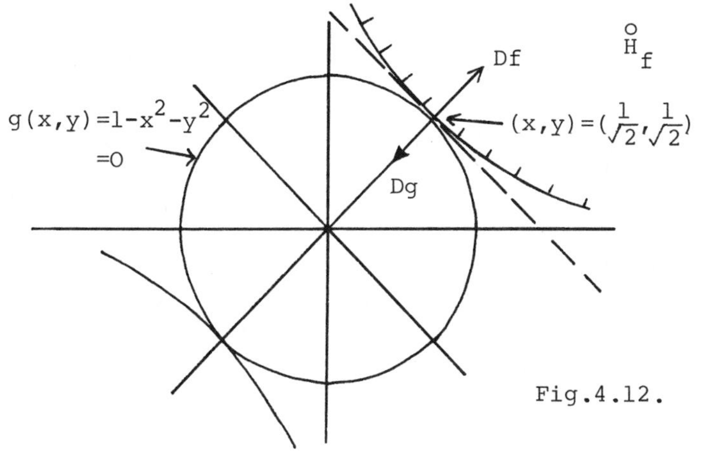

Fig.4.12.

Example 4.9

In an earlier Example 3.7 we examined the maximisation of a convex preference correspondence subject to a budget constraint of the form

$$B(p) = \{x \in \mathbb{R}^n_+ : (p,x) \leq (p,e) = I\},$$

given by an exogenous price vector $p \in \mathbb{R}^n_+$, and initial endowment vector $e \in \mathbb{R}^n_+$.

Suppose now that the preference correspondence is given by a utility function

$$f: \mathbb{R}^2_+ \to \mathbb{R} : (x,y) \to \beta \log x + (1-\beta) \log y, 0 < \beta < 1.$$

Clearly $Df(x,y) = \left(\frac{\beta}{x}, \frac{1-\beta}{y}\right)$

and so $Hf(x,y) = \begin{pmatrix} -\beta/x^2 & 0 \\ 0 & \frac{-(1-\beta)}{y^2} \end{pmatrix}$ is negative definite. Thus f is concave on $\mathbb{R}^2$.

The budget constraint is

$$g(x,y) = I - p_1x - p_2y \geq 0$$

where p_1, p_2 are the given prices of commodities x,y. The first order condition on the Lagrangian is:

$$Df(x,y) + \lambda Dg(x,y) = 0$$

ie. $\left(\frac{\beta}{x}, \frac{1-\beta}{y}\right) + \lambda(-p_1, -p_2) = 0$ and $\lambda > 0$.

Hence $\frac{p_1}{p_2} = \frac{\beta}{x} \cdot \frac{y}{1-\beta}$.

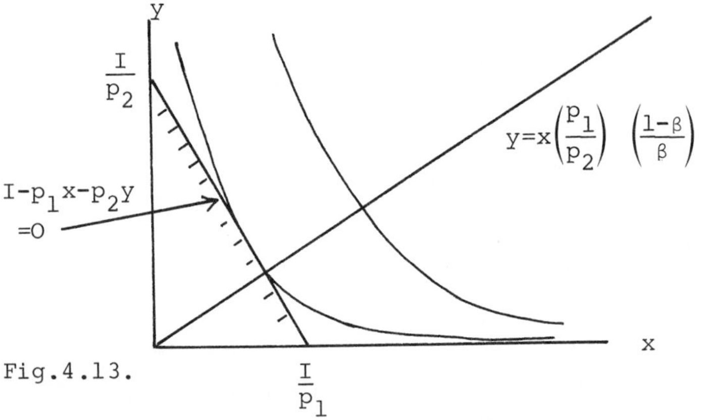

Fig.4.13.

Now f is concave and has no critical point within the constraint set. Thus (x,y) maximises L_λ iff

$y = x\left(\frac{p_1}{p_2}\right)\left(\frac{1-\beta}{\beta}\right)$ and $g(x,y) = 0$.

Thus $y = \frac{I-p_1x}{p_2}$ and so $x = \frac{I\beta}{p_1}$, $y = \frac{I(1-\beta)}{p_2}$,

and $\lambda = \frac{1}{I}$, is the marginal utility of income.

Now consider a situation where prices vary. Then optimal consumption $(x^*, y^*) = (d_1(p_1, p_2), d_2(p_1, p_2))$ where $d_1(p_1, p_2)$ is the demand for commodity x, in this case given by $d_1(p_1, p_2) = \frac{I\beta}{p_1}$, and similarly for p_2. Suppose that all prices are increased by the same proportion ie. $(p_1', p_2') = \alpha(p_1, p_2), \alpha > 0$.

In this exchange situation $I' = p_1'e_1 + p_2'e_2 = \alpha I$

$= \alpha(p_1e_1 + p_2e_2)$.

Thus $x' = \frac{I'\beta}{p_1'} = \frac{\alpha I \beta}{\alpha p_1} = x'$, and $y' = y$.

Hence $d_1(\alpha p_1, \alpha p_2) = d_1(p_1, p_2)$, and so the demand function is homogeneous in prices.

Suppose now that income is obtained from supplying labour at a wage rate w say.

Now let the supply of labour by the consumer be $e = 1-x_3$, where x_3 is leisure time and enters int the utility function.

Then $f: \mathbb{R}^3 \to \mathbb{R} : (x_1 x_2 x_3) \to \sum_{i=1}^{3} a_i \log x_i$

and the budget constraint is

$$p_1x_1 + p_2x_2 \leq (1-x_3)w.$$

or $g(x_1, x_2, x_3) = w-(p_1x_1 + p_2x_2 + wx_3) \geq 0$.

The first order condition is

$$\left(\frac{a_1}{x_1}, \frac{a_2}{x_2}, \frac{a_3}{x_3}\right) = \lambda(p_1, p_2, w), \lambda > 0.$$

Clearly the demand function will again be homogeneous, since $d(p_1, p_2, w) = d(\alpha p_1, \alpha p_2, \alpha w)$.

For this reason we may normalise the price vector. In general, in an n-commodity exchange economy let

$\Delta = \{p \in \mathbb{R}^n_+ : \| p \| = 1\}$ be the price simplex.

Here $\| \ \|$ is a convenient norm on $\mathbb{R}^n$.

In the same way if $f:\mathbb{R}^n_+ \to \mathbb{R}$ is the utility function, let

$$D^*f(x) = \frac{Df(x)}{||Df(x)||} \in \Delta .$$

Suppose then that $x^* \in \mathbb{R}^n$ is a maximum of $f:\mathbb{R}^n_+ \to \mathbb{R}$ subject to the budget constraint $(p,x) \leq I$.
As we have seen the first order condition is

$$Df(x) + \lambda Dg(x) = 0$$

where $Dg(x) = -p = (-p_1, \ldots\ldots, -p_n)$, $p \in \mathbb{R}^n_+$,
and $Df(x) = \left(\frac{\partial f}{\partial x_1}, \ldots\ldots, \frac{\partial f}{\partial x_n}\right)$.

Thus $Df(x) = \lambda(p_1, \ldots, p_n) = \lambda p \in \mathbb{R}^n_+$.

But then $D^*f(x) = \frac{p}{||p||} \in \Delta$.

Subject to boundary problems, a <u>necessary</u> condition for optimal consumer behaviour is therefore that

$$D^*f(x) = \frac{p}{||p||} .$$

As we have seen the optimality condition is that

$$\frac{\partial f}{\partial x_i} \Big/ \frac{\partial f}{\partial x_j} = \frac{p_i}{p_j}$$, for the ith and j^{th} commodity,

where $\frac{\partial f}{\partial x_i}$ is often called the <u>marginal utility</u> of the ith commodity.
Now any point y on the boundary of the budget set satisfies $(p,y) = I = \frac{1}{\lambda}(Df(x^*),x^*)$.
Hence $y \in H(p,I)$, the hyperplane separating the budget set from the preferrred set at the optimum x^*, iff $(Df(x^*),y-x^*) = 0$.

Consider now the question of maximisation of a profit function

$$\pi(x_1,\ldots,x_m,x_{m+1},\ldots,x_n) = \sum_{j=1}^{n-m} p_{m+j}x_{m+j} - \sum_{j=1}^{m} p_j x_j$$

where $(x_1,\ldots,x_m) \in \mathbb{R}^m_+$ are inputs and $(x_{m+1},\ldots,x_n)$ are outputs and $p \in \mathbb{R}^n_+$ is a non-negative price vector.

As in example 3.6, the set of <u>feasible</u> input-output combinations is given by the production set

$$G = \{x \in \mathbb{R}^n_+ : F(x) \geq 0\} \quad \text{where}$$

$F: \mathbb{R}^n_+ \to \mathbb{R}$ is a smooth function and $F(x) = 0$ when x is on the upper boundary or <u>frontier</u> of the production set G.

At a point x on the boundary, the vector which is normal to the surface $\{x: F(x) = 0\}$ is

$$DF(x) = \left(\frac{\partial F}{\partial x_1}, \ldots\ldots \frac{\partial F}{\partial x_n}\right)_x .$$

The first order condition for the Lagrangian is that

$$D\pi(x) + \lambda DF(x) = 0$$

or $(-p_1, \ldots, -p_m, p_{m+1}, \ldots, p_n) + \lambda\left(\frac{\partial F}{\partial x_1}, \ldots, \frac{\partial F}{\partial x_n}\right) = 0.$

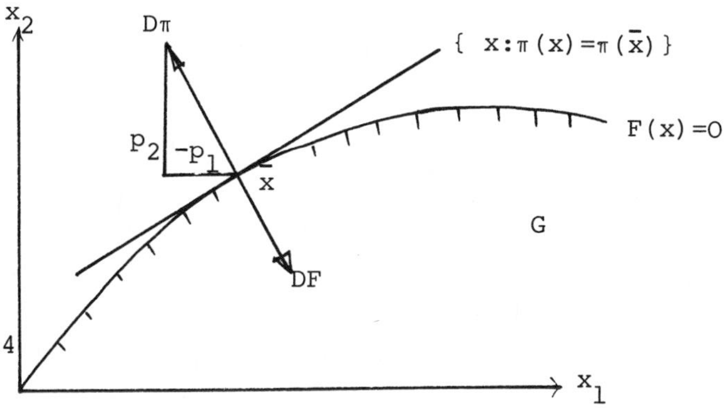

Fig.4.14

For example with two inputs (x_1 and x_2) and one output (x_3) we might express maximum possible output y in terms of x_1 and x_2 ie. $y = g(x_1, x_2)$. Then the feasible set is $\{x \in \mathbb{R}^3_+ : F(x_1, x_2, x_3) = g(x_1, x_2) - x_3 \geq 0\}$

Then $(-p_1, -p_2, p_3) + \lambda\left(\frac{\partial g}{\partial x_1}, \frac{\partial g}{\partial x_2}, -1\right) = 0$

and so $p_1 = p_3 \frac{\partial g}{\partial x_1}, p_2 = p_3 \frac{\partial g}{\partial x_2}$ or $\frac{p_1}{p_2} = \frac{\partial g}{\partial x_1} \Big/ \frac{\partial g}{\partial x_2}$.

Here $\frac{\partial g}{\partial x_j}$ is called the <u>marginal</u> <u>product</u> (with respect to commodity j for j=1,2).

For fixed $\bar{x} = (\bar{x}_1, \bar{x}_2)$ consider the locus of points in $\mathbb{R}^2_+$ such that $y = g(\bar{x})$ is a constant.

If $\left(\frac{\partial g}{\partial x_1}, \frac{\partial g}{\partial x_2}\right)_{\bar{x}} \neq 0$ at $\bar{x}$, then by the implicit function theorem (discussed in the next chapter) we can express x_2 as a function $x_2(x_1)$ of x_1, only, near $\bar{x}$.

In this case $\frac{\partial g}{\partial x_1} + \frac{dx_2}{dx_1}\frac{\partial g}{\partial x_2} = 0$

and so $\frac{\partial g}{\partial x_1} \Big/ \frac{\partial g}{\partial x_2}\Big|_{\bar{x}} = \frac{dx_2}{dx_1}\Big|_x = \frac{p_1}{p_2}$.

Thus $\frac{\partial g}{\partial x_1} \Big/ \frac{\partial g}{\partial x_2}\Big|_{\bar{x}}$ is called the <u>marginal rate of technical substitution</u> of x_2 for x_1 at the point $(\bar{x}_1, \bar{x}_2)$.

<u>Example 4.10</u>

There are two inputs K (capital) and L (labour), and one output, Y, say.

Let $g(K,L) = [dK^{-\rho} + (1-d)L^{-\rho}]^{\frac{-1}{\rho}}$

and the feasibility constraint be

$$F(K,L,Y) = g(K,L) - Y \geq 0.$$

Let $-v,-w,p$ be the prices of capital, labour and the output.

For optimality we obtain:

$$(-v,-w,p) + \lambda\left(\frac{\partial F}{\partial K}, \frac{\partial F}{\partial L}, \frac{\partial F}{\partial Y}\right) = 0.$$

On the production frontier, $g(K,L) = Y$ and so

$p = -\lambda\frac{\partial F}{\partial Y} = \lambda$ since $\frac{\partial F}{\partial Y} = -1.$

Now let $X = [dK^{-\rho} + (1-d)L^{-\rho}]$.

Then $\frac{\partial F}{\partial K} = \left(-\frac{1}{\rho}\right)\left[-\rho d K^{-\rho-1}\right] X^{-\frac{1}{\rho}-1}$.

Now $Y = X^{-\frac{1}{\rho}}$ so $Y^{1+\rho} = X^{-\frac{1}{\rho}-1}$.

Thus $\frac{\partial F}{\partial K} = d\left(\frac{Y}{K}\right)^{1+\rho}$.

Similarly $\frac{\partial F}{\partial L} = (1-d)\left(\frac{Y}{L}\right)^{1+\rho}$.

Thus $\frac{r}{w} = \frac{\partial F}{\partial K} \Big/ \frac{\partial F}{\partial L} = \frac{d}{1-d}\left(\frac{L}{K}\right)^{1+\rho}$.

In the case just of a single output, where the production frontier is given by a function

$$x_{m+1} = g(x_1,\ldots,x_m) \text{ and } (x_1,\ldots,x_m) \in \mathbb{R}^m_+$$

is the input vector, then clearly the constraint set will be a convex set if and only if g is a concave function. (See Example 3.3). In this case the solution to the Lagrangian will give an optimal solution. However when the constraint set is not convex, then some solutions to the Lagrangian problem may be local minima. See Figure 4.15 for an illustration.

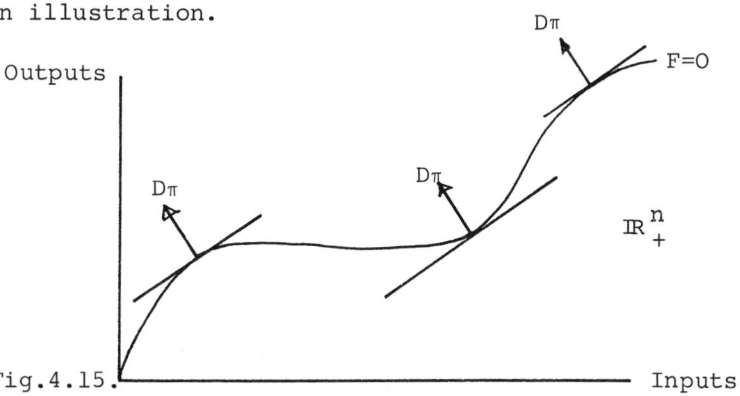

Fig.4.15.

As with the consumer, the optimum point on the production frontier is unchanged if all prices are multiplied by a positive number.

For a general consumer let $d:\mathbb{R}^n_+ \to \mathbb{R}^n_+$ be the demand map where

$$d(p_1,\ldots,p_n) = (x^*_1(p),\ldots x^*_n(p)) = x^*(p)$$

and $x^*(p)$ is any solution to the maximisation problem on the budget set

$$B(p_1,\ldots,p_n) = \{x \in \mathbb{R}^n_+ : (p,x) \leq I\}.$$

In general it need not be the case that d is single-valued, and so it need not be a function.

As we have seen, d is homogeneous in prices and so we may regard d as a correspondence

$$d:\Delta \to \mathbb{R}^n_+ .$$

Similarly for a producer let $s:\Delta \to \mathbb{R}^n_+$ where $s(p_1,\ldots,p_n) = (-x^*_1(p),\ldots,-x^*_m(p),x^*_{m+1}(p)\ldots)$ be the supply correspondence. (Here the first m values are negative because these are inputs).

Now consider a society $\{1,\ldots,i,\ldots N\}$ and commodities named $\{1,\ldots,j,\ldots n\}$. Let $e_i \in \mathbb{R}^n_+$ be the initial endowment vector of agent i, and $e = \sum_{i=1}^{N} e_i$ the total endowment of the society.

Then a price vector $p^* \in \Delta$ is a <u>market-clearing</u> <u>price equilibrium</u> when $e + \sum_{i=1}^{N} s_i(p^*) = \sum_{i=1}^{N} d_i(p^*)$ where $s_i(p^*) \in \mathbb{R}^n_+$ belongs to the set of optimal input-output vectors at price p^* for agent i, and $d_i(p^*)$ is an optimal demand vector for consumer i at price vector p^*.

As an illustration, consider a two person, two good exchange economy (without production) and let e_{ij} be the initial endowment of good j to agent i.

Let $(f_1,f_2):\mathbb{R}^2_+ \to \mathbb{R}^2$ be the C^1 - utility functions of the two players.

At $(p_1,p_2) \in \Delta$, for optimality we have

$$\left(\frac{\partial f_i}{\partial x_{i1}} , \frac{\partial f_i}{\partial x_{i2}}\right) = \lambda_i(p_1 , p_2) , \quad \lambda_i > 0.$$

But $x_{1j} + x_{2j} = e_{1j} + e_{2j}$ for j=1 or 2, in market equilibrium.

Thus $\frac{\partial f_i}{\partial x_{ij}} = - \frac{\partial f_i}{\partial x_{kj}}$ when $i \neq k$.

Hence $\frac{1}{\lambda_1}\left(-\frac{\partial f_1}{\partial x_{11}} , \frac{\partial f_1}{\partial x_{12}}\right) = (p_1,p_2)$

$= \frac{1}{\lambda_2}\left(\frac{\partial f_2}{\partial x_{11}} , - \frac{\partial f_2}{\partial x_{12}}\right)$

or $\left(\frac{\partial f_1}{\partial x_{11}} , \frac{\partial f_1}{\partial x_{12}}\right) + \lambda\left(\frac{\partial f_2}{\partial x_{11}} , \frac{\partial f_2}{\partial x_{12}}\right) = 0$

for some $\lambda > 0$. See Figure 4.16.

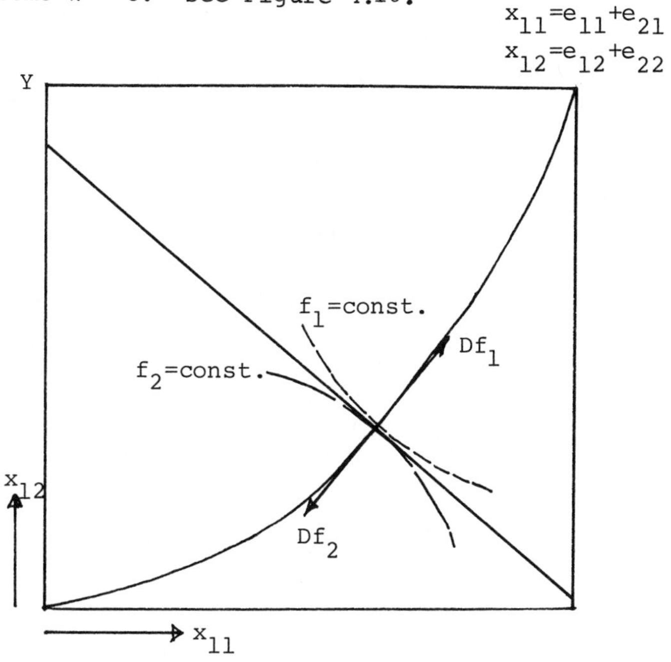

Fig.4.16.

As we shall see in the next section this implies that the result $(x_{11}, x_{12}, x_{21}, x_{22})$ of optimal individual behaviour at the market-clearing price equilibrium is a Pareto optimal outcome under certain conditions.

4.4. THE PARETO SET AND EQUILIBRIA

Consider a society $M = \{1,\ldots,m\}$ of m individuals where the preference of the ith individual in M on a convex admissible set Y in $\mathbb{R}^n$ is given by a C^1-function $u_i : Y \subset \mathbb{R}^n \to \mathbb{R}$.
Then $u = (u_1,\ldots,u_m) : Y \subset \mathbb{R}^n \to \mathbb{R}^m$ is called a C^1- profile for the society.

A point $y \in Y$ is said to be Pareto preferred (for the society M) to $x \in Y$ iff $u_i(y) > u_i(x)$ for all $i \in M$. In this case write $y \in P_M(x)$ and call $P_M : Y \to Y$ the Pareto correspondence. The (global) Pareto set for M on Y is the choice $P(u_1,\ldots,u_m) = \{y \in Y : P_M(y) = \Phi\}$.
We seek to characterise this set.

In the same way as before we shall let $H_i(x) = \{y \in Y: du_i(x)(y-x) > 0\}$ where $H_i : Y \to Y$ for each $i=1,\ldots,m$.
Given a correspondence $P:Y \to Y$ the inverse correspondence $P^{-1}:Y \to Y$ is defined by

$$P^{-1}(x) = \{y \in Y : x \in P(y)\}.$$

In section 3.3 we said a correspondence $P:Y \to Y$ (where Y is a topological space) is lower demi - continuous (ldc) iff for all $x \in Y$, $P^{-1}(x)$ is open in Y.
Clearly if $u_i : W \to \mathbb{R}$ is continuous then the preference correspondence $P_i : Y \to Y$ given by $P_i(x) = \{y : u_i(y) > u_i(x)\}$ is ldc since

$P_i^{-1}(y) = \{x : u_i(y) > u(x)\}$ is open.

We show now that when $u_i : Y \to \mathbb{R}$ is C^1 then $H_i : Y \to Y$ is ldc and as a consequence if $H_i(x) \neq \Phi$ then $P_i(x) \neq \Phi$.

Alternatively, if x is a global maximimum of u_i on Y (so $P_i(x) = \Phi$) then $H_i(x) = \Phi$ (so x is a generalised critical point). See lemma 4.8 above.

<u>Lemma 4.18</u>

If $u_i : Y \to \mathbb{R}$ is a C^1-function on the convex admissible set Y, then $H_i : Y \to Y$ is lower demi-continuous and if $H_i(x) \neq \Phi$ then $P_i(x) \neq \Phi$.

<u>Proof</u>

Suppose that $H_i(x) \neq \Phi$. Then there exists $y \in Y$ such that $du_i(x)(y-x) > 0$.

Let $h = y-x$.

By the continuity of $du_i : Y \to \mathcal{L}(\mathbb{R}^n, \mathbb{R})$ there exists a neighbourhood U of x in Y, and a neighbourhood V of h in $\mathbb{R}^n$ such that $du_i(z)(h') > 0$ for all $z \in U$, for all $h' \in V$.

Since $y \in H_i(x)$, we have $x \in H_i^{-1}(y)$.

Now $h = y-x$. Let

$$U' = \{x' \in U : y-x' \in V\}.$$

For all $x' \in U'$, $du_i(x')(y-x') > 0$.

Thus $U' \subset H_i^{-1}(y)$.

Hence $H_i^{-1}(y)$ is open.

This is true at each $y \in Y$, and so H_i is ldc.

Suppose that $H_i(x) \neq \Phi$ and $h \in H_i(x)$.

Since H_i is ldc it is possible to choose $\lambda \in (0,1)$ such that by Taylor's Theorem

$$u_i(x+\lambda h) = u_i(x) + du_i(z)(\lambda h),$$

where $du_i(z)(h) > 0$, and $z \in (x, x+\lambda h)$.

Thus $u_i(x+\lambda h) > u_i(x)$ and so $P_i(x) \neq \Phi$.

When $u = (u_1, \ldots, u_m): Y \to \mathbb{R}^m$ is a C^1-profile then define the correspondence $H_M: Y \to Y$ by

$$H_M(x) = \bigcap_{i \in M} H_i(x)$$

ie. $y \in H_M(x)$ iff $du_i(x)(y-x) > 0$ for all $i \in M$.

Lemma 4.19

If $(u_1, \ldots, u_m): Y \to \mathbb{R}^m$ is a C^1-profile then $H_M: Y \to Y$ is lower demi-continuous.
If $H_M(x) \neq \Phi$ then $P_M(x) \neq \Phi$.

Proof

Suppose that $H_M(x) \neq \Phi$. Then there exists $y \in H_i(x)$ for each $i \in M$. Thus $x \in H_i^{-1}(y)$ for all $i \in M$. But each $H_i^{-1}(y)$ is open; hence $\exists$ an open neighbourhood U_i of x in $H_i^{-1}(y)$; let $U = \bigcap_{i \in M} U_i$.
Then $x' \in U$ implies that $x' \in H_M^{-1}(y)$. Thus H_M is ldc.
As in lemma 4.18 it is then possible to choose $h \in \mathbb{R}^n$ such that for all i in M,

$$u_i(x+h) = u_i(x) + du_i(z)(h)$$

where z belongs to U, and $du_i(z)(h) > 0$.
Thus $x+h \in P_M(x)$ and so $P_M(x) \neq \Phi$.

The set $\{x: H_M(x) = \Phi\}$ is called the critical Pareto set, and is often written as θ_M, or $\theta(u_1, \ldots, u_m)$.
By lemma 4.19, $\theta(u_1, \ldots, u_m)$ contains the Pareto set $P(u_1, \ldots, u_m)$.
Moreover we can see that θ_M must be closed in Y.
To see this suppose that $H_M(x) \neq \Phi$, and $y \in H_M(x)$.
Thus $x \in H_M^{-1}(y)$. But H_M is ldc and so there is a neighbourhood U of x in Y such that $x' \in H_M^{-1}(y)$ for all $x' \in U$.
Then $y \in H_M(x')$ for all $x' \in U$, and so $H_M(x') \neq \Phi$ for all $x' \in U$.

Hence the set $\{x \in Y : H_M(x) \neq \Phi\}$ is open and so the critical Pareto set is closed.
In the same way, the Pareto correspondence $P_M : Y \to Y$ is given by $P_M(x) = \bigcap_{i \in M} P_i(x)$ where $P_i(x) = \{y : u_i(y) > u_i(x)\}$ for each $i \in M$.
Since each P_i is ldc, so must be P_M, and thus the Pareto set $P(u_1, \ldots, u_m)$ must also be closed.
Suppose now that $u_1, \ldots, u_m$ are all concave C^1- or strictly pseudo-concave functions on the convex set Y.
By lemma 4.17, for each $i \in M$, $P_i(x) \subset H_i(x)$ at each $x \in Y$.
If $x \in \theta(u_i, \ldots, u_m)$ then

$$\bigcap_{i \in M} P_i(x) \subset \bigcap_{i \in M} H_i(x) = \Phi$$

and so x must also belong to the (global) Pareto set.

A point in $P(u_1, \ldots, u_m)$ is the precise analogue, in the case of a family of functions, of a maximum point for a single function, while a point in $\theta(u_1, \ldots, u_m)$ is the analogue of a critical point of a single function $u: Y \to \mathbb{R}$, such that $du_i(x)(y-x) \leq 0$ for all $y \in Y$. In the case of a family of functions, the point belongs to the critical Pareto set θ_M, when a generalised Lagrangian $L(u_1, \ldots u_m)$ has differential $dL(x) = 0$.
This allows us to define a Hessian for the family and determine which critical Pareto points are global Pareto points.

Suppose then that $u = (u_1 \ldots, u_m) : Y \to \mathbb{R}^m$ where Y is a convex admissible set and each $u_i : Y \to \mathbb{R}$ is a C^1-function.

A generalised Lagrangian $L(\lambda, u)$ for u is a <u>semipositive</u> combination $\sum_{i=1}^{m} \lambda_i u_i$ where each $\lambda_i \geq 0$ but not all $\lambda_i = 0$.

For convenience let us write

$$\mathbb{R}^m_+ = \{x \in \mathbb{R}^m : x_i \geq 0 \text{ for } i \in M\}$$

$$\overset{\circ}{\mathbb{R}}{}^m_+ = \{x \in \mathbb{R}^m : x_i > 0 \text{ for } i \in M\}$$

and $\overline{\mathbb{R}^m_+} = \mathbb{R}^m_+ \setminus \{0\}$.

Thus $\lambda \in \overline{\mathbb{R}^m_+}$ iff each $\lambda_i \geq 0$ but not all $\lambda_i = 0$. Since each $u_i : Y \to \mathbb{R}$ is a C^1-function, the differential at x is a linear map $du_i(x) : \mathbb{R}^n \to \mathbb{R}$. Once a coordinate basis for $\mathbb{R}^n$ is chosen, $du_i(x)$ may be represented by the row vector

$$Du_i(x) = \left(\left.\frac{\partial u_i}{\partial x_i}\right|_x, \ \ldots \ \left.\frac{\partial u_i}{\partial x_n}\right|_x \right).$$

Similarly the profile $u : Y \to \mathbb{R}^m$ has differential at x represented by the (n x m) Jacobian matrix

$$Du(x) = \begin{pmatrix} Du_i(x) \\ \\ Du_m(x) \end{pmatrix} : \mathbb{R}^n \to \mathbb{R}^m.$$

Suppose now that $\lambda \in \mathbb{R}^m$.

Then define $\lambda . Du(x) : \mathbb{R}^n \to \mathbb{R}$ by

$$(\lambda . Du(x))(v) = (\lambda, Du(x)(v))$$

where $(\lambda, Du(x)(v))$ is the scalar product of the two vectors $\lambda, Du(x)(v)$ in $\mathbb{R}^m$.

Lemma 4.20

The gradient vectors $\{Du_i(x) : i \in M\}$ are linearly dependent and satisfy the equation

$$\sum_{i=1}^{m} \lambda_i Du_i(x) = 0$$

iff $[\text{Im } Du(x)]^{\perp}$ is the subspace of $\mathbb{R}^m$ spanned by $\lambda = (\lambda_1, \ldots, \lambda_m)$.

Here $\lambda \in [\text{Im } Du(x)]^{\perp}$ iff $(\lambda, w) = 0$ for all $w \in \text{Im } Du(x)$.

Proof

$$\lambda \in [\text{Im Du}(x)]^{\perp} \iff (\lambda, w) = 0 \ \forall w \in \text{Im Du}(x)$$
$$\iff (\lambda, Du(x)(v)) = 0 \ \forall v \in \mathbb{R}^n$$
$$\iff (\lambda . Du(x))(v) = 0 \ \forall v \in \mathbb{R}^n$$
$$\iff (\lambda . Du(x)) = 0 .$$

But $\lambda . Du(x) = 0 \iff \sum_{i=1}^{m} \lambda_i Du_i(x) = 0$
where $\lambda = (\lambda_1, \ldots, \lambda_m)$.

Theorem 4.21

If $u: Y \to \mathbb{R}^m$ is a C^1-profile on an admissible convex set and x belongs to the interior of Y, then $x \in \theta(u_1, \ldots, u_m)$ iff there exists $\lambda \in \mathbb{R}^m_+$ such that $dL(\lambda, u)(x) = 0$.
If x belongs to the boundary of Y and $dL(\lambda, u)(x) = 0$ then $x \in \theta(u_1, \ldots, u_m)$

Proof

Pick a coordinate basis. Suppose that there exists $\lambda \in \mathbb{R}^m_+$ such that

$$L(\lambda, u)(x) = \sum_{i=1}^{m} \lambda_i u_i(x)$$

satisfies $\sum_{i=1}^{m} \lambda_i \ Du_i(x) = 0$.
By lemma 4.20 this implies that

$$\lambda \in \left[\text{Im}(Du(x))\right]^{\perp} .$$

However suppose $x \notin \theta(u_1, \ldots, u_m)$. Then there exists $v \in \mathbb{R}^n$ such that $Du(x)(v) = w \in \overset{o}{\mathbb{R}}{}^m_+$
(ie. $(Du_i(x), v) = w_i > 0$ for all $i \in M$).
But $w \in \text{Im Du}(x)$ and $w \in \overset{o}{\mathbb{R}}{}^m_+$.

Moreover $\lambda \in \overline{\mathbb{R}^m_+}$ and so $(\lambda, w) > 0$ (since not all $\lambda_i = 0$).

This contradicts $\lambda \in [\text{Im}(Du(x))]^{\perp}$, since $(\lambda, w) \neq 0$. Hence $x \in \theta(u_1, \ldots, u_m)$.
Thus we have shown that for any $x \in Y$, if $dL(\lambda, u)(x) = 0$ for some $\lambda \in \mathbb{R}^m_+$, then $x \in \theta(u_1, \ldots, u_m)$.

Suppose now that $\{Du_i(x): i \in M\}$ are linearly independent. If x belongs to the interior of Y then for a vector $h \in \mathbb{R}^n$ there exists a vector $y = x+\theta h$, for θ sufficiently small, so that $y \in Y$ and $\forall i \in M, (Du_i(x), h) > 0$. Thus $x \notin \theta(u_1, \ldots, u_m)$.

So suppose that $DL(\lambda, u)(x) = 0$ where $\lambda \neq 0$ but $\lambda \notin \mathbb{R}^m_+$. Then for at least one $i, \lambda_i < 0$. But then there exists a vector $w \in \overset{o}{\mathbb{R}}{}^m_+$, where $w = (w_1, \ldots, w_m)$ and $w_i > 0$ for each $i \in M$, such that $(\lambda, w) = 0$. By lemma 4.20, $w \in Im(Du(x))$. Hence there exists a vector $h \in \mathbb{R}^n$ such that $Du(x)(h) = w$.
But $w \in \overset{o}{\mathbb{R}}{}^m_+$, and so $(Du_i(x), h) > 0$ for all $i \in M$. Since x belongs to the interior of Y, there exists a point $y = x+\alpha h$ such that $y \in H_i(x)$ for all $i \in M$. Hence $x \notin \Theta(u_1, \ldots, u_m)$.
Consequently if x is an interior point of Y then $x \in \Theta(u_1, \ldots, u_m)$ implies that $dL(\lambda, u)(x) = 0$ for some semipositive λ in $\mathbb{R}^m_+$.

Example 4.11

Compute the Pareto set in $\mathbb{R}^2$ when the utility functions are

$$u_1(x_1, x_2) = x_1^\alpha x_2 \qquad \text{where } \alpha \in (0,1).$$
$$u_2(x_1, x_2) = 1 - x_1^2 - x_2^2.$$

Thus maximise u_1 subject to the constraint $u_2(x_1, x_2) \geq 0$.
As in example 4.8 the first order condition is

$$(\alpha x_1^{\alpha-1} x_2, x_1^\alpha) + \lambda(-2x_1, -2x_2) = 0 .$$

$$\text{Hence } \lambda = \frac{\alpha x_1^{\alpha-1} x_2}{2x_1} = \frac{x_1^\alpha}{2x_2}$$

$$\text{or } \alpha x_2^2 = x_1^2$$

or $x_1 = \pm\sqrt{\alpha}\; x_2$.

If $x_1 = -\sqrt{\alpha}\; x_2$ then $\lambda = \dfrac{x_1^{\alpha}\sqrt{\alpha}}{2(-x_1)} < 0$

and so such a point does not belong to the critical Pareto set. Thus $(x_1,x_2)\in\theta(u_1,u_2)$ iff $x_1=x_2\sqrt{\alpha}$. Note that if $x_1=x_2=0$ then the Lagrangian may be written as $L(\lambda,u)(0,0) = \lambda_1 u_1(0,0) + \lambda_2 u_2(0,0)$ where $\lambda_1 = 0$ and λ_2 is any positive number. In the positive quadrant $\mathbb{R}^2_+$, the critical Pareto set and global Pareto set coincide.

Finally to maximise u_1 on the set $\{(x_1,x_2):u_2(x_1,x_2) \geq 0\}$ we simply choose λ such that $u_2(x_1,x_2) = 0$.

Thus $x_1^2 + x_2^2 = \alpha x_2^2 + x_2^2 = 1$ or $x_2 = \dfrac{1}{\sqrt{1+\alpha}}$

and so $(x_1,x_2) = \left(\sqrt{\dfrac{\alpha}{1+\alpha}}, \dfrac{1}{\sqrt{1+\alpha}}\right)$.

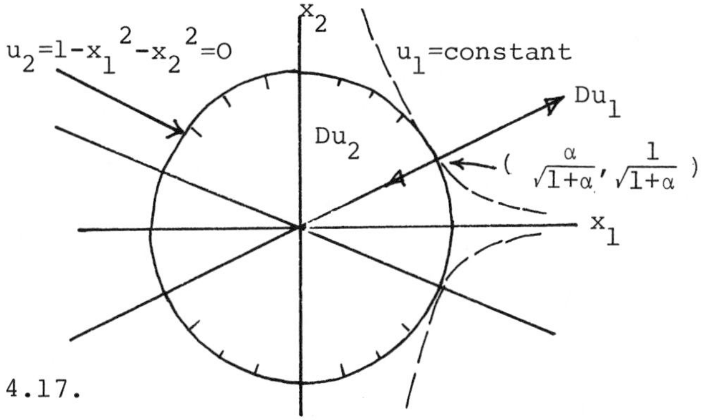

Fig.4.17.

In the next chapter we shall examine the critical Pareto set $\theta(u_1,\ldots,u_m)$ and demonstrate that the set belongs to a singularity "manifold" which can be topologically characterised to be of "dimension" m-1. This allows us then to examine the price equilibria of an exchange economy.

Note that in the example of a two person exchange economy studied in section 4.3.2, we showed that the result of individual optimising behaviour at an equilibrium price vector led to an outcome, x, such that

$$Du_1(x) + \lambda Du_2(x) = 0$$

where $\lambda > 0$. As we have shown here this market clearing equilibrium must belong to the critical Pareto set $\Theta(u_1,u_2)$. Moreover when both u_1 and u_2 are concave then this outcome belongs to the global Pareto set. We develop this in the following theorem.

<u>The Welfare Theorem for an Exchange Economy</u>

In an exchange economy where each individual in the society $M = \{1,\ldots,i,\ldots m\}$ has initial endowment $e_i \in \mathbb{R}^n_+$ and if

i) the demand $x_i^*(p) \in \mathbb{R}^n_+$ of agent i at each price $p \in \mathbb{R}^n$ is such that $x_i^*(p)$ maximises the C^1-utility function $u_i : \mathbb{R}^n \to \mathbb{R}$ on the budget set $B(p) = \{x \in \mathbb{R}^n_+ : (p,x) \leq (p,e_i)\}$ by

a) $Du_i(x_i^*(p)) = \lambda_i p \ , \lambda_i > 0,$

b) $(p, x_i^*(p)) = (p, e_i),$

ii) p* is a market clearing price equilibrium so that $\sum_{i=1}^{m} x_i^*(p^*) = \sum_{i=1}^{m} e_i \in \mathbb{R}^n,$

<u>then</u> $x^* = (x_1^*(p^*),\ldots,x_m^*(p)) \in \Theta(u_1,\ldots,u_m)$. Moreover if each u_i is either concave, or strictly pseudo-concave then x* belongs to the Pareto set.

<u>Proof</u>

We need to define the set of outcomes first of all. The states that can result from exchange are

$$(x_1, \ldots, x_i, \ldots, x_m) \in (\mathbb{R}^n_+)^m = \mathbb{R}^{nm}_+,$$

where $x_i = (x_{i1}, \ldots, x_{in}) \in \mathbb{R}^n_+$ is an allocation for agent i. However there are n resource constraints

$$\sum_{i=1}^{m} x_{ij} = \sum_{i=1}^{m} e_{ij} = e_{.j}, \text{ for } j=1,\ldots,n,$$

where $(e_{i1}, \ldots, e_{in}) \in \mathbb{R}^n_+$ is the set of initial endowments of agent i.

Thus the set Y of feasible outcomes is a hyperplane of dimension n(m-1) in $\mathbb{R}^{nm}_+$ through the point $(e_1, \ldots, e_m)$.

As coordinates for any point $x \in Y$ we may choose $x = (x_{11}, \ldots, x_{1n}, x_{21}, \ldots, x_{2n}, \ldots, x_{(m-1)1}, \ldots, x_{(m-1)n})$ where it is implicit that the bundle of commodities available to agent m is

$$x_m = (x_{m1}, \ldots, x_{mn}) \text{ where } x_{mj} = e_{.j} - \sum_{i=1}^{m-1} x_{ij}.$$

Now define $u_i^*: Y \to \mathbb{R}$, the extended utility function of i on Y, by

$$u_i^*(x) = u_i(x_{i1}, \ldots, x_{in}).$$

For $i \in M$, it is clear that the direction gradient of i on Y is

$$Du_i^*(x) = \left(0, \ldots 0, \frac{\partial u_i}{\partial x_{i1}}, \ldots, \frac{\partial u_i}{\partial x_{in}}, 0, \ldots 0\right)$$

$$= (\;..\; 0, \;..\; Du_i(x) \;..\; , 0).$$

For agent m, $\dfrac{\partial u_m^*}{\partial x_{ij}} = - \dfrac{\partial u_m}{\partial x_{mj}}$ for $i=1,\ldots,m-1$;

thus $Du_m^*(x)$

$$= -\left(\frac{\partial u_m}{\partial x_{m1}}, \ldots, \frac{\partial u_m}{\partial x_{mn}}, \ldots\right)$$

$$= - (Du_m(x), \ldots\ldots, Du_m(x)).$$

If p* is a market-clearing price equilibrium, then by definition $\sum_{i=1}^{m} x_i^*(p^*) = \sum_{i=1}^{m} e_i$.

Thus $x^*(p^*) = (x_1^*(p^*),\ldots,x_{m-1}^*(p^*))$ belongs to Y. But each x_i^* is a critical point of $u_i:\mathbb{R}_+^n \to \mathbb{R}$ on the budget set and $Du_i(x_i^*(p^*)) = \lambda_i p^*$.
Thus the Jacobian for $u^* = (u_1^*,\ldots,u_m^*):Y \to \mathbb{R}^m$ at $x^*(p^*)$ is

$$Du^*(x^*) = \begin{bmatrix} \lambda_1 p^* & 0 \ . \ . & 0 \\ 0 & \lambda_2 p^* & \\ \cdot & \cdot & \\ \cdot & \cdot & \lambda_{m-1}p^* \\ -\lambda_m p^* & -\lambda_m p^* & -\lambda_m p^* \end{bmatrix}$$

Thus $\frac{1}{\lambda_1} Du_1^*(x^*) + \frac{1}{\lambda_2} Du_2^*(x^*) \ldots + \frac{1}{\lambda_m} Du_m^*(x^*) = 0$.
But each $\lambda_i > 0$ for $i=1,\ldots,m$.
Then $dL(\mu,u)(x^*(p^*)) = 0$ where

$$\underline{L(\mu,u)(x)} = \sum_{i=1}^m \mu_i u_i(x) \text{ and } \mu_i = \frac{1}{\lambda_i} \text{ and}$$

$\mu \in \mathbb{R}_+^m$.

By theorem 4.21 , $x^*(p^*)$ belongs to the critical Pareto set.
Clearly,if for each i, $u_i:\mathbb{R}_+^n \to \mathbb{R}$ is concave C^1- or strictly pseudo-concave then $u_i^*:Y \to \mathbb{R}$ will be also. By previous results, the critical and global Pareto set will coincide, and so $x^*(p^*)$ will be Pareto optimal.

One can show that the market-clearing equilibrium is Pareto optimal very much more simply. By definition $x^*(p^*)$ is characterised by

a) $\sum_{i=1}^m x_i^*(p^*) = \sum_{i=1}^m e_i$

b) If $u_i(x_i) > u_i(x_i^*(p^*))$ then $(p^*,x_i) > (p^*,e_i)$ (by the optimality condition for agent i: see example 3.5).

But then if $x_i^*(p^*)$ is not Pareto optimal, there exists a vector $x = (x_1,\ldots,x_m) \in \mathbb{R}_+^{nm}$ such that

$u_i(x_i) > u_i(x_i^*(p^*))$ for $i = 1,\ldots,m$.

By (b) $\quad (p^*,x_i) > (p^*,e_i)$ for each i

and so $\sum_{i=1}^{m}(p^*,x_i) = (p^*, \sum_{i=1}^{m} x_i) > (p^*, \sum_{i=1}^{m} e_i)$.

But if $x \in \mathbb{R}_+^{nm}$ is feasible $\sum_{i=1}^{m} x_i \leq \sum_{i=1}^{m} e_i$

which implies $(p^*, \sum_{i=1}^{m} x_i) \leq (p^*, \sum_{i=1}^{m} e_i)$.

By contradiction $x^*(p^*)$ must belong to the Pareto optimal set.

However the Welfare Theorem gives a deeper insight into the nature of market-clearing equilibria. The coefficients μ_i of the Lagrangean $L(\mu,u)$ of the social optimisation problem turn out to be inverse to the coefficients λ_i in the individual optimisation problems, where λ_i is equal to the marginal utility of income for the ith agent. This in turn suggests that it is possible for an agent to transform his utility function from u_i to u_i' in such a way as to decrease λ_i and thus increase μ_i, the "weight" of the ith agent in the social optimisation problem. This is called the <u>problem of preference manipulation</u> and is currently an unresolved research problem (see Satterthwaite and Sonnenschein, 1981).

Secondly the weights μ_i can be regarded as functionally dependent on the initial endowment vector $(e_1,\ldots,e_m) \in \mathbb{R}_+^{nm}$. Thus the question of market equilibrium could be examined in terms of the functions $\mu_i : \mathbb{R}_+^{nm} \to \mathbb{R}$, $i=1,\ldots,m$. It is possible that one or a number of agents could destroy or exchange commodities so as to increase their weights. This is termed the problem of <u>resource manipulation</u> or the transfer paradox (see Balasko,1978, and Polemarchakis,1982).

We also have not shown the existence of a market-clearing price equilibrium. In the next chapter however we shall examine the nature of the price equilibria.

Example 4.10

To illustrate these observations consider a two person (i=1,2) exchange economy with two commodities (j=1,2).

As in Example 4.9, assume the preference of the ith agent is given by a utility function

$f_i : \mathbb{R}^2_+ \to \mathbb{R} : f_i(x,y) = \beta_i \log x + (1-\beta_i) \log y$

where $0 < \beta_i < 1$.

Let the initial endowment vector of i be $e_i = (e_{i1}, e_{i2})$.

At the price vector $p = (p_1, p_2)$, demand by agent i is $d_i(p_1,p_2) = \left(\frac{I_i \beta_i}{p_1}, \frac{I_i(1-\beta_i)}{p_2}\right)$ where $I_i = p_1 e_{i1} + p_2 e_{i2}$ is the value at p of his endowment.

Thus agent i "desires" to change his initial endowment

$$(e_{i1}, e_{i2}) \to (e'_{i1}, e'_{i2}) = \left(\beta_i e_{i1} + \frac{\beta_i e_{i2} p_2}{p_1},\right.$$
$$\left.(1-\beta_i)e_{i2} + (1-\beta_i)\frac{e_{i1}p_1}{p_2}\right).$$

Another way of interpreting this is that i optimally divides his expenditure between the first and second commodities in the ratio $\beta:(1-\beta)$.

Thus agent i offers to sell $(1-\beta_i)e_{i1}$ units of commodity 1 for $(1-\beta_i)e_{i1}p_1$ monetary units and buy $(1-\beta_i)e_{i1}\frac{p_1}{p_2}$ units of the second commodity, and to sell $\beta_i e_{i2}$ units of the second commodity and buy $\beta_i e_{i2}\frac{p_2}{p_1}$ units of the first commodity.

At the price vector (p_1, p_2) the amount of the first commodity on offer is $(1-\beta_i)e_{11}+(1-\beta_2)e_{21}$ and the amount on request is $\beta_1 e_{12} p_2^* + \beta_2 e_{22} p_2^*$; here p_2^* is the ratio $p_2 : p_1$ of relative prices. For (p_1, p_2) to be a market-clearing price equilibrium we require

$$e_{11}(1-\beta_1)+e_{21}(1-\beta_2) = p_2^*(e_{12}\beta_1+e_{22}\beta_2).$$

Clearly if all endowments are increased by a multiple $\alpha > 0$, then the equilibrium relative price vector is unchanged. Thus p_2^* is uniquely determined and so the final allocations (e'_{11}, e'_{12}), (e'_{21}, e'_{22}) can be determined.
As we showed in example 4.9, the coefficients λ_i for the individual optimisation problems satisfy $\lambda_i = {}^1/I_i$, where λ_i is the marginal utility of income for agent i.
By the previous analysis, the weights μ_i in the social optimisation problem satisfy $\mu_i = I_i$.
After some manipulation of the price equilibrium equation we find

$$\frac{\mu_i}{\mu_k} = \frac{e_{i1}(e_{i2}+\beta_k e_{k2})+e_{i2}(1-\beta_k)e_{k1}}{e_{k1}(e_{k2}+\beta_i e_{i2})+e_{k2}(1-\beta_i)e_{i1}}.$$

Clearly if agent i can increase the ratio $\mu_i : \mu_k$ then the relative utility of i vis-a-vis k is increased. However since the relative price equilibrium is uniquely determined in this case, it is not possible for agent i, say, to destroy some of his initial endowments (e_{i1}, e_{i2}) to manipulate the outcome. The interested reader is referred to Balasko(1978) for further discussion.

In this example the relative price equilibrium is unique, but this need not always occur. Consider the two person, two commodity case illustrated below in Figure 4.18. As in the Welfare Theorem, the set of feasible outcomes Y is the subset of $\mathbb{R}^4_+ = (x_{11}, x_{12}, x_{21}, x_{22})$ such that

$$x_{11}+x_{21} = e_{.1}$$
$$x_{12}+x_{22} = e_{.2},$$

and this is a two-dimensional hyperplane through the point $(e_{11}, e_{12}, e_{21}, e_{22})$. Thus Y can be represented in the usual two-dimensional Edgeworth box where point A, the most preferred point for agent 1, satisfies $(x_{11}, x_{12}) = (e_{.1}, e_{.2})$.

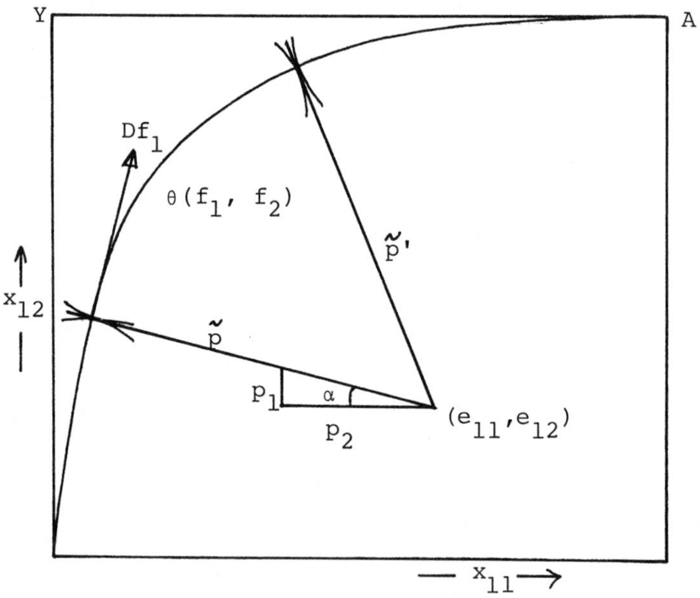

Fig.4.18.

The price ray $\tilde{p}$ is that ray through (e_{11}, e_{12}) where $\tan \alpha = p_1/p_2$. Clearly (p_1, p_2) is an equilibrium price vector if the price ray intersects the critical Pareto set $\theta(f_1, f_2)$ at a point (x_{11}, x_{12}) in Y where $\tilde{p}$ is tangential to the indifference curves for f_1 and f_2 through (x_{11}, x_{12}). At such a point we then have $Df_1(x_{11}, x_{12}) + \mu Df(x_{11}, x_{12}) = 0$.

As Figure 4.18 indicates there may well be a second price ray $\tilde{p}'$ which satisfies the tangency property. Indeed it is possible that there exists a family of such rays, or even an open set V in the price simplex such that each p in V is a market clearing equilibrium.

To be more formal let $X = \mathbb{R}^n_+$ be the commodity space. An <u>initial endowment</u> is a vector $e = (e_1, \ldots, e_m) \in X^m$. A C^r utility function is a C^r-function $u = (u_1, \ldots, u_m): X \to \mathbb{R}^m$.
Now let $C_r(X, \mathbb{R}^m)$ be the set of C^r-profiles, and endow $C_r(X, \mathbb{R}^m)$ with a topology in the following way. (See Hirsch, 1976, p.35 for the subtleties of this, the <u>Whitney</u>, topology).
A neighbourhood of $f \in C_r(X, \mathbb{R}^m)$ is a set $\{g \in C_r(X, \mathbb{R}^m): \| d^r g(x) - d^r f(x) \| < \varepsilon(x)\}$
where $\varepsilon(x) > 0$ for all $x \in X$.
Write $C^r(X, \mathbb{R}^m)$ for $C_r(X, \mathbb{R}^m)$ with this topology.
A property K is called <u>generic</u> iff it is true for all profiles which belong to a <u>residual</u> set in $C^r(X, \mathbb{R}^m)$. Here residual means that the set is the countable intersection of open dense sets in $C^r(X, \mathbb{R}^m)$ - see §3.1.2.
In particular if a property is generic then it means that almost all profiles in $C^r(X, \mathbb{R}^m)$ have that property.

An <u>exchange economy</u> is a pair $(e, u) \in X^m \times C^r(X, \mathbb{R}^m)$.
As before the feasible outcome set is

$$Y = \{(x_1, \ldots, x_m) \in X^m: \sum_{i=1}^m x_i = \sum_{i=1}^m e_i\}$$

and a price vector p belongs to the simplex

$\Delta = \{p \in X: \| p \| = 1\}$, where Δ is an object of dimension n-1.

As in the welfare theorem, the demand by i at $p \in \Delta$ satisfies: $x_i^*(p)$ maximises u_i on $B(p) = \{x \in X: (p,x) \leq (p,e_i)\}$.

Thus, as we have observed under appropriate boundary conditions, we may assume $x_i^*(p)$ satisfies

i) $(p, x_i^*(p)) = (p,e_i)$

ii) $D^* u_i (x_i^*(p)) = p \in \Delta$ (see page 216). Thus $(x^*(p^*),p^*) = (x_1^*(p^*),\ldots,x_m^*(p^*),p^*) \in X^m \times \Delta$ is a market or Walrasian equilibrium iff $x^*(p^*)$ is the demand vector at p^* and satisfies

$$\sum_{i=1}^{m} x_i^* (p^*) = \sum_{i=1}^{m} e_i \in \mathbb{R}^n_+.$$

The economy (e,u) is regular iff (e,u) is such that the set of Walrasian equilibria is finite.

Smale's Theorem on Generic Existence of Regular Economies

There is a residual set U in $C^r(X,\mathbb{R}^m)$ such that for every profile $u \in U$, there is a dense set $V \in X^m$ with the property that (e,u) is a regular economy whenever $(e,u) \in V \times U$.

The proof of this theorem is discussed in the next chapter (and the interested reader might consult Smale, 1974). However we can give a flavour of the proof here.

Consider a point $(e,x,p) \in X^m \times X^m \times \Delta$. This space is of dimension $2nm + (n-1)$.

Now there are n resource restrictions

$$\sum_{i=1}^{m} x_{ij} = \sum_{i=1}^{m} e_{ij}$$ for $j=1,\ldots,n$, together with $(m-1)$ budget restrictions $(p,x_i) = (p, e_i)$ for $i=1,\ldots,m-1$.

Note that the budget restriction for the mth

agent is redundant.

Let $\Gamma = \{(e,x,p) \in X^m \times X^m \times \Delta\}$ be the set of points satisfying these various restrictions. Then Γ will be of dimension $2nm + (n-1) - [n+m-1] = 2nm-m$.

However, we also have m distinct vector equations $D^*u_i(x) = p$, $i=1,\ldots,m$.
Since these vectors are normalised, each one consists of (n-1) separate equations. Chapter 5 shows that singularity theory implies that for every profile u in a residual set, each of these constraints is independent. Together these m(n-1) constraints reduces the dimension of Γ by m(n-1). Hence the set of points in Γ satisfying the first order optimality conditions is a smooth object Z_u of dimension

$$2nm - m - m(n-1) = nm.$$

Now consider the projection

$$Z_u \subset X^m \times (X^m \times \Delta) \to X^m : (e,x,p) \to e,$$

and note that both Z_u and X^m have dimension nm.

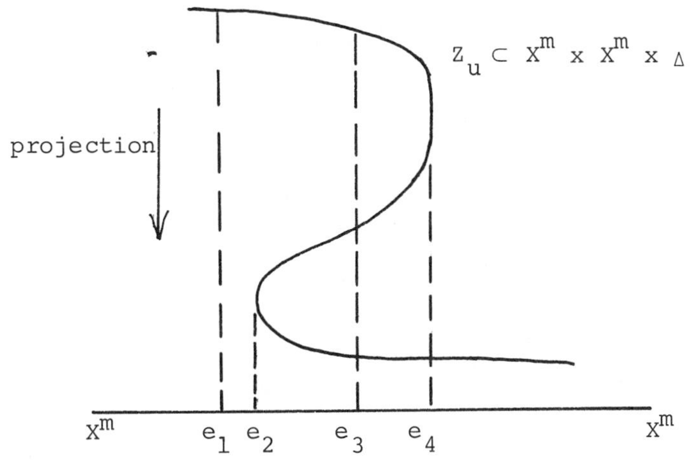

Fig.4.19.

A regular economy (e,u) is one such that the projection map proj: $Z_u \to X^m$: $(e,x,p) \to e$ has differential with maximal rank nm. Call e a <u>regular value</u> in this case. From singularity theory it is known that for all u in the residual set U, the set of regular values of the projection map is dense in X^m. Thus when $u \in U$, and e is regular, the set of Walrasian equilibria for (e,u) will be finite. Figure 4.19 illustrates this. At e_1 there is only one Walrasian equilibrium, while at e_3 there are three. Moreover in a neighborhood of e_3 the Walrasian equilibria move continuously with e. At e_4 the Walrasian equilibrium set is one-dimensional. As e moves from the right past e_2 the number of Walrasian equilibria drops suddenly from 3 to 1, and displays a discontinuity. (See Debreu, 1966 for further discussion). Note that the points (x,p) satisfying $(e,x,p) \in (\text{proj})^{-1}(e)$ need not be Walrasian equilibria in the classical sense, since we have considered only the first order conditions. It is clearly the case that with a non-convex preference correspondence, the first order conditions are not sufficient. However, Smale's theorem shows the existence of extended Walrasian equilibria. The same difficulty occurs in the proof that a Walrasian equilibrium gives a Pareto optimal point in Y.

Let $\overset{o}{\Theta}(u) = \overset{o}{\Theta}(u_1, \ldots\ldots, u_m)$ be the set of points satisfying the first order condition $dL(\lambda,u) = 0$ where $\lambda \in \mathbb{R}^m_+$. Suppose that we solve this such that $\lambda_1 \neq 0$.

Then we may write $Du_1(x) + \sum_{i=2}^{m} \frac{\lambda_i}{\lambda_1} Du_i(x) = 0$.

Clearly there are (m-1) degrees of freedom in this solution and indeed $\overset{o}{\Theta}(u_1, \ldots, u_m)$ can be shown

Note however that this is not a necessary condition. As we know from the previous section it might well be the case for some point x on the boundary of the admissible set Y that $dL(x) \neq 0$ yet there exists no $y \in Y$ such that

$$dg(x)(x-y) \geq 0 \text{ and } df(x)(x-y) > 0.$$

Figure 4.10 illustrates such a case when

$$Y = \{(x,y) \in \mathbb{R}^2 : x \geq 0, y \geq 0\}.$$

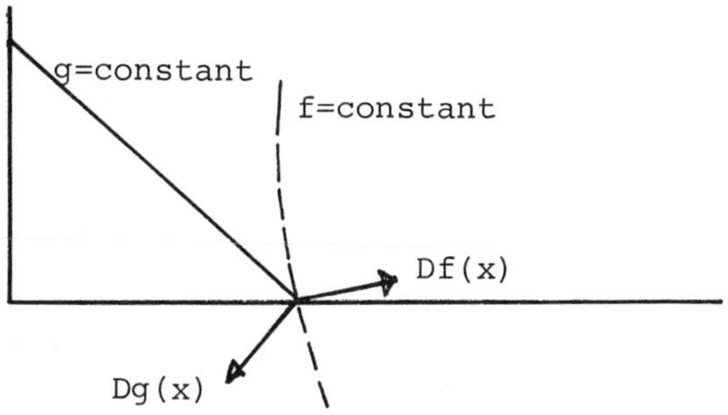

Fig.4.10.

We shall refer to this possibility as the boundary problem.

As we know we may represent the linear maps $df(x), dg(x)$ by the direction gradients, or vectors normal to the indifference surfaces, labelled $Df(x), Dg(x)$.

When $df(x), dg(x)$ satisfy $df(x)+\lambda dg(x) = 0$, $\lambda > 0$, then the direction gradients are positively dependent and satisfy $Df(x) + \lambda Dg(x) = 0$.

In the example $Df(x)$ and $Dg(x)$ are not positively dependent, yet x is a solution to the optimisation problem.

It is often common to make some boundary assumption so that the solution does not belong to the boundary of the feasible or admissible set Y.

In the more general optimisation problem $(f,g):Y \to \mathbb{R}^{m+1}$, the Kuhn Tucker theorem implies that a global saddle point (x^*, λ^*) to the

Lagrangian $L_\lambda(f,g) = f+\sum\lambda_i g_i$

gives a solution x* to the optimisation problem. Aside from the boundary problem, we may find the global maxima of $L_\lambda(f,g)$ by finding the critical points of $L_\lambda(f,g)$.

Thus we must choose x* such that

$$df(x^*) + \sum_{i=1}^{m} \lambda_i dg_i(x^*) = 0$$

Once a coordinate system is chosen this is equivalent to finding x*, and coefficients $\lambda_1,\ldots,\lambda_m$ all non-negative such that

$$Df(x^*) + \sum_{i=1}^{m} \lambda_i Dg_i(x^*) = 0.$$

The Kuhn Tucker theorem also showed that if x* is such that $g_i(x^*) > 0$ then $\lambda_i = 0$ and if $g_i(x^*) = 0$ then $\lambda_i > 0$.

Example 4.7

Maximise the function $f:\mathbb{R} \to \mathbb{R} : x \to x^2 : x \geq 0$

$x \to 0 : x < 0$

subject to $g_1(x) = x \geq 0$ and $g_2(x) = 1-x \geq 0$.

Now $L_\lambda(x) = x^2 + \lambda_1 x + \lambda_2(1-x)$;

$$\frac{\partial L}{\partial x} = 2x + \lambda_1 - \lambda_2 = 0, \quad \frac{\partial L}{\partial \lambda_1} = x = \frac{\partial L}{\partial \lambda_2} = 1-x=0.$$

Clearly these equations have no solution. By inspection the solution cannot satisfy $g_1(x) = 0$. Hence choose $\lambda_1 = 0$ and solve

$$L\lambda(x) = x^2 + \lambda(1-x).$$

Then $\frac{\partial L}{\partial x} = 2x - \lambda$, $\frac{\partial L}{\partial \lambda} = 1-x = 0$.

Thus $x = 1$ and $\lambda = 2$ is a solution.

Suppose now that $f,g_1,\ldots,g_m$ are all concave functions on the convex admissible set

$Y = \{x \in \mathbb{R}^n : x_i \geq 0, i=1,\ldots,n\}$.

Obviously if $z = \alpha y + (1-\alpha)x$

then $L_\lambda(f,g)(z) = f(z) + \sum_{i=1}^{m} \lambda_i g_i(z)$

$$\geq \alpha f(y) + (1-\alpha) f(x)$$

$$+ \sum_{i=1}^{m} \lambda_i \; [\alpha g_i(y) + (1-\alpha) g_i(x)]$$

$$= \alpha L_\lambda(f,g)(y) + (1-\alpha) L_\lambda(f,g)(x) .$$

Thus $L_\lambda(f,g)$ is a concave function.
By lemma 4.11, x^* is a global maximum of $L_\lambda(f,g)$ iff $dL(f,g)(x^*) = 0$ (aside from the boundary problem).

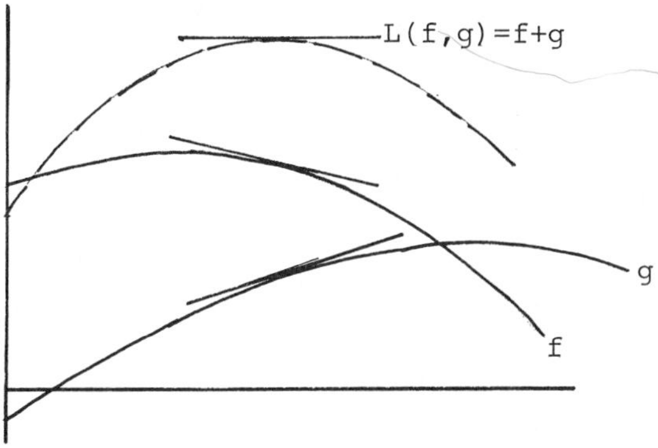

Fig.4.11.

For more general functions, to find the global maximum of the Lagrangian $L_\lambda(f,g)$, and thus the optimum to the problem (f,g), we find the critical points of $L_\lambda(f,g)$. Those critical points which have negative definite Hessian will then be local maxima of $L_\lambda(f,g)$. However we still have to examine critical points where the Hessian of the Lagrangian is negative semi-definite and then examine local maxima to find the global maxima. Even in this general case, any solution x^* to the problem (f,g) must be a global maximum for a suitably chosen Lagrangian $L_\lambda(f,g)$, and thus must satisfy the first order condition

$$Df(x^*) + \sum_{i=1}^{m} \lambda_i Dg_i(x^*) = 0$$

(again subject to the boundary problem).

Example 4.8

Maximise $f:\mathbb{R}^2 \to \mathbb{R}:(x,y) \to xy$
subject to the constraint $g(x,y) = 1-x^2-y^2 \geq 0$.
We seek a solution to the first order condition:

$$DL(x,y) = Df(x,y) + \lambda\, Dg(x,y) = 0.$$

Thus $(y,x) + \lambda(-2x,-2y) = 0$
or $\lambda = y/_{2x} = x/_{2y}$ so $x^2 = y^2$.
For $x = -y$, $\lambda < 0$ and so $Df(x,y) = |\lambda| Dg(x,y)$, (corresponding to a minimum of f on the feasible set $g(x,y) \geq 0$).
Thus we choose $x = y$ and $\lambda = \frac{1}{2}$.
For (x,y) on the boundary of the constraint set we require $1-x^2-y^2 = 0$. Hence $x=y= \pm \frac{1}{\sqrt{2}}$.
The Lagrangian is therefore $L=xy+\frac{1}{2}(1-x^2-y^2)$ with differential (with respect to x,y)

$$DL(x,y) = (y-x,x-y) \text{ and Hessian}$$

$$HL(x,y) = \begin{pmatrix} -1 & 1 \\ 1 & -1 \end{pmatrix}.$$

The eigenvalues of HL are -2,0 corresponding to eigenvectors (1,-1) and (1,1) respectively.
Hence HL is negative semi-definite, and so for example the point $\left(\frac{1}{\sqrt{2}}, \frac{1}{\sqrt{2}}\right)$ is a local maximum for the Lagrangian. As we have observed in Example 3.4(vi) the function $f(x,y) = xy$ is not quasi-concave on $\mathbb{R}^2$, and hence it is not the case that $P_f \subset H_f$. However on $\mathbb{R}^2_+ = \{(x,y) \in \mathbb{R}^2 : x \geq 0, y \geq 0\}$ f is quasi-concave, and so the optimality condition $H_g(x,y) \cap H_f(x,y) = \Phi$ is sufficient for an optimum.

Note also that $Df(x,y) = (y,x)$ and so the origin (0,0) is a critical point of f.
However setting $DL(x,y) = 0$ at $(x,y) = (0,0)$

to be a geometric object of dimension (m-1) "almost always". (See Smale, 1973). However $\overset{o}{\theta}(u)$ will contain points that are the "social" equivalents of the minima of a real-valued function.

For example consider Figure 4.20, of a two agent two commodity exchange economy.

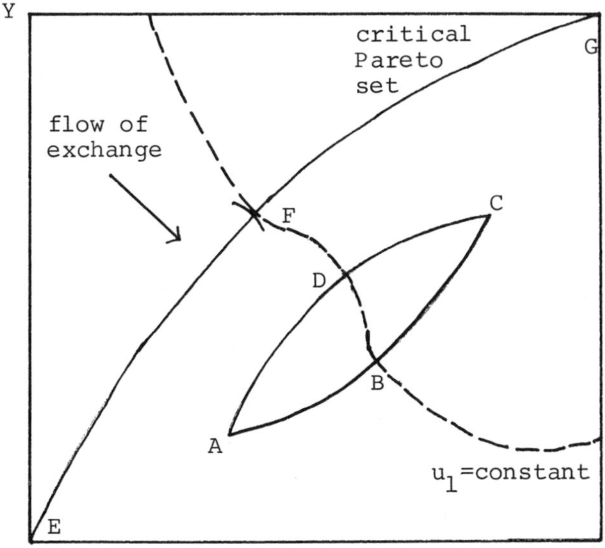

Fig.4.20.

Agent 1 has non-convex preference, and the critical Pareto set consists of three components ABC, ADC and EFG.

On ADC although the utilities satisfy the first order condition, there exist nearby points that both agents prefer.

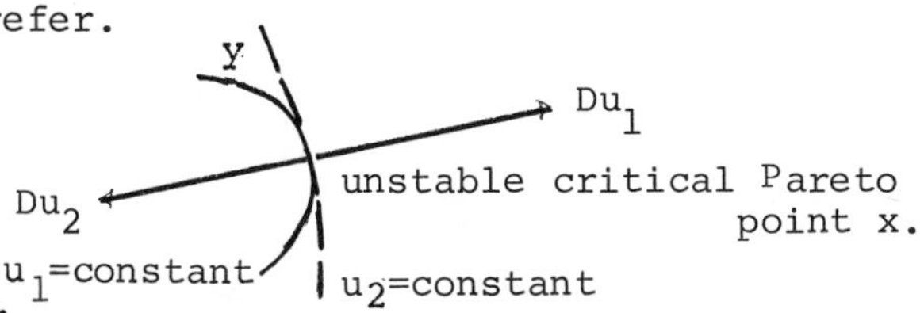

Fig.4.21.

Fig.4.22.

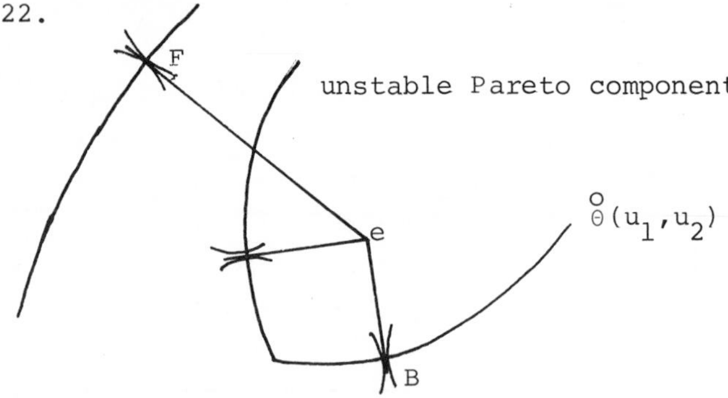

For example, both agents prefer a nearby point y to x. In Figure 4.22 from an initial endowment such as $e = (e_{11}, e_{12})$, there exists three Walrasian extended equilibria, but at least one can be excluded. Note that if e is the initial endowment vector, then the Walrasian equilibrium B which is accessible by exchange along the price vector may be Pareto inferior to a Walrasian equilibrium, F, which is not readily accessible.

Example 4.11

Consider the example due to Smale (1975). Let $Y = \mathbb{R}^2$ and suppose

$$u_1(x,y) = y - x^2$$

$$u_2(x,y) = \frac{-y}{x^2+1} .$$

Then

$$Du_1(x,y) = (-2x,1)$$

$$Du_2(x,y) = \left(\frac{2xy}{(x^2+1)^2}, \frac{-1}{x^2+1}\right) .$$

Let $DL_\lambda(x,y) = \lambda_1(-2x,1) + \lambda_2\left(\frac{2xy}{(x^2+1)^2}, \frac{-1}{x^2+1}\right)$.

Clearly one solution will be x = 0, in which case

$\lambda_1(0,1) + \lambda_2(0,-1) = 0$ or $\lambda_1 = \lambda_2 = 1.$

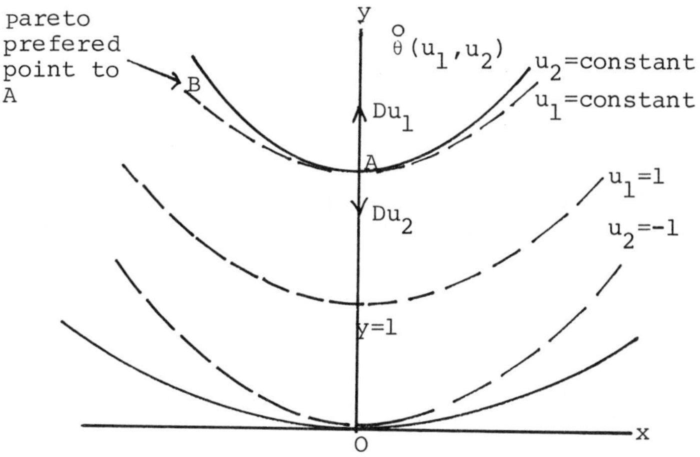

Fig. 4.23

The Hessian for L at x = 0 is then

$$HL(0,y) = D^2u_1(0,y) + D^2u_2(0,y)$$
$$= \begin{pmatrix} -2 & 0 \\ 0 & 0 \end{pmatrix} + \begin{pmatrix} 2y & 0 \\ 0 & 0 \end{pmatrix}$$

which is negative semi-definite for $2(y-1) < 0$ or $y < 1$.

It is also possible that individual utilities may not be defined simply on the commodity space X, but on the feasible space Y. In such situations of externalities or public goods, market exchange need not lead to Pareto optimal outcomes, and the problem of preference manipulation or the "free-rider problem" may occur in a severe form. The application of the differential procedures that have been outlined here to the study of such generalised economies is an exciting and rapidly developing field of mathematical economics.

Chapter 5
SINGULARITY THEORY AND GENERAL EQUILIBRIUM

In the last section of the previous chapter we introduced the critical Pareto set $\theta(u)$ of a smooth profile for a society, and the notion of a regular economy. Both ideas relied on the concept of a singularity of a smooth function $f:X \to \mathbb{R}^m$, where a singularity is a point analogous to the critical point of a real-valued function.

In this short and final chapter we introduce the fundamental result in singularity theory, that the set of singularity points of a smooth function almost always has a particular geometric structure, and then go on to use this result to discuss Smale's Theorem on the generic existence of regular economies. We shall make no effort to prove these results, but rather aim at providing some geometric understanding of the ideas behind the theorems. References are given in the text to the original sources.

5.1 SINGULARITY THEORY

In chapter 4 we showed that when $f:X \to \mathbb{R}$ was a C^2-function on a normed vector space, then knowledge of the first and second differential of f at a critical point gave information about the local behaviour (near x) of the function. In this section we discuss the case of a differentiable function $f:X \to Y$ between general normed vector spaces, and consider regular points (where the differential has maximal rank) and singularity points (where the differential has non-maximal rank). For both kinds of points we can characterise the behaviour of the function in a topological sense.

5.1.1. Regular Points: The Inverse and Implicit Function Theorems

Suppose that $f:X \to Y$ is a function between normed vector spaces and that for all x' in a neighbourhood U of the point x the differential df(x') is defined. By the results of §3.2, if df(x') is bounded, or if X is finite-dimensional, then df(x') will be a continuous linear function. Suppose now that X and Y have the same finite dimension (n) and df(x') has rank n at all $x' \in U$. Then we know that $df(x')^{-1}: Y \to X$ is a linear map and thus continuous. We shall call f a C^1-diffeomorphism on U in this case.

In general, when Y is an infinite-dimensional vector space, even when $df(x')^{-1}$ exists it need not be continuous. However when X and Y are complete, normed vector spaces then the existence of $df(x')^{-1}$ is sufficient to guarantee that $df(x')^{-1}$ is continuous.

Here a normed vector space X is called complete iff any sequence (x_n) converges to a point in X. More formally a Cauchy sequence is a sequence (x_n) such that for any $\varepsilon > 0$ there exists some number

$n(\varepsilon)$ such that $r,s > n(\varepsilon)$ implies that $\|x_r - x_s\| < \varepsilon$. If (x_n) is a sequence with a limit x_o in X then clearly (x_n) must be a Cauchy sequence. On the other hand a Cauchy sequence need not in general converge to a point in the space X. If <u>every</u> Cauchy sequence has a limit in X, then X is called <u>complete</u>. A complete normed vector space is called a <u>Banach</u> space. Clearly $\mathbb{R}^n$ is a Banach space. Suppose now that X,Y are normed vector spaces of the same dimension, $f:U \subset X \to Y$ is a C^r-differentiable function on U, and df(x) has a continuous inverse $[df(x)]^{-1}$ at x. We call f a C^r-diffeomorphism at x. Then we can show that f has an inverse $f^{-1}:f(U) \to U$ with differential $df^{-1}(f(x)) = [df(x)]^{-1}$. Moreover there exists a neighbourhood V of x in U such that f is a C^r-diffeomorphism on V. In particular this means that f has an inverse $f^{-1}:f(V) \to V$ with continuous differential $df^{-1}(f(x')) = [df(x')]^{-1}$ for all $x' \in V$, <u>and</u> that f^{-1} is C^r-differentiable on V. To prove the theorem we need to ensure that $[df(x)]^{-1}$ is not only linear but continuous, and it is sufficient to assume X and Y are Banach spaces.

<u>Inverse Function Theorem</u>

Suppose $f:U \subset X \to Y$ is C^r-differentiable, where X and Y are Banach spaces of dimension n. Suppose that the linear map $df(x):X \to Y$, for $x \in U$, is an isomorphism with inverse $[df(x)]^{-1}:Y \to X$. Then there exists open neighbourhoods V of x in U and V' of f(x) such that $f:V \to V'$ is a bijection with inverse $f^{-1}:V' \to V$. Moreover f^{-1} is itself C^r-differentiable on V', and for all $x' \in V$, $df^{-1}(f(x')) = [df(x')]^{-1}$. f is called a <u>local</u>

C^r-diffeomorphism.

Outline of Proof

Let $t = df(x):X \to Y$. Since $[df(x)]^{-1}$ exists and is continuous, $t^{-1}:Y \to X$ is linear and continuous.

It is possible to choose a neighbourhood V' of f(x) in f(U) and a closed ball V in U centred at x, such that, for each $y \in V'$, the function $g_y:V \subset U \subset X \to V \subset X$ defined by $g_y(x') = x' - t^{-1}[f(x') - y]$ has a fixed point.

That is to say for each $y \in V'$, there exists $x' \in V$ such that $g_y(x') = x'$. But then $t^{-1}[f(x')-y] = 0$. Since, by hypothesis, t^{-1} is an isomorphism, its kernel = {0}, and so f(x') = y. Thus for each $y \in V'$ we establish $g_y(x') = x'$ is equivalent to $f(x') = y$. Define $f^{-1}(y) = g_y(x') = x'$, which gives the inverse function on V'. To show f^{-1} is differentiable proceed as follows.

Note that $dg_y(x') = Id - t^{-1} \circ df(x')$, is independent of y. Now $dg_y(x')$ is a linear and continuous function from X to X and is thus bounded. Since X is Banach, it is possible to show that $\mathcal{L}(X,X)$, the set of continuous maps from X to X, is also Banach. Thus if $u \in \mathcal{L}(X,X)$ so is $(Id-u)^{-1}$.

Now $dg_y(x') \in \mathcal{L}(X,X)$ and so $(Id-dg_y(x'))^{-1} \in \mathcal{L}(X,X)$. But then $t^{-1} \circ df(x')$ has a continuous linear inverse. Now $t^{-1} \circ df(x'):X \to Y \to X$ and t^{-1} has a continuous linear inverse. Thus df(x') has a continuous linear inverse, for all $x' \in V$.

This is the fundamental theorem of differential calculus. Notice that the theorem asserts that if $f:\mathbb{R}^n \to \mathbb{R}^n$ and df(x) has rank n at x, then df(x') has rank n for all x' in a neighbourhood of x.

Example 5.1

i) For a simple example, consider the function $\exp:\mathbb{R} \to \mathbb{R}_+ : x \to e^x$. Clearly for any finite $x \in \mathbb{R}$, $d(\exp)(x) = e^x \neq 0$, and so the rank of the differential is 1. The inverse $\phi:\mathbb{R}_+ \to \mathbb{R}$ must satisfy

$$d\phi(y) = [d(\exp)(x)]^{-1} = \frac{1}{e^x}$$

where $y = \exp(x) = e^x$. Thus $d\phi(y) = \frac{1}{y}$.

Clearly ϕ must be the function $\log_e : y \to \log_e y$.

ii) Consider $\sin: (0,2\pi) \to [-1,+1]$.

Now $d(\sin)(x) = \cos x$.

If $x \neq \frac{\pi}{2}$ or $\frac{3\pi}{2}$ then $d(\sin)(x) \neq 0$. Hence there exists neighbourhoods V of x and V' of sin x and an inverse $\phi:V' \to V$ such that

$$d\phi(y) = \frac{1}{\cos x} = \frac{1}{\sqrt{1-y^2}} .$$

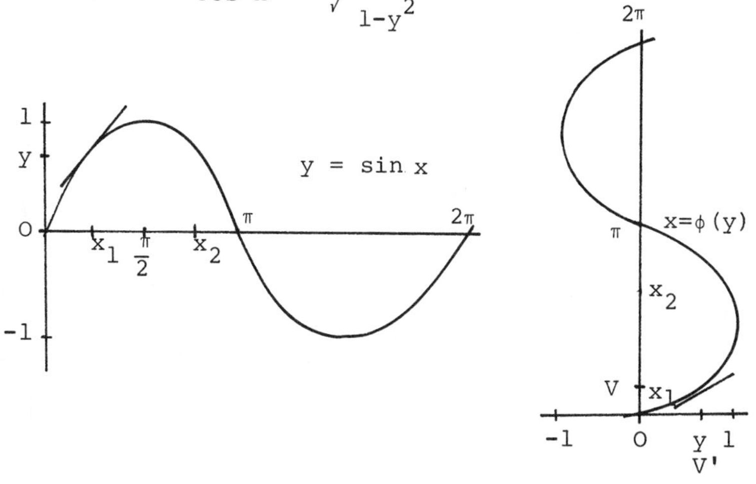

Fig. 5.1

This inverse ϕ is only locally a function. As Figure 5.1 makes clear even when sin x = y, there exists distinct values x_1, x_2 such that $\sin(x_1) =$

$\sin(x_2) = y$.

However $d(\sin)(x_1) \neq d(\sin)(x_2)$.

The figure also shows that there is a neighbourhood V' of y such that $\phi: V' \to V$ is single-valued and differentiable on V'. Suppose now $x = \pi/_2$. Then $d(\sin)(\frac{\pi}{2}) = 0$. Moreover there is no neighbourhood V of $\Pi/_2$ such that $\sin: (\pi/_2 - \varepsilon, \pi/_2 + \varepsilon) = V \to V'$ has an inverse function.

Note one further consequence of the theorem .

For h small, we may write

$$f(x+h) = f(x) + df(x) \circ [df(x)]^{-1} (f(x+h) - f(x)).$$

$$= f(x) + df(x)\psi(h)$$

where $\psi(h) = [df(x)]^{-1}(f(x+h) - f(x))$.

Now by a linear change of coordinates we can diagonalise $df(x)$. So that in the case $f = (f_1, \ldots, f_n): \mathbb{R}^n \to \mathbb{R}^n$ we can ensure $\left.\frac{\partial f_i}{\partial x_j}\right|_x = \partial_{ij}$ where $\partial_{ij} = 1$ if $i=j$ and 0 if $i \neq j$.

Hence $f(x+h) = f(x) + (\psi_1(h), \ldots, \psi_n(h))$.

There is therefore a C^r-diffeomorphic change of coordinates ϕ near x such that $\phi(\underline{0}) = x$ and

$$f(\phi(h_1, \ldots, h_n)) = f(x) + (h_1, \ldots, h_n).$$

In other words by choosing coordinates appropriately f may be represented by its linear differential.

Suppose now that $f: U \subset \mathbb{R}^n \to \mathbb{R}^m$ is a C^1-function. The maximal rank of df at a point x in U is min(n,m), and if indeed df(x) has maximal rank then x is called a <u>regular point</u> of f, and f(x) a <u>regular value</u>. In this case we write $x \in S_0(f)$.

The inverse function theorem showed that when $n=m$ and $x \in S_0(f)$ then f could be regarded as an identity function near x.

In particular this means that there is a neighbourhood U of x such that $f^{-1}[f(x)] \cap U = \{x\}$ is an isolated point.

In the case that $n \neq m$ then we use the inverse function theorem to characterise f at regular points.

<u>Implicit Function Theorem for Vector Spaces</u>

i) (Surjective Version) Suppose that $f: U \subset \mathbb{R}^n \to \mathbb{R}^m, n \geq m$, and rank $(df(x)) = m$, with $f(x) = \underline{0}$ for convenience. If f is C^r-differentiable at x, then there exists a C^r-diffeomorphism $\phi: \mathbb{R}^n \to \mathbb{R}^n$ on a neighbourhood of the origin such that

$$\phi(\underline{0}) = x$$

and $f \circ \phi(h_1, \ldots, h_n) = (h_1, \ldots, h_m)$.

ii) (Injective Version) If $f: U \subset \mathbb{R}^n \to \mathbb{R}^m$, $n \leq m$, rank $df(x) = n$, with $f(\underline{0}) = p$, and f is C^r-differentiable at x then there exists a C^r-diffeomorphism $\psi: \mathbb{R}^m \to \mathbb{R}^m$ such that $\psi(p) = \underline{0}$ and

$$\psi f(h_1, \ldots, h_n) = (h_1, \ldots, h_n, 0 \ldots, 0).$$

<u>Proof</u>

i) Now $df(x) = [B \quad C]$, with respect to some coordinate system, where B is an $(m \times m)$ non singular matrix and C is an $(n-m) \times m$ matrix.

Define $F: \mathbb{R}^n \to \mathbb{R}^n$ by

$$F(x_1, \ldots, x_n) = (f(x_1, \ldots, x_n), x_{m+1}, \ldots, x_n).$$

Clearly $DF(x)$ has rank n, and by the inverse function theorem there exists an inverse ϕ to F near x.

Hence $F \circ \phi(h_1, \ldots, h_n) = (h_1, \ldots, h_n)$.

But then $f \circ \phi(h_1, \ldots, h_n) = (h_1, \ldots, h_m)$.

Part (ii) follows similarly.

As an application of the theorem, suppose $f:\mathbb{R}^m \times \mathbb{R}^{n-m} \to \mathbb{R}^m$. Write x for a vector in $\mathbb{R}^m$, and y for a vector in $\mathbb{R}^{n-m}$, and let $df(x,y) = [B \quad C]$ where B is an m x m matrix and C is an (n-m) x m matrix. Suppose that B is invertible, at $(\bar{x},\bar{y})$, and that $f(\bar{x},\bar{y}) = 0$. Then the implicit function theorem implies that there exists an open neighbourhood U of $\bar{y}$ in $\mathbb{R}^{n-m}$ and a differentiable function $g:U \to \mathbb{R}^m$ such that $g(y') = x'$ and $f(g(y'),y') = 0$ for all $y' \in V$.

To see this define $F:\mathbb{R}^m \times \mathbb{R}^{n-m} \to \mathbb{R}^m \times \mathbb{R}^{n-m}$ by $F(x,y) = (f(x,y),y)$.

Clearly $dF(\bar{x},\bar{y}) = \begin{bmatrix} B & C \\ O & I \end{bmatrix}$ and so $dF(\bar{x},\bar{y})$ is invertible. Thus there exists a neighbourhood V of $(\bar{x},\bar{y})$ in $\mathbb{R}^n$ on which F has a diffeomorphic inverse G. Now $F(\bar{x},\bar{y}) = (0,\bar{y})$. So there is a neighbourhood V' of $(0,\bar{y})$ and a neighbourhood V of $(\bar{x},\bar{y})$ s.t. $G:V \subset \mathbb{R}^n \to V' \subset \mathbb{R}^n$ is a diffeomorphism.

Let $g(y')$ be the x coordinate of $G(0,y')$ for all y' such that $(0,y') \in V'$.

Clearly $g(y')$ satisfies $G(0,y') = (g(y'),y')$ and so

$$F \circ G(0,y') = F(g(y'),y') = (f(g(y'),y'),y') = (0,y').$$

Now if $(x,y') \in V'$ then $y' \in U$ where U is open in $\mathbb{R}^{n-m}$. Hence for all $y' \in U$, $g(y')$ satisfies $f(g(y'),y') = 0$. Since G is differentiable, so must be $g:U \subset \mathbb{R}^{n-m} \to \mathbb{R}^m$. Hence $x'=g(y')$ <u>solves</u> $f(x',y')=0$.

Example 5.2

i) Let $f:\mathbb{R}^3 \to \mathbb{R}^2$ where $f_1(x,y,z)=x^2+y^2+z^2-3$
$f_2(x,y,z)=x^3y^3z^3-x+y-z$.

At $(x,y,z) = (1,1,1)$, $f_1=f_2=0$.

We seek a function $g: \mathbb{R} \to \mathbb{R}^2$ such that $f(g_1(z), g_2(z), z) = 0$ for all z in a neighbourhood of 1.

Now $df(x,y,z) = \begin{pmatrix} 2x & 2y & 2z \\ 3x^2y^3z^3-1 & 3x^3y^2z^3+1 & 3x^3y^3z^2-1 \end{pmatrix}$

and so $df(1,1,1) = \begin{pmatrix} 2 & 2 & 2 \\ 2 & 4 & 2 \end{pmatrix}$.

The matrix $\begin{pmatrix} 2 & 2 \\ 2 & 4 \end{pmatrix}$ is non-singular.

Hence there exists a diffeomorphism $G: \mathbb{R}^3 \to \mathbb{R}^3$ such that $G(0,0,1) = (1,1,1)$, and $G(0,0,z') = (g_1(z'), g_2(z'), z')$ for z' near 1.

ii) In a simpler example suppose

$f: \mathbb{R}^2 \to \mathbb{R} : (x,y) \to (x-a)^2 + (y-b)^2 - 25 = 0$,

and $df(x,y) = (2(x-a), 2(y-b))$.

Now let $F(x,y) = (x, f(x,y))$, where $F: \mathbb{R}^2 \to \mathbb{R}^2$, and suppose $y \neq b$.

Then $dF(x,y) = \begin{pmatrix} 1 & 0 \\ \frac{\partial f}{\partial x} & \frac{\partial f}{\partial y} \end{pmatrix}$

$= \begin{pmatrix} 1 & 0 \\ 2(x-a) & 2(y-b) \end{pmatrix}$

with inverse $dG(x,y) = \frac{1}{2(y-b)} \begin{pmatrix} 2(y-b) & 0 \\ -2(x-a) & 1 \end{pmatrix}$.

Define $g(x')$ to be the y-coordinate of $G(x',0)$.

Then $F \circ G(x',0) = F(x', g(x')) = F(x', f(x',y')) = (x',0)$, and so $y' = g(x')$ for $f(x',y') = 0$ and y' sufficiently close to y.

Now $\left.\frac{dg}{dx}\right|_{x'} = \left.\frac{dG_2}{\partial x}\right|_{(x',g')} = -\frac{(x'-a)}{(y'-b)}$.

Note that in Example 5.2(i), the "solution" $g(z) = (x,y)$ to the smooth constraint $f(x,y,z) = 0$ is, in a topological sense, a one-dimensional object.

In the same way in example 5.2(ii) the solution $y = g(x)$ is a one-dimensional object.

More specifically say that an open set V in $\mathbb{R}^n$ is an r-dimensional smooth manifold iff there exists a diffeomorphism $\phi: V \subset \mathbb{R}^n \to U \subset \mathbb{R}^r$.

When $f: \mathbb{R}^n \to \mathbb{R}^m$ and rank $(df(x)) = m \leq n$ then say that f is a submersion at x.
If rank $(df(x)) = n \leq m$ then say f is an immersion at x.

Suppose now that $f: X^n \to Y^m$ is a map between the smooth manifolds X,Y. Since X and Y can be "embedded" in Euclidean spaces they inherit appropriate topologies. In this fashion we may determine whether f has a differential df at each point in X (See Chillingsworth,1976, for the full details). If the differential df is continuous at every $x \in X$ then we shall write $f \in C_1(X,Y)$ and, as before call f a C^1-map. The implicit function theorem also holds for members of $C_1(X,Y)$.

Implicit function theorem for manifolds

Suppose that $f: X^n \to Y^m$ is a C^1-function between smooth manifolds of dimension n,m respectively.

i) if $n \geq m$ and f is a submersion at x (ie rank $df(x) = m$) then $f^{-1}(f(x))$ is (locally) a smooth manifold in X of dimension (n-m).
Moreover, if Z is a manifold in Y^n of dimension r, and f is a submersion at each point in $f^{-1}(Z)$ then $f^{-1}(Z)$ is a submanifold of X of dimension n-m+r.

ii) if $n \leq m$ and f is an immersion at x (ie rank $df(x) = n$) then there is a neighbourhood U of x in X such that f(U) is an n-dimensional manifold in Y and in particular f(U) is open in Y.

The proof of this theorem is considerably beyond the scope of this book, but the interested reader should look at Golubitsky and Guillemin (1973, page 9) or Hirsch (1976,page 22).
This theorem is a smooth analogue of the isomorphism theorem for linear functions given in §2.2. For a linear function $T:\mathbb{R}^n \to \mathbb{R}^m$ when $n \geq m$ and T is surjective, then $T^{-1}(y)$ has the form x_0+K where K is the (n-m)-dimensional kernel.
Conversely if $T:\mathbb{R}^n \to \mathbb{R}^m$ and $n \leq m$ when T is injective then image(T) is an n-dimensional subspace of $\mathbb{R}^m$. More particularly if U is an n-dimensional open set in $\mathbb{R}^n$ then T(U) is also an n-dimensional open set in $\mathbb{R}^m$.

Example 5.3

To illustrate, consider example 5.2(ii) again. When $y \neq b$, df has rank 1 and so there exists a "local" solution $y' = g(x')$ such that $f(x',g(x'))=0$. In other words

$$f^{-1}(0) = \{(x',g(x')) \in \mathbb{R}^2 : x' \in U\},$$

which essentially is a copy of U but deformed in $\mathbb{R}^2$. Thus $f^{-1}(0)$ is "locally" a one-dimensional manifold. Indeed the set $S^1 = \{(x,y):f(x,y) = 0\}$ itself is a 1-dimensional manifold in $\mathbb{R}^2$.
If $y \neq b$, and $(x,y) \in S^1$ then there is a neighbourhood U of x and a diffeomorphism $g:S^1 \to \mathbb{R} : (x',y') \to g(y')$ and this parametrises S^1 near (x,y).
If $y=b$, then we can do the same thing through a local solution $x' = h(y')$ satisfying $f(h(y'),y') = 0$.

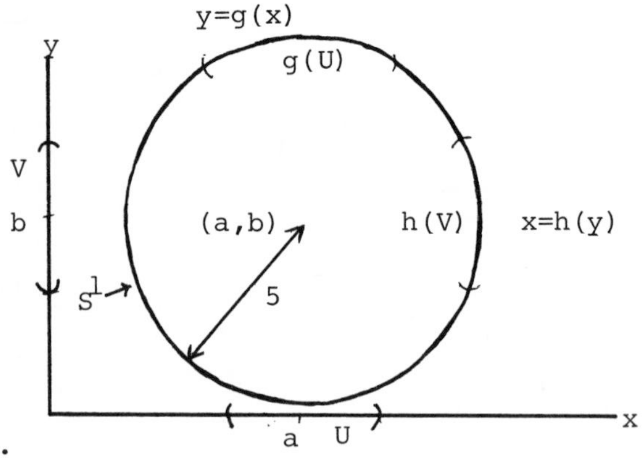

Fig.5.2.

5.1.2. Singular Points and Transversality

When $f:X^n \to Y^m$ is a C^1-function between smooth manifolds, and rank $df(x)$ is maximal $(=\min(n,m))$ then as before write $x \in S_o(f)$.
The set of singular points of f is $S(f) = X \setminus S_o(f)$.
Let $z = \min(n,m)$ and say that x is a corank r singularity, or $x \in S_r(f)$, if rank $(df(x)) = z-r$.

Clearly $S(f) = \bigcup_{r>1} S_r(f)$.

In this section we shall examine the corank r singularity sets of a C^1-function and show that they have a nice geometric structure.

In the case of a C^2-function $f:X^n \to \mathbb{R}$, either x will be regular (in $S_o(f)$) or a critical point (in $S_1(f)$) where $df(x) = 0$. We called a critical point of f non-degenerate iff $d^2f(x)$ is non-singular. A C^2-function all of whose critical points are non degenerate is called a Morse function. A Morse function can be locally characterised near a critical point.

A local system of coordinates at a point x in X

is a smooth assignment

$y \overset{\phi}{\to} (h_1,\ldots,h_n)$ for every y in some neighbourhood U of x in X.

Lemma 5.1 (Morse)

If $f:X^n \to \mathbb{R}$ is C^2 and x is a non-degenerate critical point of index k, then there exists a local system of coordinates at x such that f is given by

$$y \overset{\phi}{\to} (h_1,\ldots,h_n) \overset{g}{\to} f(x) - \sum_{i=1}^{k} h_1^2 + \sum_{i=k+1}^{n} h_i^2 .$$

As before the index of the critical point is the number of negative eigenvalues of the Hessian Hf at x. The C^2-function g has Hessian

$$Hg(0) = \begin{pmatrix} -2 & & & & \\ & \ddots & & & \\ & & -2 & & \\ & & & 2 & \\ & & & & \ddots \end{pmatrix}$$

with k negative eigenvalues. Essentially the Morse lemma implies that when x is a non-degenerate critical point of f then f is topologically equivalent to the function g with a similar Hessian at the point.

If f is a Morse function then all its critical points are non-degenerate. Moreover if $x \in S_1(f)$ then there exists a neighbourhood U of x such that x is the only critical point of f in U.

To see this note that for $y \in U$,

$df(y) = dg(h_1,\ldots,h_n) = (-2h_1,\ldots,2h_n) = 0$ iff $h_1 = \ldots = h_n = 0$, or $y = x$. Thus each critical point of f is isolated, and so $S_1(f)$ is the union of a set of isolated points and thus a zero-dimensional object.

As we shall see almost any smooth function

can be approximated arbitrarily closely by a Morse function.

To examine the regular points of a differentiable function $f:X \to \mathbb{R}$, we have the Sard lemma.

First of all a set V in a topological space X is called <u>nowhere dense</u> if its closure, clos(V), contains no non-empty open set. Alternatively $X \setminus \text{clos}(V)$ is dense.
If X is a complete metric space then the union of a countable collection of closed nowhere dense sets is nowhere dense. This also means that a residual set (the intersection of a countable collection of open dense sets) is dense. See §3.1.2.
A set V is of <u>measure zero</u> in X iff for any $\varepsilon > 0$ there exists a family of cubes, with volume less than ε, covering V. If V is closed, of measure zero, then it is nowhere dense.

<u>Lemma 5.2</u> (Sard)

If $f:X^n \to \mathbb{R}$ is a C^r-map where $r \geq n$, then the set $f(S_1(f))$ of critical values of f has measure zero in $\mathbb{R}$. Thus $f(S_0(f))$, the set of regular values of f, is the countable intersection of open dense sets and thus dense.

To illustrate this consider Figure 5.3.

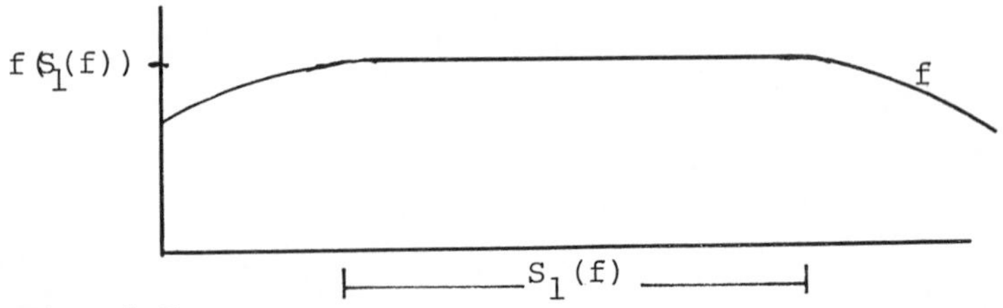

Fig. 5.3

f is a quasi-concave C^1-function $f:\mathbb{R} \to \mathbb{R}$. The set of critical points of f, namely $S_1(f)$, clearly does not have measure zero, since $S_1(f)$ has a non-empty interior. Thus f is not a Morse function. However $f(S_1(f))$ is an isolated point in the image.

Example 5.4

To illustrate the Morse lemma let $Z = S^1 \times S^1$ be the torus (the skin of a doughnut) and let $f:Z \to \mathbb{R}$ be the height function

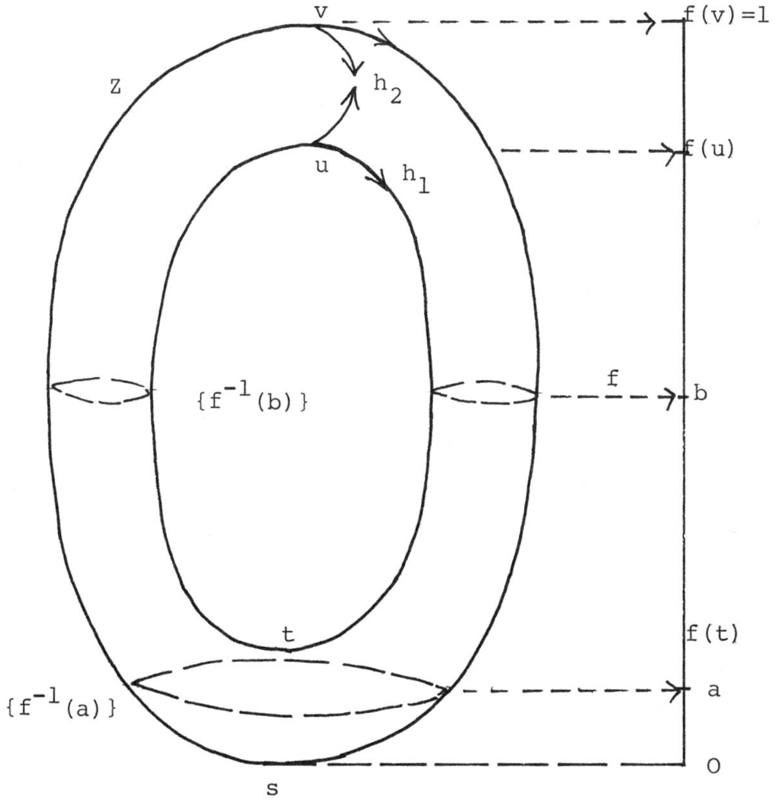

Fig. 5.4

Point s, at the bottom of the torus, is a minimum of the function, and so the index of s = 0.
Let f(s) = 0.
Then near s, f can be represented by

$$(h_1,h_2) \rightarrow 0 + h_1^2 + h_2^2$$

Note that the Hessian of f at s is $\begin{bmatrix} 2 & 0 \\ 0 & 2 \end{bmatrix}$,

and so is positive definite.
The next critical point, t, is clearly a saddle, with index 1, and so we can write

$$(h_1,h_2) \rightarrow f(t) + h_1^2 - h_2^2 .$$

Again $Hf(t) = \begin{bmatrix} 2 & 0 \\ 0 & -2 \end{bmatrix}$.

Suppose now that $a \in (f(s),f(t))$. Clearly a is a regular value, and so any point $x \in Z$ satisfying $f(x) = a$ is a regular point, and f is a submersion at x. By the implicit function theorem $f^{-1}(a)$ is a one-dimensional manifold. Indeed it is a single copy of the circle, S^1.

The next critical point is the saddle, u, near which f is represented as

$$(h_1,h_2) \rightarrow f(u) - h_1^2 + h_2^2.$$

Now for $b \in (f(t),f(u))$, $f^{-1}(b)$ is a one-dimensional manifold, but this time it is <u>two</u> copies of S^1.
Finally v is a local maximum and f is represented near v by

$$(h_1,h_2) \rightarrow f(v) - h_1^2 - h_2^2.$$

To examine the singularity set S(f) of a smooth function $f:X \rightarrow Y$ we introduce the idea of <u>transversality</u>.

A linear manifold V in $\mathbb{R}^n$ of dimension v is of the form $x_0 + K$, where K is a vector subspace of

$\mathbb{R}^n$ of dimension v. Intuitively if V and W are linear manifolds in $\mathbb{R}^n$ of dimension v,w then they typically will not intersect if $v+w \leq n$.
On the other hand if $v+w \geq n$ then $V \cap W$ will typically be of dimension v+w-n.
For example two lines in $\mathbb{R}^2$ will intersect in a point of dimension 1+1-2.
Another way of expressing this is to define the codimension of V in $\mathbb{R}^n$ to be n-v. Then the codimension of $V \cap W$ in W will typically be $w-(v+w-n) = n-v$, the same codimension.

Suppose now that $f: X^n \to Y^m$ where X,Y are vector spaces of dimension n,m respectively.
Let Z be an z-dimensional linear manifold in Y.
Say that f is transversal to Z iff for all $x \in X$, either i) $f(x) \notin Z$ or ii) the image of df(x), regarded as a vector subspace of Y^m, together with Z span Y. In this case write $f \pitchfork Z$.
The same idea can be extended to the case when X,Y,Z are all manifolds. Wherever $f \pitchfork Z$ then if $x \in f^{-1}(Z)$, f will be a submersion at x, and so $f^{-1}(Z)$ will be a smooth manifold in X of codimension equal to the codimension of Z in Y. Another way of interpreting this is that the number of constraints which determine Z in Y will be equal to the number of constraints which determine $f^{-1}(Z)$ in X.
Thus $\dim(f^{-1}(Z)) = n - (m-z)$.

In the previous chapter we put a topology - the Whitney C^p-topology - on the set of C^p-differentiable maps $X^n \to Y^m$, and called this $C^p(X,Y)$. In this topological space a residual set is dense. The fundamental theorem of singularity theory is that transversal intersection is generic.

Thom Transversality Theorem

Let X^n, Y^m be manifolds and Z^z a submanifold of Y. Then the set

$$\{f \in C_p(X,Y) : f \pitchfork Z\} = \pitchfork(X,Y;Z)$$

is a residual (and thus dense) set in the topological space $C^p(X,Y)$.

Note that if $f \in \pitchfork(X,Y;Z)$ then $f^{-1}(Z)$ will be a manifold in X of dimension n-m+z.
Moreover if $g \in C_p(X,Y)$ but g is not transversal to Z, then there exists some C^p-map, as near to g as we please in the C^p topology, which is transversal to Z. Thus transversal intersection is typical or generic.
Suppose now that $f: X^n \to Y^m$, and corank df(x) = r, so rank df(x) = min(n,m) - r. In this case we said that $x \in S_r(f)$, the corank r singularity set of f. We seek to show that $S_r(f)$ is a manifold in X, and compute its dimension.

Suppose X^n, Y^m are vector spaces. As before $\mathcal{L}(X,Y)$ is the normed vector space of linear maps from X to Y. Let $\mathcal{L}_r(X,Y)$ be the subset of $\mathcal{L}(X,Y)$ consisting of linear maps with corank r.

Lemma 5.3

$\mathcal{L}_r(X,Y)$ is a submanifold of $\mathcal{L}(X,Y)$ of codimension (n-z+r)(m-z+r) where z=min(n,m).

Proof

Choose bases such that a corank r linear map S is represented by a matrix $\begin{pmatrix} A & B \\ C & D \end{pmatrix}$

where rank(A) = k = z-r.
Let U be a neighbourhood of S in $\mathcal{L}(X,Y)$, such that for all $S' \in U$, corank(S') = r.

Define $F: U \to \mathcal{L}(\mathbb{R}^{n-k}, \mathbb{R}^{m-k})$ by

$$F(S') = D' - C'(A')^{-1}B'.$$

Now $S' \varepsilon F^{-1}(0)$ iff $\text{rank}(S') = k$, where O is the zero map. The codimension of O in $\mathcal{L}(\mathbb{R}^{n-k}, \mathbb{R}^{m-k})$ is $(n-k)(m-k)$. Since F is a submersion $F^{-1}(0) = \mathcal{L}_r(X,Y)$ is of codimension

$$(n-z+r)(m-z+r)$$

Now if $f \in C_p(X,Y)$, then $df \in C_{p-1}(X, \mathcal{L}(X,Y))$. If $df(x) \in \mathcal{L}_r(X,Y)$ then $x \in S_r(f)$. By the Thom Transversality Theorem, there is a residual set in $C^{p-1}(X, \mathcal{L}(X,Y))$ such that $df(x)$ is transversal to $\mathcal{L}_r(X,Y)$. But then $S_r(f) = df^{-1}(\mathcal{L}_r(X,Y))$ is a submanifold of X of codimension $(n-z+r)(m-z+r)$. Thus we have:

<u>The Singularity Theorem</u>

There is a residual set V in $C^p(X,Y)$ such that for all $f \in V$, the corank r singularity set of f is a submanifold in X of codimension $(n-z+r)(m-z+r)$.

If $f: X^n \to \mathbb{R}$ then $\text{codim } S_1(f) = (n-1+m)(1-1+1) = n$. Hence generically the set of critical points will be zero-dimensional, and so critical points will be isolated. Now a Morse function has isolated, non-degenerate critical points. Let $M^p(X)$ be the set of Morse functions with the topology induced from $C^p(X, \mathbb{R})$.

<u>Morse Theorem</u>

The set $M^p(X)$ of C^p-differentiable Morse functions with non-degenerate critical points, is an open dense set in $C^p(X, \mathbb{R})$. Moreover if $f \in M^p(X)$, then the critical points of f are isolated.

More generally if $f:X^n \to Y^m$ with $m \leq n$ then in the generic case, $S_1(f)$ is of codimension $(n-m+1)(m-m+1) = n-m+1$ in X and so $S_1(f)$ will be of dimension $(m-1)$.

Suppose now that $n > 2m-4$, and $n \geq m$. Then $2n-2m+4 > n$ and so $r(n-m+r) > n$ for $r \geq 2$. But codimension $(S_r(f)) = r(n-m+r)$, and since codimension $(S_r(f)) >$ dimension X, $S_r(f) = \Phi$ for $r \geq 2$.

Submanifold Theorem

If Z^z is a submanifold of Y^m and $z < m$ then Z is nowhere dense in Y (here $z = \dim(Z)$ and $m = \dim(Y)$).

In the case $n \geq m$, the singularity set $S(f)$ will generically consist of a union of the various co-rank r singularity submanifolds, for $r \geq 1$. The highest dimension of these is $m-1$. We shall call a $S(f)$ a stratified manifold of dimension $(m-1)$. Note also that $S(f)$ will then be nowhere dense in X. We also require the following theorem.

Morse Sard Theorem

If $f:X^n \to Y^m$ is a C^p-map, where $p > n-m$, then $f(S(f))$ has measure zero in Y and $f(S_o(f))$ is residual and therefore dense in Y.

We are now in a position to apply these results to the critical Pareto set. Suppose then that $u = (u_1,\ldots,u_m):X^n \to \mathbb{R}^m$ is a smooth profile on the manifold of feasible states X.
Say $x \in \overset{o}{\theta}(u_1,\ldots,u_m) = \overset{o}{\theta}(u)$ iff $dL(\lambda,u)(x) = 0$

where $L(\lambda,u) = \sum_{i=1}^{m} \lambda_i u_i$ and $\lambda \in \overline{\mathbb{R}^m_+}$.

By lemma 4.21, $\theta(u)$ contains $\overset{o}{\theta}(u)$ but possibly also contains further points on the boundary of X. However we shall regard $\overset{o}{\theta}(u)$ as the differential analogue of the Pareto set. By lemma 4.19, $\overset{o}{\theta}(u)$ must be closed in X. Moreover when $n \geq m$ then the differentials $\{du_i(x) : i \in M\}$ must be linearly dependent. Hence $\overset{o}{\theta}(u)$ must belong to S(u). But also S(u) will be nowhere dense in X. Thus we obtain the following theorem (Smale, 1973).

<u>Pareto Theorem</u>

There exists a residual set U in $C^1(X,\mathbb{R}^m)$, for $\dim(X) \geq m$, such that for any profile $u \in V$, the closed critical Pareto set $\overset{o}{\theta}(u)$ belongs to the nowhere dense stratified singularity manifold S(u) of dimension (m-1). Moreover if $\dim(X) > 2m-4$, then $\theta(u)$ is itself a manifold of dimension (m-1), for all $u \in C^1(X,\mathbb{R}^m)$.

As we have already observed this result implies that $\theta(u)$ can generally be regarded as an (m-1) dimensional object parametrised by (m-1) coefficients $\{\lambda_2/\lambda_1, \ldots, \lambda_m/\lambda_1\}$ say. Since points in $\overset{o}{\theta}(u)$ are characterised by first order conditions alone, it is necessary to examine the Hessian of L to find the Pareto optimal points.

5.2. GENERIC EXISTENCE OF REGULAR ECONOMIES

In this brief final section we outline a proof of Smale's Theorem on the Generic Existence of Regular Economies (see Smale, 1974).

As in section 4.4, let $u = (u_1, \ldots, u_m) : X \to \mathbb{R}^m$ be a smooth profile, where $X = \mathbb{R}^n_+$, the commodity space facing each individual. Let $e=(e_1, \ldots, e_m) \in X^m$ be an initial endowment vector. Given u, define the Walras manifold to be the set

$$Z_u = \{(e,x,p)\} \in X^m \times X^m \times \Delta\}$$

(where Δ is the price simplex)
such that (x,p) is a Walrasian equilibrium for the economy (e,u).
Thus $(x,p) = ((x_1, \ldots, x_m, p)$ satisfies :

i) individual optimality: $D^*u_i(x_i) = p$ for $i \in M$,

ii) individual budget constraints: $(p, x_i) = (p, e_i)$ for $i \in M$,

iii) social resource constraints: $\sum_{i=1}^{m} x_{ij} = \sum_{i=1}^{m} e_{ij}$ for each $j = 1, \ldots, n$.

We seek to show that there is a residual set U in $C^r(X, \mathbb{R}^m)$ such that the Walras manifold is a smooth manifold of dimension mn.
Now define the Debreu projection

$$\pi : Z_u \subset X^m \times X^m \times \Delta \to X^m : (e,x,p) \to e.$$

Note that both Z_u and X^m will then have dimension mn.
By the Morse Sard Theorem the set

$$V = \{e \in X^m : d\pi \text{ has rank nm at } (e,x,p)\}$$

is dense in X^m.

Say the economy (e,u) is regular if $\pi(e,x,p) = e$ is a regular value of π (or rank $d\pi$ = mn) for all $(x,p) \in X^m \times \Delta$ such that $(e,x,p) \in Z_u$.
When e is a regular value of π, then by the inverse function theorem,

$$\pi^{-1}(e) = \{(e,x,p)^1, (e,x,p)^2, \ldots (e,x,p)^k\}$$

is a zero-dimensional object, and thus will consist of a finite number of isolated points.
Thus for each $e \in V$, the Walrasian equilibria

associated with e will be finite in number. Moreover there will exist a neighbourhood N of e in V such that the Walrasian equilibria move continuously with e in N.

Proof of the generic regularity of the Debreu projection

Define $\psi_u : X^m \times \Delta \rightarrow \Delta^{m+1}$ where $u \in C^r(X, \mathbb{R}^m)$

by $\psi_u(x,p) = (D^*u_1(x_1), \ldots, D^*u_m(x_m), p)$

where $x = (x_1, \ldots, x_m)$ and $u = (u_1, \ldots, u_m)$.

Let I be the diagonal $\{(p,\ldots,p) \in \Delta^{m+1}\}$ in Δ^{m+1}.

If $(x,p) \in \psi_u^{-1}(I)$ then for each $i, D^*u_i(x_i) = p$ and so the first order individual optimality conditions are satisfied. By the Thom Transversality Theorem there is a residual set (in fact an open dense set) of profiles U such that ψ_u is transversal to I for each $u \in U$. But then the codimension of $\psi_u^{-1}(I)$ in $X^m \times \Delta$ equals the codimension of I in Δ^{m+1}.

Now Δ and I are both of dimension (n-1) and so codimension (I) in Δ^{m+1} is $(m+1)(n-1)-(n-1)=m(n-1)$.

Thus $\dim(X^m \times \Delta)-\dim(\psi_u^{-1}(I)) = (m+1)(n-1)-(n-1)$

and $\dim(\psi_u^{-1}(I)) = mn+(n-1)-m(n-1)$

$= n+m-1$, for all $u \in U$.

Now let $e \in X^m$ be the initial endowment vector and

$$Y(e) = \{(x_1,\ldots,x_m) \in X^m : \sum_{i=1}^{m} x_i = \sum_{i=1}^{m} e_i\}$$

be the set of feasible outcomes, a hyperplane in $\mathbb{R}_+^{nm}$ of dimension $n(m-1)$. For each i, let $B_i(p) = \{x_i \in X : (p,x_i) = (p,e_i)\}$, the ith budget set at the price vector p.

Define $\Sigma(e) = \{(x,p) \in X^m \times \Delta : x \in Y(e), x_i \in B_i(p), \forall i \in M\}$ and $\Gamma = \{(e,x,p) : e \in X^m, (x,p) \in \Sigma(e)\}$.

Now Γ is a submanifold of $X^m \times X^m \times \Delta$ of dimension $2mn-m$, and at each point the projection is a regular map (ie.the rank of the differential of $(e,x,p) \to (x,p)$ is maximal).

To see this define $\phi: X^m \times X^m \times \Delta \to \mathbb{R}^n \times \mathbb{R}^{m-1}$ by $\phi(e,x,p) = \left(\sum_{i=1}^{m} x_i - \sum_{i=1}^{m} e_i, (p,x_1)-(p,e_1), \ldots \right.$

$$\left. (p,x_{m-1}) - (p,e_{m-1}) \right).$$

Clearly if $\phi(e,x,p) = \underline{O}$ then $x \in Y$ and $x_i \in B_i(p)$ for each i.

But $\underline{O}$ is of codimension $n+m-1$ in $\mathbb{R}^n \times \mathbb{R}^{m-1}$; thus $\phi^{-1}(\underline{O})$ is of the same codimension in $X^{2m} \times \Delta$.

Thus $\dim(X^{2m} \times \Delta) - \dim \phi^{-1}(\underline{O}) = n+m-1$

and $\dim \phi^{-1}(\underline{O}) = 2nm+(n-1)-(n+m-1) = 2mn-m$.

In a similar fashion for $(x,p) \in \Sigma(e)$, $\phi(e,x,p) = \underline{O}$, and so

$$\dim(X^m \times \Delta) - \dim \phi^{-1}(\underline{O}) = n+m-1$$

and thus $\Sigma(e)$ is a submanifold of dimension

$$nm+(n-1) - (n+m-1) = mn-m.$$

Finally define $Z_u = \{(e,x,p) \in \Gamma : \psi_u(x,p) \in I\}$.

For each $u \in U$, Z_u is a submanifold of $X^{2m} \times \Delta$ of dimension mn.

To see this consider

$$f_u: \Gamma \to X^m \times X^m \times \Delta \to X^m \times \Delta \overset{\psi_u}{\to} \Delta^{m+1}.$$

As we observed for all $u \in U$, ψ_u is transversal to I in Δ^{m+1}. But the codimension of I in Δ^{m+1} is $m(n-1)$. Since f_u will be transversal to I,

$$\dim(\Gamma) - \dim(f_u^{-1}(I)) = m(n-1);$$

hence $\dim(f_u^{-1}(I)) = 2mn-m-m(n-1) = mn$

and $f_u^{-1}(I) = Z_u$.

Thus for all $u \in U$, the Debreu projection

$$\pi: Z_u \to X^m .$$

will be a C^1-map between manifolds of dimension mn, and the Morse Sard Theorem gives the result.

Thus we have shown that for each smooth profile u in an open dense set U, there exists an open dense set V of initial endowments such that (e,u) is a regular economy for all $e \in V$.

The result is also related to the existence of a demand function for an economy.

A demand function for i (with utility u_i) is the function

$$f_i : \Delta \times \mathbb{R}_+ \to X$$

where $f_i(p,I)$ is that $x_i \in X$ which maximises u_i on $B_i(p,I) = \{x \in X : (p,x) = I\}$.

Now define $\phi_i : X \to \Delta \times \mathbb{R}_+$ by $\phi_i(x) = (D^*u_i(x), (D^*u_i(x), x))$.

But the optimality condition is precisely that $D^*u_i(x) = p$ and $(D^*u_i(x), x) = (p,x) = I$.

Thus when ϕ_i has maximal rank, it is locally invertible (by the inverse function theorem) and so locally defines a demand function.

On the other hand if f_i is a C^1-function then ϕ_i must be locally invertible (by f_i).

If this is true for all the agents, then $\psi_u : X^m \times \Delta \to \Delta^{m+1}$ must be transversal to I.

Consequently if $u = (u_1, \ldots, u_m)$ is such that each u_i defines a C^1-demand function $f_i : \Delta \times \mathbb{R}_+ \to X$ then $u \in U$, the open dense set of the regular economy theorem.

As a final note suppose that $u \in U$ and e is a critical value of the Debreu projection. Then it is possible that $\pi^{-1}(e) = e \times W$ where W is a continuum of Walrasian equilibria. Another possibility is that there is a continuum of singular or catastrophic endowments C, so that as the endowment vector crosses C the number of Walrasian equilibria changes suddenly. As we discussed in section 4.4, at a "catastrophic" endowment, stable and unstable Walrasian equilibria may merge (See Balasko,1975).

Another question is whether for every smooth profile,u, and every endowment vector, e, there exists a Walrasian equilibrium (x,p). This is equivalent to the requirement that for every u the projection $Z_u \rightarrow X^m$ is <u>onto</u> X^m.
In this case for each e there will exist some $(e,x,p) \in Z_u$. This is clearly necessary if there is to exist a market clearing price equilibrium p for the economy (e,u).

The usual general equilibrium arguments to prove existence of a market clearing price equilibrium typically rely on convexity properties of preference (see Hildenbrand and Kirman,1976). However weaker assumptions on preference permit the use of topological arguments to show the existence of an extended Walrasian equilibrium associated with each economy.

FURTHER READING

For a nice introductory treatment of the mathematical procedures developed in this book the reader might like to refer to S. Glaister, Mathematical Methods for Economists, (Blackwell, Oxford, 1972).

Economic applications of these techniques can be found in the following articles and books.

The classical book on social choice theory and the analysis of the rationality properties of preference relations is:

A.K. Sen, Collective Choice and Social Welfare (Holden-Day, San Francisco, 1970).

For the proof that an acyclic lower demi-continuous preference correspondence has a choice see:

M. Walker, "On the Existence of Maximal Elements", Journal of Economic Theory 16, (1977),470-474.

For a lucid account of economic equilibrium theory, including the separating hyperplane theorem, see:

W. Hildenbrand and A.P. Kirman, Introduction to Equilibrium Analysis (North Holland, Amsterdam, 1976).

For the Kuhn Tucker Theorem see:

G. M. Heal, The Theory of Economic Planning (North Holland, Amsterdam, 1973).

The discussion on the Pareto set and regular economies is very much dependent on Smale's original results. For the critical Pareto set and regular economies see:

S. Smale, Global Analysis and Economics I: Pareto Optimum and a Generalization of Morse Theory, Dynamical Systems, ed. by M. Peixoto (Academic Press, New York, 1973).

S. Smale, Global Analysis and Economics IIA: Extension of a Theorem of Debreu, Journal of Mathematical Economics 1, (1974), 1-14.

S. Smale, Optimizing Several Functions, Manifolds, Tokyo, 1973, ed. by Akio Hattori, (Tokyo, 1975).

G. Debreu, The Application to Economics of Differential Topology and Global Analysis, American Economic Review 66, (1976), 280-287.

Y. Balasko, Some Results on Uniqueness and on Stability of Equilibrium in General Equilibrium Theory, Journal of Mathematical Economics 2, (1975), 95-118.

There have recently been a number of attractive presentations of singularity theory, including:

D.R.J. Chillingsworth, Differential Topology with a View to Applications, (Pitman, London 1976).

M. Hirsch, Differential Topology, (Springer Verlag Berlin, 1976).

M. Golubitsky and V. Guillemin, Stable Mappings and their Singularities, (Springer Verlag, 1973).

For recent developments of the idea of manipulation see:

M.A. Satterthwaite and H. Sonnenschein, Strategy Proof Allocation Mechanisms at Differentiable Points, Review of Economic Studies 48, (1981), 587-597.

D. Gale, Exchange Equilibrium and Coalitions, Journal of Mathematical Economics 1, (1974), 63-66.

R. Guesnerie and J.J. Laffont, Advantageous Reallocations of Initial Resources, Econometrica 46, (1978), 835-841.

Y. Balasko, The Transfer Problem and the Theory of Regular Economies, International Economic Review 19, (1978), 687-694.

H.M. Polemarchakis, On the Transfer Problem, Mimeographed, Columbia University 1982.

Z. Safra, Manipulation by Reallocating Initial Endowments, Journal of Mathematical Economics, 12, (1983), 1-17.

R. Guesnerie and J.J. Laffont, On the Robustness of Strategy Proof Mechanisms, Journal of Mathematical Economics, 10, (1982), 5-15.

REVIEW EXERCISES

Chapter 1

1.1. Consider the relations

$$P = \{(2,3),(1,4),(2,1),(3,2)(4,4)\}$$

and $Q = \{(1,3),(4,2),(2,4),(4,1)\}$

Compute $Q \circ P$, $P \circ Q$, $(P \circ Q)^{-1}$ and $(Q \circ P)^{-1}$. Let ψ_Q and ψ_P be the mappings associated with these two relations. Are either ψ_Q or ψ_P functions, and are they surjective and/or injective?

1.2. Suppose that each member i of a society $N = \{1,\ldots,n\}$ has weak and strict preferences (R_i, P_i) on a set X of feasible states. Define the weak Pareto rule, Q, on X by xQy iff xR_iy $\forall_i \in N$, and xP_jy for some $j \in N$. Show that if each $R_i, i \in N$, is transitive then Q is transitive. Hence show that the Pareto choice set $C_Q(X)$ is non empty.

1.3. Show that the set $\Theta = \{e^{i\theta} : 0 \leq \theta \leq 2\pi\}$, of all 2 x 2 matrices representing rotations, is a subgroup of $(M^*(2), o)$, under matrix composition, o.

Chapter 2

2.1. With respect to the usual basis for $\mathbb{R}^3$, let $x_1 = (1,1,0)$, $x_2 = (0,1,1)$, $x_3 = (1,0,1)$. Show that $\{x_1, x_2, x_3\}$ are linearly independent.

2.2. Suppose $f : \mathbb{R}^5 \to \mathbb{R}^4$ is a linear transformation, with a 2-dimensional kernel. Show that there exists some vector $z \in \mathbb{R}^4$, such that for any vector $y \in \mathbb{R}^4$ there exists a vector $y_0 \in \text{Im}(f)$ such that $y = y_0 + \lambda z$ for some $\lambda \in \mathbb{R}$.

2.3. Find all solutions to the equations $A(x) = b_i$, for $i = 1,2,3$,

where $A = \begin{pmatrix} 1 & 4 & 2 & 3 \\ 3 & 1 & -1 & 1 \\ 1 & -1 & 4 & 6 \end{pmatrix}$

and $b_1 = \begin{pmatrix} 7 \\ 3 \\ 4 \end{pmatrix}$, $b_2 = \begin{pmatrix} 1 \\ 1 \\ 1 \end{pmatrix}$ and $b_3 = \begin{pmatrix} 3 \\ 2 \\ 1 \end{pmatrix}$.

2.4. Find all solutions to the equation $A(x) = b$

where $A = \begin{pmatrix} 6 & -1 & 1 & 4 \\ 1 & 1 & 3 & -1 \\ 3 & 4 & 1 & 2 \end{pmatrix}$

and $b = \begin{pmatrix} 4 \\ 3 \\ 7 \end{pmatrix}$.

2.5. Let $F: \mathbb{R}^4 \to \mathbb{R}^2$ be the linear transformation represented by the matrix

$$\begin{pmatrix} 1 & 5 & -1 & 3 \\ -1 & 0 & -4 & 2 \end{pmatrix}$$

Compute the set $F^{-1}(y)$, when $y = \begin{pmatrix} 4 \\ 1 \end{pmatrix}$.

2.6. Find the kernel and image of the linear transformation, A, represented by the matrix

$$\begin{pmatrix} 3 & 7 & 2 \\ 4 & 10 & 2 \\ 1 & -2 & 5 \end{pmatrix}.$$

Find new bases for the domain and codomain of A so that A is expressible as a matrix

$\begin{pmatrix} I & 0 \\ 0 & 0 \end{pmatrix}$ with respect to these bases.

2.7. Find the kernel of the linear transformation, A, represented by the matrix

$$\begin{pmatrix} 1 & 3 & 1 \\ 2 & -1 & -5 \\ -1 & 1 & 3 \end{pmatrix}.$$

Use the dimension theorem to compute the image of A. Does the equation $A(x)=b$ have a solution when $b = \begin{pmatrix} 1 \\ 1 \\ 1 \end{pmatrix}$?

2.8. Find the eigenvalues and eigenvectors of

$$\begin{pmatrix} 2 & -1 \\ 1 & 4 \end{pmatrix}.$$

Is this matrix positive or negative definite or neither?

2.9. Diagonalize the matrix

$$\begin{pmatrix} 4 & 1 & 1 \\ 1 & 8 & 0 \\ 1 & 10 & 2 \end{pmatrix}$$

2.10. Compute the eigenvalues and eigenvectors of

$$\begin{pmatrix} 1 & 0 & 0 \\ 0 & 0 & 1 \\ 0 & 1 & 0 \end{pmatrix}$$

and thus diagonalize the matrix.

Chapter 3

3.1. Show that if A is a set in a topological space $(X,\mathcal{T})$ then the interior, Int(A), of A is open and the closure, Clos(A), is closed. Show that Int(A) $\subset$ A $\subset$ Clos(A). What is the interior and what is the closure of the set [a,b) in $\mathbb{R}$, with the Euclidean topology? What is the boundary of [a,b)? Determine the limit points of [a,b)

3.2. If two metrics d_1,d_2 on a space X are equivalent write $d_1 \sim d_2$. Show that $\sim$ is an equivalence relation on the set of all metrics on X. Thus show that the cartesian, Euclidean and city block topologies on $\mathbb{R}^n$ are equivalent.

3.3. Show that the set, $L(\mathbb{R}^n,\mathbb{R}^m)$, of linear transformations from $\mathbb{R}^n$ to $\mathbb{R}^m$ is a normed vector space with norm

$\|f\| = \sup_{x\in\mathbb{R}^n} \{\frac{\|f(x)\|}{\|x\|} : \|x\| \neq 0\}$, with respect to the Euclidean norms on $\mathbb{R}^n$ and $\mathbb{R}^m$. In particular verify that $\|\ \|$ satisfies the three norm properties. Describe an open neighbourhood of a member f of $L(\mathbb{R}^n,\mathbb{R}^m)$ with respect to the induced topology on $L(\mathbb{R}^n,\mathbb{R}^m)$. Let M(n,m) be the set of n x m matrices with the natural topology (see page 123), and let

$$M : L(\mathbb{R}^n, \mathbb{R}^m) \to M(n,m)$$

be the matrix representation with respect to bases for $\mathbb{R}^n$ and $\mathbb{R}^m$. Discuss the continuity of M with respect to these topologies for $L(\mathbb{R}^n, \mathbb{R}^m)$ and $M(n,m)$.

3.4. Determine, from first principles, whether the following functions are continuous on their domain:

i) $\mathbb{R}_+ \to \mathbb{R} : x \to \log_e x$;
ii) $\mathbb{R} \to \mathbb{R}_+ : x \to x^2$;
iii) $\mathbb{R} \to \mathbb{R}_+ : x \to e^x$;
iv) $\mathbb{R} \to \mathbb{R} : x \to \cos x$;
v) $\mathbb{R} \to \mathbb{R} : x \to x \cos \frac{1}{x}$.

3.5. What is the image of the interval $[-1,1]$ under the function $x \to \cos \frac{1}{x}$? Is the image compace?

3.6. Determine which of the following sets are convex:

i) $X_1 = \{(x_1,x_2) \in \mathbb{R}^2 : 3x_1^2 + 2x_2^2 \le 6\}$;
ii) $X_2 = \{(x_1,x_2) \in \mathbb{R}^2 : x_1 \le 2, x_2 \le 3\}$;
iii) $X_3 = \{(x_1,x_2) \in \mathbb{R}_+^2 : x_1 x_2 \le 1\}$;
iv) $X_4 = \{(x_1,x_2) \in \mathbb{R}_+^2 : x_2 - 3 \ge -x_1^2\}$.

3.7. In $\mathbb{R}^2$, let $B_c(x,r_1)$ be the <u>cartesian</u> open ball of radius r_1 about x, and $B_E(y,r_2)$ the <u>Euclidean</u> ball of radius r_2 about x. Show that these two sets are convex. For fixed $x,y \in \mathbb{R}^2$ obtain necessary and sufficient restrictions on r_1, r_2 so that these two open balls may be strongly separated by a hyperplane.

3.8. Determine whether the following functions are convex, quasi-concave, or concave:

i) $\mathbb{R} \to \mathbb{R}_+ : x \to e^x$;
ii) $\mathbb{R} \to \mathbb{R} : x \to x^7$;
iii) $\mathbb{R}^2 \to \mathbb{R} : (x,y) \to xy$;
iv) $\mathbb{R} \to \mathbb{R} : x \to {}^1/_x$;
v) $\mathbb{R}^2 \to \mathbb{R} : (x,y) \to x^2 - y$.

Chapter 4

4.1. Suppose that $f: \mathbb{R}^n \to \mathbb{R}^m$ and $g: \mathbb{R}^m \to \mathbb{R}^k$ are both C^r-differentiable. Is $g \circ f: \mathbb{R}^n \to \mathbb{R}^k$ C^r-differentiable? If so, why?

4.2. Find and classify the critical points of the following functions:
i) $\mathbb{R}^2 \to \mathbb{R} : (x,y) \to x^2 + xy + 2y^2 + 3$;
ii) $\mathbb{R}^2 \to \mathbb{R} : (x,y) \to -x^2 + xy - y^2 + 2x + y$;
iii) $\mathbb{R}^2 \to \mathbb{R} : e^{2x} - 2x + 2y$.

4.3. Determine the critical points, and the Hessian at these points, of the function
$\mathbb{R}^2 \to \mathbb{R} : (x,y) \to x^2 y$.
Compute the eigenvalues and eigenvectors of the Hessian at critical points, and show how this allows the determination of the nature of the critical points.

4.4. Show that the origin is a critical point of the function
$\mathbb{R}^3 \to \mathbb{R} : (x,y,z) \to x^2 + 2y^2 + 3z^2 + xy + xz$.
Determine the nature of this critical point by examining the Hessian.

4.5. Determine the set of critical points of the function $\mathbb{R}^2 \to \mathbb{R}: (x,y) \to -x^2y^2 + 4xy - 4x^2$.

4.6. Maximise the function $\mathbb{R}^2 \to \mathbb{R}: (x,y) \to x^2y$ subject to the constraint $1-x^2-y^2 = 0$.

4.7. Maximise the function $\mathbb{R}^2 \to \mathbb{R}: (x,y) \to a\log x + b\log y$, subject to the constraint $px+qy \leq I$, where $p,q,I \in \mathbb{R}_+$.

Chapter 5

5.1. Show that if dimension $(X) \geq m$, then for almost every smooth profile $u=(u_1,\ldots,u_m):X \to \mathbb{R}^m$ it is the case that Pareto optimal points in the interior of X can be parametrised by at most (m-1) strictly positive coefficients $\{\lambda_1,\ldots,\lambda_{m-1}\}$.

5.2. Consider a two agent, two good exchange economy, where the initial endowment of good j by agent i is e_{ij}. Suppose that each agent, i, has utility function $u_i:(x_{i1},x_{i2}) \to a\log x_{i1} + b\log x_{i2}$. Compute the Pareto set in the feasible set $Y = \{(x_{11},x_{12}) \in \mathbb{R}^2_+ : 0 \leq x_{ij} \leq e_{ij} + e_{2j}, j=1,2\}$.

INDEX